LUTHER'S CATECHISM

The Small Catechism of Dr. Martin Luther
and
an Exposition for Children and Adults
Written in Contemporary English

David P. Kuske

NORTHWESTERN PUBLISHING HOUSE
Milwaukee, Wisconsin

Produced by the Board for Parish Services
Wisconsin Evangelical Lutheran Synod
Copyright © 1982, 1989, 1998

Northwestern Publishing House
1250 N. 113th St., Milwaukee, WI 53226-3284
All rights reserved.
3rd edition 1998
Printed in the United States of America

ISBN 0-8100-0874-2

CONTENTS

PREFACE

Dr. Martin Luther wrote the Small Catechism so that all Christians might have a short and simple summary of the main truths that the Bible teaches.

The first part of this book is a translation of the Small Catechism, which Luther wrote in German in 1529. The second part of this book is an exposition or explanation of what Luther wrote.

In the exposition, each part of Luther's Small Catechism is explained in a question and answer form. After each question there are Scripture passages that give the Bible's answer to the question. The words in italics in each passage indicate the part of the passage that is most important for answering the question. The answer merely summarizes what the Scripture passages teach.

At various points in the exposition there are explanations of terms and customs that are well-known in our Lutheran church. Throughout the exposition there are diagrams which illustrate the main points which were taught in that section.

May you study this book carefully and regularly, and may you return to it often to review and deepen your knowledge of the main truths that the Bible teaches.

David P. Kuske

LUTHER'S SMALL CATECHISM

The Ten Commandments

As the head of the family should teach them in the simplest way to those in his household.

THE FIRST COMMANDMENT

You shall have no other gods.

What does this mean?

We should fear, love, and trust in God above all things.

THE SECOND COMMANDMENT

You shall not misuse the name of the Lord your God.

What does this mean?

We should fear and love God that we do not use his name to curse, swear, lie, or deceive, or use witchcraft, but call upon God's name in every trouble, pray, praise, and give thanks.

THE THIRD COMMANDMENT

Remember the Sabbath day by keeping it holy.

What does this mean?

We should fear and love God that we do not despise preaching and his Word, but regard it as holy and gladly hear and learn it.

THE FOURTH COMMANDMENT

Honor your father and mother, that it may go well with you and that you may enjoy long life on the earth.

What does this mean?

We should fear and love God that we do not dishonor or anger our parents and others in authority, but honor, serve, and obey them, and give them love and respect.

THE FIFTH COMMANDMENT

You shall not murder.

What does this mean?

We should fear and love God that we do not hurt or harm our neighbor in his body, but help and befriend him in every bodily need.

THE SIXTH COMMANDMENT

You shall not commit adultery.

What does this mean?

We should fear and love God that we lead a pure and decent life in words and actions, and that husband and wife love and honor each other.

THE SEVENTH COMMANDMENT

You shall not steal.

What does this mean?

We should fear and love God that we do not take our neighbor's money or property, or get it by dishonest dealing, but help him to improve and protect his property and means of income.

THE EIGHTH COMMANDMENT

You shall not give false testimony against your neighbor.

What does this mean?

We should fear and love God that we do not tell lies about our neighbor, betray him, or give him a bad name, but defend him, speak well of him, and take his words and actions in the kindest possible way.

THE NINTH COMMANDMENT

You shall not covet your neighbor's house.

What does this mean?

We should fear and love God that we do not scheme to get our neighbor's inheritance or house, or obtain it by a show of right, but do all we can to help him keep it.

THE TENTH COMMANDMENT

You shall not covet your neighbor's wife, workers, animals, or anything that belongs to your neighbor.

What does this mean?

We should fear and love God that we do not force or entice away our neighbor's spouse, workers, or animals, but urge them to stay and do their duty.

THE CONCLUSION

What does God say about all these commandments?

He says, "I, the LORD your God, am a jealous God, punishing the children for the sin of the fathers to the third and fourth generation of those who hate me, but showing love to a thousand generations of those who love me and keep my commandments."

What does this mean?

God threatens to punish all who transgress these commandments. Therefore we should fear his anger and not disobey what he commands.

But he promises grace and every blessing to all who keep these commandments. Therefore we should love and trust in him and gladly obey what he commands.

The Creed

As the head of the family should teach it in the simplest way to those in his household.

THE FIRST ARTICLE
(Creation)

I believe in God the Father almighty, maker of heaven and earth.

What does this mean?

I believe that God created me and all that exists, and that he gave me my body and soul, eyes, ears, and all my members, my mind and all my abilities.
And I believe that God still preserves me by richly and daily providing clothing and shoes, food and drink, property and home, spouse and children, land, cattle, and all I own, and all I need to keep my body and life. God also preserves me by defending me against all danger, guarding and protecting me from all evil. All this God does only because he is my good and merciful Father in heaven, and not because I have earned or deserved it. For all this I ought to thank and praise, to serve and obey him.
This is most certainly true.

THE SECOND ARTICLE
(Redemption)

I believe in Jesus Christ, his only Son, our Lord, who was conceived by the Holy Spirit, born of the virgin Mary, suffered under Pontius Pilate, was crucified, died, and was buried. He descended into hell. The third day he rose again from the dead. He ascended into heaven and is seated at the right hand of God the Father almighty. From there he will come to judge the living and the dead.

4

What does this mean?

I believe that Jesus Christ, true God, begotten of the Father from eternity, and also true man, born of the virgin Mary, is my Lord.

He has redeemed me, a lost and condemned creature, purchased and won me from all sins, from death, and from the power of the devil, not with gold or silver but with his holy, precious blood and with his innocent suffering and death.

All this he did that I should be his own, and live under him in his kingdom, and serve him in everlasting righteousness, innocence, and blessedness, just as he has risen from death and lives and rules eternally.

This is most certainly true.

THE THIRD ARTICLE
(Sanctification)

I believe in the Holy Spirit; the holy Christian church, the communion of saints; the forgiveness of sins; the resurrection of the body; and the life everlasting. Amen.

What does this mean?

I believe that I cannot by my own thinking or choosing believe in Jesus Christ, my Lord, or come to him.

But the Holy Spirit has called me by the gospel, enlightened me with his gifts, sanctified and kept me in the true faith. In the same way he calls, gathers, enlightens, and sanctifies the whole Christian church on earth, and keeps it with Jesus Christ in the one true faith.

In this Christian church he daily and fully forgives all sins to me and all believers.

On the Last Day he will raise me and all the dead and give eternal life to me and all believers in Christ.

This is most certainly true.

The Lord's Prayer

*As the head of the family should teach it in the simplest way
to those in his household.*

THE ADDRESS

Our Father in heaven.

What does this mean?

With these words God tenderly invites us to believe that he is our
true Father and that we are his true children, so that we may pray
to him as boldly and confidently as dear children ask their dear
father.

THE FIRST PETITION

Hallowed be your name.

What does this mean?

God's name is certainly holy by itself, but we pray in this petition that
we too may keep it holy.

How is God's name kept holy?

God's name is kept holy when his Word is taught in its truth and
purity and we as children of God lead holy lives according to it. Help
us to do this, dear Father in heaven! But whoever teaches and lives
contrary to God's Word dishonors God's name among us. Keep us
from doing this, dear Father in heaven!

THE SECOND PETITION

Your kingdom come.

What does this mean?

God's kingdom certainly comes by itself even without our prayer,
but we pray in this petition that it may also come to us.

How does God's kingdom come?

God's kingdom comes when our heavenly Father gives his Holy Spirit, so that by his grace we believe his holy Word and lead a godly life now on earth and forever in heaven.

THE THIRD PETITION

Your will be done on earth as in heaven.

What does this mean?

God's good and gracious will certainly is done without our prayer, but we pray in this petition that it may be done among us also.

How is God's will done?

God's will is done when he breaks and defeats every evil plan and purpose of the devil, the world, and our sinful flesh, which try to prevent us from keeping God's name holy and letting his kingdom come. And God's will is done when he strengthens and keeps us firm in his Word and in the faith as long as we live. This is his good and gracious will.

THE FOURTH PETITION

Give us today our daily bread.

What does this mean?

God surely gives daily bread without our asking, even to all the wicked, but we pray in this petition that he would lead us to realize this and to receive our daily bread with thanksgiving.

What, then, is meant by daily bread?

Daily bread includes everything that we need for our bodily welfare, such as food and drink, clothing and shoes, house and home, land and cattle, money and goods, a godly spouse, godly children, godly workers, godly and faithful leaders, good government, good weather, peace and order, health, a good name, good friends, faithful neighbors, and the like.

THE FIFTH PETITION

Forgive us our sins, as we forgive those who sin against us.

What does this mean?

We pray in this petition that our Father in heaven would not look upon our sins or because of them deny our prayers; for we are worthy of none of the things for which we ask, neither have we deserved them, but we ask that he would give them all to us by grace; for we daily sin much and surely deserve nothing but punishment.

So we too will forgive from the heart and gladly do good to those who sin against us.

THE SIXTH PETITION

Lead us not into temptation.

What does this mean?

God surely tempts no one to sin, but we pray in this petition that God would guard and keep us, so that the devil, the world, and our flesh may not deceive us or lead us into false belief, despair, and other great and shameful sins; and though we are tempted by them, we pray that we may overcome and win the victory.

THE SEVENTH PETITION

But deliver us from evil.

What does this mean?

In conclusion, we pray in this petition that our Father in heaven would deliver us from every evil that threatens body and soul, property and reputation, and finally when our last hour comes, grant us a blessed end and graciously take us from this world of sorrow to himself in heaven.

THE DOXOLOGY

For the kingdom, the power, and the glory are yours now and forever. Amen.

What does this mean?

We can be sure that these petitions are acceptable to our Father in heaven and are heard by him, for he himself has commanded us to pray in this way and has promised to hear us. Therefore we say, "Amen. Yes, it shall be so."

The Sacrament of Holy Baptism

As the head of the family should teach it in the simplest way to those in his household.

THE INSTITUTION OF BAPTISM

First: *What is Baptism?*

Baptism is not just plain water, but it is water used by God's command and connected with God's Word.

Which is that word of God?

Christ our Lord says in the last chapter of Matthew, "Go and make disciples of all nations, baptizing them in the name of the Father and of the Son and of the Holy Spirit."

THE BLESSINGS OF BAPTISM

Second: *What does Baptism do for us?*

Baptism works forgiveness of sin, delivers from death and the devil, and gives eternal salvation to all who believe this, as the words and promises of God declare.

What are these words and promises of God?

Christ our Lord says in the last chapter of Mark, "Whoever believes and is baptized will be saved, but whoever does not believe will be condemned."

THE POWER OF BAPTISM

Third: *How can water do such great things?*

It is certainly not the water that does such things, but God's Word which is in and with the water and faith which trusts this Word used with the water.
For without God's Word the water is just plain water and not Baptism. But with this Word it is Baptism, that is, a gracious water of life and a washing of rebirth by the Holy Spirit.

Where is this written?

Saint Paul says in Titus, chapter 3, "[God] saved us through the washing of rebirth and renewal by the Holy Spirit, whom he poured out on us generously through Jesus Christ our Savior, so that, having been justified by his grace, we might become heirs having the hope of eternal life. This is a trustworthy saying."

THE MEANING OF BAPTISM FOR OUR DAILY LIFE

Fourth: *What does baptizing with water mean?*

Baptism means that the old Adam in us should be drowned by daily contrition and repentance, and that all its evil deeds and desires be put to death. It also means that a new person should daily arise to live before God in righteousness and purity forever.

Where is this written?

Saint Paul says in Romans, chapter 6, "We were . . . buried with [Christ] through baptism into death in order that, just as Christ was raised from the dead through the glory of the Father, we too may live a new life."

The Use of the Keys and Confession

*As the head of the family should teach them in the simplest way
to those in his household.*

THE KEYS

First: *What is the use of the keys?*

The use of the keys is that special power and right which Christ gave to his church on earth: to forgive the sins of penitent sinners but refuse forgiveness to the impenitent as long as they do not repent.

Where is this written?

The holy evangelist John writes in chapter 20, "[Jesus] breathed on [his disciples] and said, 'Receive the Holy Spirit. If you forgive anyone his sins, they are forgiven; if you do not forgive them, they are not forgiven.' "

THE PUBLIC USE OF THE KEYS

Second: *How does a Christian congregation use the keys?*

A Christian congregation with its called servant of Christ uses the keys in accordance with Christ's command by forgiving those who repent of their sin and are willing to amend, and by excluding from the congregation those who are plainly impenitent that they may repent. I believe that when this is done, it is as valid and certain in heaven also, as if Christ, our dear Lord, dealt with us himself.

Where is this written?

Jesus says in Matthew, chapter 18, "Whatever you bind on earth will be bound in heaven, and whatever you loose on earth will be loosed in heaven."

CONFESSION

First: *What is confession?*

Confession has two parts. The one is that we confess our sins; the other, that we receive absolution or forgiveness from the pastor as from God himself, not doubting but firmly believing that our sins are thus forgiven before God in heaven.

Second: *What sins should we confess?*

Before God we should plead guilty of all sins, even those we are not aware of, as we do in the Lord's Prayer.
But before the pastor we should confess only those sins which we know and feel in our hearts.

Third: *How can we recognize these sins?*

Consider your place in life according to the Ten Commandments. Are you a father, mother, son, daughter, employer, or employee? Have you been disobedient, unfaithful, or lazy? Have you hurt anyone by word or deed? Have you been dishonest, careless, wasteful, or done other wrong?

Fourth: *How will the pastor assure a penitent sinner of forgiveness?*

He will say, "By the authority of Christ, I forgive you your sins in the name of the Father and of the Son and of the Holy Spirit. Amen."

The Sacrament of Holy Communion

As the head of the family should teach it in the simplest way to those in his household.

THE INSTITUTION OF HOLY COMMUNION

First: *What is the Sacrament of Holy Communion?*

It is the true body and blood of our Lord Jesus Christ under the bread and wine, instituted by Christ for us Christians to eat and to drink.

Where is this written?

The holy evangelists Matthew, Mark, Luke, and the apostle Paul tell us: Our Lord Jesus Christ, on the night he was betrayed, took bread; and when he had given thanks, he broke it and gave it to his disciples, saying, "Take and eat; this is my body, which is given for you. Do this in remembrance of me."

Then he took the cup, gave thanks, and gave it to them, saying, "Drink from it, all of you; this is my blood of the new covenant, which is poured out for you for the forgiveness of sins. Do this, whenever you drink it, in remembrance of me."

THE BLESSINGS OF HOLY COMMUNION

Second: *What blessing do we receive through this eating and drinking?*

That is shown us by these words: "Given" and "poured out for you for the forgiveness of sins."

Through these words we receive forgiveness of sins, life, and salvation in this sacrament.

For where there is forgiveness of sins, there is also life and salvation.

THE POWER OF HOLY COMMUNION

Third: *How can eating and drinking do such great things?*

It is certainly not the eating and drinking that does such things, but the words "Given" and "poured out for you for the forgiveness of sins."

These words are the main thing in this sacrament, along with the eating and drinking.

And whoever believes these words has what they plainly say, the forgiveness of sins.

THE RECEPTION OF HOLY COMMUNION

Fourth: *Who, then, is properly prepared to receive this sacrament?*

Fasting and other outward preparations may serve a good purpose, but he is properly prepared who believes these words: "Given" and "poured out for you for the forgiveness of sins."

But whoever does not believe these words or doubts them is not prepared, because the words "for you" require nothing but hearts that believe.

The Nicene Creed

We believe in one God, the Father, the Almighty, maker of heaven and earth, of all that is, seen and unseen.

We believe in one Lord, Jesus Christ, the only Son of God, eternally begotten of the Father, God from God, Light from Light, true God from true God, begotten, not made, of one being with the Father. Through him all things were made. For us and for our salvation, he came down from heaven, was incarnate of the Holy Spirit and the virgin Mary, and became fully human. For our sake he was crucified under Pontius Pilate. He suffered death and was buried. On the third day he rose again in accordance with the Scriptures. He ascended into heaven and is seated at the right hand of the Father. He will come again in glory to judge the living and the dead, and his kingdom will have no end.

We believe in the Holy Spirit, the Lord, the giver of life, who proceeds from the Father and the Son, who in unity with the Father and the Son is worshiped and glorified, who has spoken through the prophets. We believe in one holy Christian and apostolic Church. We acknowledge one baptism for the forgiveness of sins. We look for the resurrection of the dead and the life of the world to come. Amen.

Daily Prayers

*How the head of the family should teach those in his household
to pray morning and evening, to ask a blessing,
and to say grace at meals.*

MORNING PRAYER

In the name of God the Father, Son, and Holy Spirit. Amen.
I thank you, my heavenly Father, through Jesus Christ, your dear
Son, that you have kept me this night from all harm and danger.
Keep me this day also from sin and every evil, that all my doings and
life may please you. Into your hands I commend my body and soul
and all things. Let your holy angel be with me, that the wicked foe
may have no power over me. Amen.

EVENING PRAYER

In the name of God the Father, Son, and Holy Spirit. Amen.
I thank you, my heavenly Father, through Jesus Christ, your dear
Son, that you have graciously kept me this day. Forgive me all my
sins, and graciously keep me this night. Into your hands I commend
my body and soul and all things. Let your holy angel be with me, that
the wicked foe may have no power over me. Amen.

TO ASK A BLESSING

The eyes of all look to you, O Lord, and you give them their food at
the proper time. You open your hand and satisfy the desires of every
living thing. Amen.

Lord God, heavenly Father, bless us through these gifts which we
receive from your bountiful goodness, through Jesus Christ, our
Lord. Amen.

TO SAY GRACE

Give thanks to the Lord, for he is good; his love endures forever.
Amen.

Lord God, heavenly Father, we thank you for all your gifts, through
Jesus Christ, our Lord. Amen.

Table of Duties

PASTORS

A pastor must be above reproach, the husband of but one wife, temperate, self-controlled, respectable, hospitable, able to teach, not given to much wine, not violent but gentle, not quarrelsome, not a lover of money. He must manage his own family well and see that his children obey him with proper respect. He must not be a recent convert. He must hold firmly to the trustworthy message as it has been taught, so that he can encourage others by sound doctrine and refute those who oppose it. (See 1 Timothy 3:2,3,4,6; Titus 1:9.)

WHAT WE OWE TO OUR PASTORS AND TEACHERS

Anyone who receives instruction in the Word must share all good things with his instructor. (See Galatians 6:6.)

In the same way, the Lord has commanded that those who preach the gospel should receive their living from the gospel. (See 1 Corinthians 9:14.)

The elders who direct the affairs of the church well are worthy of double honor, especially those whose work is preaching and teaching. For the Scripture says, "The worker deserves his wages." (See 1 Timothy 5:17,18.)

Obey your leaders and submit to their authority. They keep watch over you as men who must give an account. Obey them so that their work will be a joy, not a burden, for that would be of no advantage to you. (See Hebrews 13:17.)

GOVERNMENT

Everyone must submit himself to the governing authorities, for there is no authority except that which God has established. The authorities that exist have been established by God. Consequently, he who rebels against the authority is rebelling against what God has instituted, and those who do so will bring judgment on themselves. For he is God's servant to do you good. But if you do wrong, be afraid, for he does not bear the sword for nothing. He is God's servant, an agent of wrath to bring punishment on the wrongdoer. (See Romans 13:1,2,4.)

HUSBANDS

Husbands, be considerate as you live with your wives, and treat them with respect as the weaker partner and as heirs with you of the gracious gift of life, so that nothing will hinder your prayers. Husbands, love your wives and do not be harsh with them. (See 1 Peter 3:7; Colossians 3:19.)

WIVES

Wives, submit to your husbands as to the Lord, like Sarah, who obeyed Abraham and called him her master. You are her daughters if you do what is right and do not give way to fear. (See Ephesians 5:22; 1 Peter 3:6.)

PARENTS

Fathers, do not exasperate your children; instead, bring them up in the training and instruction of the Lord. Fathers, do not embitter your children, or they will become discouraged. (See Ephesians 6:4; Colossians 3:21.)

CHILDREN

Children, obey your parents in the Lord, for this is right. "Honor your father and mother"—which is the first commandment with a promise—"that it may go well with you and that you may enjoy long life on the earth." (See Ephesians 6:1-3.)

EMPLOYEES

Obey your earthly masters with respect and fear, and with sincerity of heart, just as you would obey Christ. Obey them not only to win their favor when their eye is on you, but like slaves of Christ, doing the will of God from your heart. Serve wholeheartedly, as if you were serving the Lord, not men, because you know that the Lord will reward everyone for whatever good he does. (See Ephesians 6:5-8.)

EMPLOYERS

Treat your employees in the same way. Do not threaten them, since you know that he who is both their Master and yours is in heaven, and there is no favoritism with him. (See Ephesians 6:9.)

YOUNG PEOPLE

Young men, be submissive to those who are older. Clothe yourselves with humility toward one another, because "God opposes the proud but gives grace to the humble." Humble yourselves, therefore, under God's mighty hand, that he may lift you up in due time. (See 1 Peter 5:5,6.)

WIDOWS

The widow who is really in need and left all alone puts her hope in God and continues night and day to pray and to ask God for help. But the widow who lives for pleasure is dead even while she lives. (See 1 Timothy 5:5,6.)

A WORD FOR ALL

Love your neighbor as yourself. This is the sum of all the commandments. (See Romans 13:8-10; Galatians 5:14.) And continue praying for everyone. (See 1 Timothy 2:1.)

Let each his lesson learn with care,
And all the household well shall fare.

MARTIN LUTHER, THE AUTHOR OF THE SMALL CATECHISM

The Need for a Reformation

For the first 500 years after the time of Christ, the Christian church continued to grow and spread in spite of persecutions and attacks by false teachers. About A.D. 600 two things happened that were very harmful for the Christian church: one was the Mohammedan conquest, and the other was the rise of the bishop of Rome.

The army of the Mohammedans conquered North Africa, Palestine, Syria, and Asia Minor. This conquest destroyed Christian churches in all these places.

In Western Europe the bishop of Rome became the leader of the Christian church. He was head of the church in Spain, France, England, Germany, and Italy. He became known as the Pope and claimed that he was appointed by Christ to rule over everyone, including kings. The Pope did not use his power to serve Christ. Instead, he introduced anti-Christian doctrines. One was purgatory. Another was that salvation is not by faith alone but also by good works. In addition, he led people to believe that they could receive God's grace only through the bishops and priests whom he appointed. When some people showed that what the Pope was teaching was wrong according to the Bible, he ordered punishment for everyone who read the Bible without his permission.

As a result of the conquest by the Mohammedans and the rise of the Pope, the truth of the gospel had almost disappeared. A reformation was needed to restore the Bible to its proper place and to bring back the truth about salvation. God used Luther to bring about this reformation.

Luther's Birth (1483) and Education

In 1483, nine years before Columbus discovered America, Luther was born in the small town of Eisleben, Germany. His parents were poor, but they knew that Martin was a bright boy, so they sent him to school. When Luther was 14 years old, he had to leave home in order to continue his education. Together with some of the other boys who didn't have much money, Luther had to earn some of his meals by singing at the homes of wealthy people. In spite of this he did so well in his studies that his teachers encouraged him to go on to college.

By this time Luther's father was earning enough money to pay some of Martin's expenses, so Luther went to the University of Erfurt. Luther studied to become a lawyer and again did very well as a student. He gained the respect of all who knew him and enjoyed the company of his fellow students. In 1505 he graduated with a master of arts degree. But Luther was not really happy.

Luther, the Monk (1505)

When Luther was a child, his parents taught him to pray to the saints, to respect the Pope and the Roman Catholic Church, and to do good works. Although Luther did all these things quite faithfully, his sins still troubled him very much. He knew that God was angry with man because of sin. So he lived in constant fear that death would mean that he must face the terrible punishment of God for his sins. To find peace for his soul, he decided to enter a monastery and become a monk.

In the monastery Luther followed all the rules that were supposed to make his life as a monk more holy. He even tortured himself by sleeping on a hard floor and by beating his body. In 1507 he became a priest and celebrated his first Mass. But none of this gave Luther the peace of mind that he was seeking.

Luther at Wittenberg (1508)

Dr. Staupitz, the head of the monastery, decided to send Luther to Wittenberg to ready himself to teach the Bible at the new university that the Elector (Ruler) of Saxony had just started. Staupitz hoped that this new assignment would give Luther more opportunity to study the Bible. He also hoped that teaching would keep Luther so busy that he would have much less time to think about his sins.

Already while Luther was in the monastery, Staupitz had told Luther that in Jesus he could find the peace he was seeking.

Luther's study of God's Word as a professor at Wittenberg gradually led him to know the love of God in Christ. Through the Bible he finally found the peace he had been seeking so urgently.

Luther soon earned the reputation of being a very good teacher and preacher. Students came from many places to be in his classes. People came in such large numbers to hear him preach that he was given the assignment to preach in the Town Church in Wittenberg. It was not only the forceful way Luther taught and preached but also the "new" things he said that made people want to hear him.

"Forgiveness of sins," he said, "is not something which we earn for ourselves by our own good deeds. Rather, it is a free gift which God gives to us as a result of all that Jesus did for us as our Savior. Salvation, therefore, is completely and only by faith in Jesus."

Luther's Ninety-Five Theses (1517)

This "new" teaching of Luther, which was really a return to the simple truth of God's Word, did not cause any great excitement until 1517. In that year an event took place that marked the beginning of the Reformation.

To raise money for the building of St. Peter's Church in Rome, the Pope allowed the sale of indulgences all over Germany. Luther objected to these worthless pieces of paper that promised people release from the punishment of their sins in purgatory in exchange for a payment of money. He wrote ninety-five theses, or statements, in Latin which showed that the sale of these indulgences was contrary to the Bible. On October 31, 1517, Luther nailed his theses on the door of the Castle Church. This church door was often used for the posting of public announcements in Wittenberg.

Luther's purpose in posting these statements was merely to challenge someone from the university to debate them with him. That is why he wrote them in Latin. The Ninety-five Theses, however, were quickly translated, printed, and spread over much of Germany and other parts of Europe. Wherever they were spread, they stirred up much excitement.

Finally, the Pope ordered Luther to appear in Rome to answer charges of false teaching. Luther's ruler, the Elector (Ruler) of Saxony, used his influence to insist that Luther's case be settled in Germany instead.

Luther at the Diet of Worms and the Wartburg (1521)

In 1518 Luther appeared before Cardinal Cajetan, whom the Pope had sent as his representative. Cajetan would not discuss the Ninety-five Theses with Luther. Instead, he demanded that Luther admit his writings were wrong. Luther said he could not do this unless Cardinal Cajetan could show him from the Bible that he was wrong. A year later, in a debate with a German church scholar named Dr. Eck, Luther said that it was not necessary to obey the Pope in order to be saved.

As a result of these statements, the Pope sent out an official notice called a papal bull (from *bulla,* meaning seal) which said that Luther would no longer be a member of the Roman Catholic Church and that all his writings should be burned if he did not retract.

In 1521 Emperor Charles summoned Luther to come to a meeting of the German princes called the Diet of Worms. The emperor hoped that at this assembly he could end the religious differences between the German princes, so that they would help him stop the invasion of the Turks. He told Luther that he did not want to hear a debate on Bible teaching but only an admission from Luther that his teachings were wrong.

After prayerfully thinking over his answer for a day, Luther said, "Unless you can prove from the Bible that I have made wrong statements, I cannot and I will not take back anything. My conscience is bound by the Word of God. Here I stand. I cannot do otherwise. God help me. Amen."

Because of Luther's refusal, the emperor declared him an "outlaw" whom anyone could kill after 20 days. Elector Frederick, however, saved Luther by having him kidnapped and taken to a secluded castle called the Wartburg. Luther stayed in hiding at the Wartburg for about a year. During this time he translated the New Testament into German, so that all his countrymen could read the Word of God for themselves.

Luther's Return to Wittenberg and Death (1546)

Luther was able to return to Wittenberg in 1522 because God was keeping Emperor Charles busy with serious problems in the other parts of his empire. It was not until after Luther's death more than 20 years later in 1546 that the emperor again was able to turn his attention to dealing with the Lutherans in Germany. By that time God had enabled Luther and his helpers to establish the Reformation so firmly that the emperor was not able to destroy it.

The last 20 years of Luther's life were very busy. He taught regularly at the University of Wittenberg and preached in the Town Church. Together with his helpers, he published a translation of both the Old and New Testaments in German and constantly worked to improve it so that the Bible could be read and understood by everyone. He wrote hymns so that people could sing the truths they learned from the Bible. He wrote many letters to people about the Bible and its teachings. He wrote explanations of Bible books called commentaries and hundreds of essays on what the Bible says about many different religious topics.

Luther married a former nun, Katherine von Bora, and the Lord blessed them with six children.

On February 18, 1546, Luther died. His body was placed in a vault just beneath the pulpit in the Castle Church.

Luther and the Small Catechism

Luther often showed his deep concern for the Christian training of young people. He urged people to provide and support Christian schools for their children. When Luther found that many pastors and parents did not know how to instruct children in the main teachings of the Bible, he wrote the Small Catechism.

Luther's chief purpose in writing the catechism was to lead children to know and believe that the only way of salvation is by faith in Jesus. He wanted the catechism to be simple, yet to include all the main teachings of the Bible. The six main parts of the Small Catechism (listed in the order in which we will study them) are

1. The Ten Commandments
2. The Creed
3. The Sacrament of Holy Baptism
4. The Sacrament of Holy Communion
5. The Use of the Keys and Confession
6. The Lord's Prayer

Our Use of the Catechism

The Lutheran Church has always considered the catechism the very least that every Christian should know about Bible teachings. For over 400 years the catechism has served well as the basic book for teaching both young and old. Everything written in the catechism is based on the Bible. In the explanation of Luther's catechism which follows, we will compare the words of Luther's catechism with the Bible to assure ourselves that the catechism truly teaches God's Word. Then we can memorize and use the words of the catechism as a simple summary of the main truths that God teaches us in his Word. This summary will also serve as a foundation on which we can continue to build as we seek to strengthen our faith by Bible study throughout our entire lives.

Though the catechism is simple, we need to study it carefully to know and understand better the Bible truths that it summarizes. Once Luther asked his son Hans how much he knew. Hans answered rather proudly, "The whole catechism, Papa, because I know that by heart." "Is that so!" Luther said. "If you really understand that much, you are wiser than I am. I still have to study it every day." May we, like the author of the Small Catechism, treasure the Bible truths it teaches us and study them diligently!

THE BIBLE

We Need the Bible

1. How do we know there is a God?

1) Hebrews 3:4. For every house is *built by someone,* but God is the builder of everything.

2) Psalm 19:1-4. (The psalmist emphasizes how all the heavenly bodies tell all men that there is a God. Note especially verse 1: "The heavens declare the glory of God; *the skies proclaim* the work of his hands.")

3) Psalm 14:1. The fool says in his heart, "There is no God."

1. We know there is a God from the things he created.

2. What do we know about God from the things he created?

4) Acts 14:17. He has shown *kindness* by giving you rain from heaven and crops in their seasons; he provides you with plenty of food and fills your hearts with joy.

5) Psalm 104. (The psalmist speaks of all the wonderful things God created. Note especially verse 24: "How many are your works, O LORD! In *wisdom* you made them all; the earth is full of your creatures.")

6) Romans 1:20. Since the creation of the world God's invisible qualities—his eternal power and divine nature—have been clearly seen, being understood from what has been made, so that men are without excuse.

2. From the things God created we know that he is kind, wise, eternal, powerful, and divine.

3. What do we know about God from our consciences?

7) Romans 2:14,15. When Gentiles, who do not have the law, do by nature things required by law, they are a law for themselves,

KNOWLEDGE ABOUT GOD

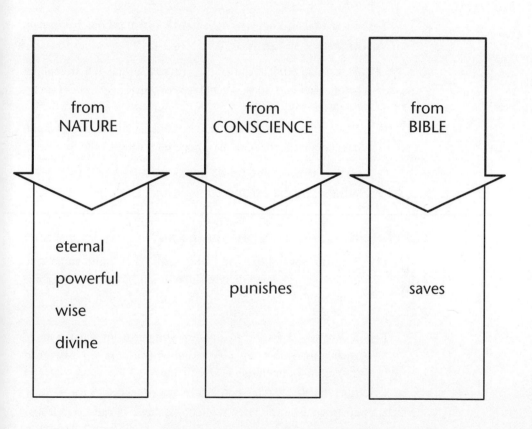

from NATURE

eternal

powerful

wise

divine

from CONSCIENCE

punishes

from BIBLE

saves

even though they do not have the law, since they show that the requirements of the law are written on their hearts, their consciences also bearing witness, and *their thoughts now accusing,* now even defending them.

8) Romans 1:32. *They know* God's righteous decree that those who do such things *deserve death.*

3. From our consciences we know that God will punish us for our sins.

4. What can we never know about God from his creation or our consciences?

9) Acts 16:29,30. The jailer . . . rushed in and fell trembling before Paul and Silas . . . and asked, "Sirs, *what must I do to be saved?"*

10) 1 Corinthians 2:9. *No eye* has seen, *no ear* has heard, *no mind* has conceived what God has prepared for those who love him.

4. From God's creation or our consciences we can never know what God has done to save us.

5. Why, then, do we need the Bible?

11) 2 Corinthians 4:6. God, who said, "Let light shine out of darkness," made his light shine in our hearts to give us *the light of the knowledge of the glory of God* in the face of Christ.

12) 2 Timothy 3:15. From infancy you have known the holy *Scriptures, which are able to make you wise for salvation* through faith in Christ Jesus.

13) Acts 16:29-32. The jailer . . . asked, "Sirs, what must I do to be saved?" They replied, "Believe in the Lord Jesus, and *you will be saved*—you and your household." Then *they spoke the word of the Lord to him* and to all the others in his house.

5. We need the Bible as a light that reveals to us what God has done to save us.

The Bible Has Two Major Parts

6. What is the Old Testament?

14) Hebrews 1:1. *In the past* God spoke to our forefathers through the prophets.

15) Acts 3:18. God fulfilled *what he had foretold* through all the prophets, saying that his Christ would suffer.

6. The Old Testament is that part of the Bible which was written before Christ came and tells about God's promise of a Savior.

7. What is the New Testament?

16) Acts 3:18. *God fulfilled* what he had foretold through all the prophets, saying that his Christ would suffer.

17) Hebrews 9:15. Christ is the mediator of *a new covenant . . . now that he has died* as a ransom to set them free from the sins committed under the first covenant.

18) John 20:31. These are written that you may believe that *Jesus is the Christ,* the Son of God, and that by believing you may have life in his name.

7. The New Testament is that part of the Bible which was written after Christ came and tells how God fulfilled his promise in Jesus.

8. Whom did God use to give us the Old and New Testaments?

19) Hebrews 1:1,2. In the past God spoke to our forefathers *through the prophets . . .* but in these last days he has spoken to us by his Son.

20) 2 Peter 3:2. I want you to recall the words spoken in the past by the holy prophets and the command given by our Lord and Savior *through your apostles.*

8. God used his prophets to give us the Old Testament and Jesus' apostles to give us the New Testament.

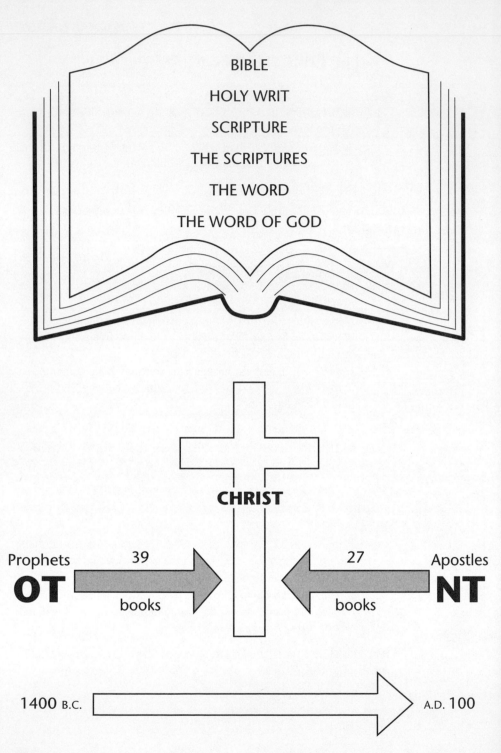

BIBLE

HOLY WRIT

SCRIPTURE

THE SCRIPTURES

THE WORD

THE WORD OF GOD

CHRIST

Prophets
OT
39
books

27
books
Apostles
NT

1400 B.C.

A.D. 100

The Books of the Bible

The word "Bible" comes from the Greek word *biblia,* which means "books." The Bible contains 66 books, which were written by about 40 men between 1400 B.C. and A.D. 100. Other names that are given to the Bible are the Scripture(s) and the Word of God.

The Old Testament has 39 books, which were written in the Hebrew language. The New Testament has 27 books, which were written in the Greek language. We read the Bible in an English translation. Some of the more reliable translations are the King James Version (KJV), the New International Version (NIV), the New King James Version (NKJV), An American Translation (AAT), and the New American Standard Bible (NASB).

The books of the Old Testament are

Historical Books

Genesis	(JEN-eh-sis)	Gen. or Ge
Exodus	(EK-suh-duss)	Exod. or Ex
Leviticus	(le-VI-tee-kuss)	Lev. or Lev
Numbers	(NUM-burrs)	Num. or Nu
Deuteronomy	(do-turr-ON-oh-mee)	Deut. or Dt
Joshua	(JOSH-uh-ah)	Josh. or Jos
Judges	(JUJ-es)	Judg. or Jdg
Ruth	(ROOTH)	Ruth or Ru
1 and 2 Samuel	(SAM-you-ell)	Sam. or Sa
1 and 2 Kings	(KINGZ)	Kings or Ki
1 and 2 Chronicles	(KRON-ih-kulz)	Chron. or Ch
Ezra	(EZZ-ruh)	Ezra or Ezr
Nehemiah	(knee-uh-MY-uh)	Neh. or Ne
Esther	(ESS-tur)	Esther or Est

Poetical Books

Job	(JOBE) or (JOHB)	Job
Psalms	(SAHMS)	Ps. or Ps
Proverbs	(PROV-urbz)	Prov. or Pr
Ecclesiastes	(eh-KLEE-zih-AS-teez)	Eccles. or Ecc
Song of Songs, or Song of Solomon	(SOLL-uh-mun)	Song of Sol. or SS

Prophetical Books

Isaiah	(eye-ZAY-uh)	Isa. or Isa
Jeremiah	(jerr-uh-MY-uh)	Jer. or Jer
Lamentations	(lamb-en-TAY-shunz)	Lam. or La
Ezekiel	(ee-ZEEK-ih-ell)	Ezek. or Eze
Daniel	(DAN-yell)	Dan. or Da
Hosea	(hoe-ZEE-uh)	Hos. or Hos
Joel	(JOE-ull)	Joel
Amos	(AY-muss)	Amos or Am
Obadiah	(oh-bah-DIE-uh)	Obad. or Ob
Jonah	(JOE-nuh)	Jon. or Jnh
Micah	(MY-kuh)	Mic. or Mic
Nahum	(NAY-hum)	Nah. or Na
Habakkuk	(ha-BACK-uk)	Hab. or Hab
Zephaniah	(zef-uh-NIGH-uh)	Zeph. or Zep
Haggai	(HAG-eye)	Hag. or Hag
Zechariah	(zeck-uh-RYE-uh)	Zech. or Zec
Malachi	(MAH-luh-kigh)	Mal. or Mal

The books of the New Testament are

Historical Books

Matthew	(MATH-you)	Matt. or Mt
Mark	(MARK)	Mark or Mk
Luke	(LOOHK)	Luke or Lk
John	(JON)	John or Jn
Acts	(ACTS)	Acts or Ac

Epistles

Romans	(ROW-manz)	Rom. or Ro
1 and 2 Corinthians	(core-IN-thee-enz)	Cor. or Co
Galatians	(gah-LAY-shunz)	Gal. or Gal
Ephesians	(ee-FEE-shunz)	Eph. or Eph
Philippians	(fil-LIP-ih-unz)	Phil. or Php
Colossians	(cul-LOSH-unz)	Col. or Col
1 and 2 Thessalonians	(thess-ah-LOAN-ee-unz)	Thess. or Th
1 and 2 Timothy	(TIM-uh-thee)	Tim. or Ti
Titus	(TIE-tuss)	Titus or Tit
Philemon	(fil-LEE-mun)	Philem. or Phm
Hebrews	(HE-bruz)	Heb. or Heb
James	(JAMZ)	James or Jas
1 and 2 Peter	(PEA-tur)	Pet. or Pe

| 1, 2, and 3 John | (JON) | John or Jn |
| Jude | (JEWD) | Jude |

Prophetical Book

| Revelation | (rev-eh-LAY-shun) | Rev. or Rev |

The Bible Is God's Word

9. What is the Bible?

21) Mark 7:10,11,13. Moses said . . . But you say . . . Thus you nullify the *word of God.*

22) 1 Thessalonians 2:13. When you received the word of God, which you heard from us, you accepted it *not as the word of men,* but as *it actually is, the word of God.*

23) 1 Peter 1:23. You have been born again, not of perishable seed, but of imperishable, through the *living* and enduring word of God.

24) Hebrews 4:12. The word of God is *living* and *active. Sharper* than any double-edged sword, it *penetrates* even to dividing soul and spirit, joints and marrow; it *judges* the thoughts and attitudes of the heart.

9. The Bible is the living and powerful Word of God.

10. How can all the words of the Bible be God's Word if human writers wrote them?

25) 2 Peter 1:21. Prophecy *never* had its origin *in the will of man,* but men spoke from God as they were *carried along by the Holy Spirit.*

26) 2 Samuel 23:2. *The Spirit* of the LORD *spoke through me; his word* was on my tongue.

27) John 14:26. The Counselor, the Holy Spirit, whom the Father will send in my name, will *teach* you *all things* and will *remind* you of *everything* I have said to you.

28) 1 Corinthians 2:12,13. We have not received the spirit of the world but the Spirit who is from God, that we may understand what God has freely given us. This is what we speak, *not in words* taught us by human wisdom *but in words* taught by the Spirit.

29) 2 Timothy 3:16. All Scripture is *God-breathed.*

10. All the words of the Bible are God's Word because the Holy Spirit taught the human writers not only the thoughts but even the words they wrote. (verbal inspiration)

11. Of what are we assured by the fact that the Bible is God's Word?

30) Numbers 23:19. God is not a man, that he should lie.

31) John 10:35. [Jesus answered them,] "The Scripture *cannot be broken.*"

32) John 17:17. Your word is truth.

11a. The fact that the Bible is God's Word assures us that the Bible has no errors but is true in everything it says.

33) Psalm 119:114,116. You are my refuge and my shield; I have put *my hope in your word.* Sustain me according to *your promise,* and I will live; do not let my hopes be dashed.

34) Numbers 23:19. God is not a man, that he should lie, nor a son of man, that he should change his mind. Does he speak and then not act? *Does he promise and not fulfill?*

35) 1 Corinthians 2:4,5. My message and my preaching were not with wise and persuasive words, but with a demonstration of the Spirit's power, so that your faith might *not rest on men's wisdom, but on God's power.*

11b. The fact that the Bible is God's Word assures us that we can trust all the promises of the Bible because we know God will keep them.

12. What does God forbid anyone to do with the Bible since it is his Word?

36) Deuteronomy 4:2. *Do not add* to what I command you.

37) Revelation 22:18. I warn everyone who hears the words of the prophecy of this book: If *anyone adds anything* to them, God will add to him the plagues described in this book.

38) Jeremiah 14:14. Then the LORD said to me, "The prophets are prophesying lies in my name. I have not sent them or appointed them or spoken to them. They are prophesying to you *false visions,* divinations, idolatries and the *delusions of their own minds.*"

VERBAL INSPIRATION

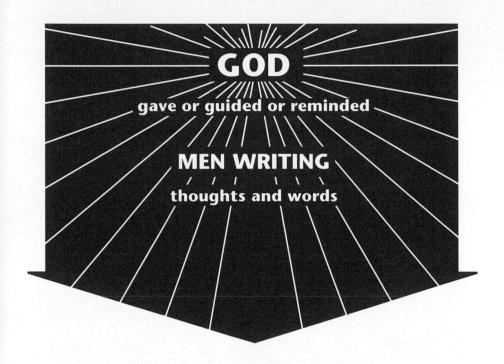

GOD

gave or guided or reminded

MEN WRITING

thoughts and words

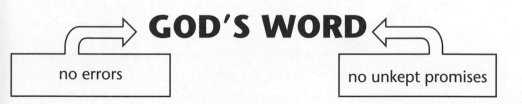

no errors

GOD'S WORD

no unkept promises

Don't Add!

Don't Subtract!

Don't Change the Meaning!

39) Matthew 15:9. They worship me in vain; their teachings are but *rules taught by men.*

40) 2 Peter 2:3. In their greed these teachers will exploit you with *stories they have made up.*

12a. God forbids anyone to add his own ideas, visions, or teachings to the Bible.

41) Deuteronomy 4:2. Do not add to what I command you and *do not subtract* from it.

42) Revelation 22:19. If anyone *takes words away from* this book of prophecy, God will take away from him his share in the tree of life.

43) 2 Timothy 4:3. The time will come when men will *not put up with sound doctrine.* Instead, to suit their own desires, they will gather around them a great number of teachers to say *what their itching ears want to hear.*

12b. God forbids anyone to subtract from the Bible by leaving out what he doesn't want to believe or teach.

44) John 10:35. The Scripture *cannot be broken.*

45) Jude 4. They are godless men, who *change* the grace of our God into a license for immorality and deny Jesus Christ our only Sovereign and Lord.

46) 2 Peter 3:16. His letters contain some things that are hard to understand, which ignorant and unstable people *distort,* as they do the other Scriptures, to their own destruction.

47) 2 Peter 1:16. We did not follow *cleverly invented stories* when we told you about the power and coming of our Lord Jesus Christ.

12c. God forbids anyone to change the Bible by twisting its meaning or by saying that it is a collection of cleverly invented stories.

The Two Main Bible Teachings

13. What are the two main Bible teachings?

48) John 1:17. The *law* was given through Moses; grace and truth came through Jesus Christ.

49) Romans 1:16. I am not ashamed of the *gospel,* because it is the power of God for the salvation of everyone who believes.

13. The two main Bible teachings are the law and the gospel.

14. What does God teach us by the law?

50) Matthew 19:17-19. If you want to enter life, obey the *commandments.* . . . *Do not* murder, *do not* commit adultery, *do not* steal, *do not* give false testimony, *honor* your father and mother, and *love* your neighbor as yourself.

51) James 2:8. If you really keep *the royal law* found in Scripture, "Love your neighbor as yourself," you are *doing right.*

52) Romans 7:7. I *would not have known* what sin was except through the law. For I *would not have known* what coveting really was if the law had not said, "*Do not* covet."

14. By the law God teaches us what he wants us to do and not to do.

15. When we examine our lives according to God's law, what else does the law teach us?

53) Galatians 3:10. Cursed is everyone who does not *continue* to do *everything* written in the Book of the Law.

54) Romans 3:22,23. There is no difference, for *all* have sinned and *fall short* of the glory of God.

55) Romans 3:20. Therefore no one will be declared righteous in his sight by observing the law; rather, through the law we *become conscious of sin.*

56) Romans 6:23. *The wages* of sin is *death.*

57) Matthew 25:41-46. (Jesus says that those who are cursed for their sins will be punished eternally in hell.)

15. When we examine our lives according to God's law, it also teaches us that we are all sinners who deserve God's punishment of death and damnation.

16. What does God teach us by the gospel?

58) Colossians 2:13,14. When you were dead in your sins . . . God made you alive with Christ. *He forgave us all our sins,* having canceled the written code, with its regulations, that was against

God's Word
TEACHES

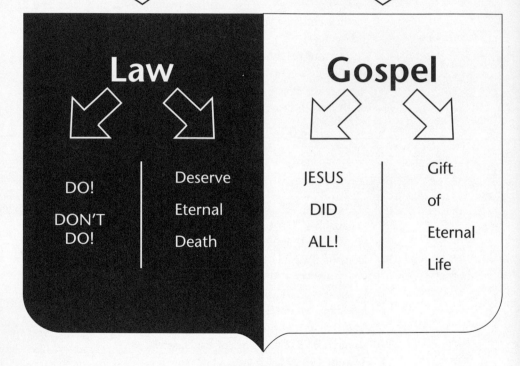

Law

DO!
DON'T
DO!

Deserve
Eternal
Death

Gospel

JESUS
DID
ALL!

Gift
of
Eternal
Life

**JESUS IS OUR
ONLY HOPE
OF
SALVATION**

us and that stood opposed to us; he took it away, *nailing it to the cross.*

59) Luke 2:10,11. The angel said to them, "Do not be afraid. I bring you *good news* of great joy that will be *for all the people.* Today in the town of David *a Savior* has been born to you; he is Christ the Lord."

60) John 3:16. God so *loved the world* that he *gave his one and only Son,* that whoever believes in him shall not perish but have eternal life.

16a. By the gospel God teaches us the good news that in his love he sent Jesus to take away the sins of all people.

61) John 3:16. God so loved the world that he gave his one and only Son, that *whoever believes* in him shall not perish but have *eternal life.*

62) Romans 1:16. I am not ashamed of the gospel, because it is the power of God for the *salvation* of everyone who believes.

16b. By the gospel God teaches us that everyone who believes in Jesus has eternal life and salvation.

17. What, then, is the chief purpose of the Bible?

63) 2 Timothy 3:15. From infancy you have known the holy Scriptures, which are *able to make you wise for salvation* through faith in Christ Jesus.

64) John 20:31. These are written *that you may believe* that Jesus is the Christ, the Son of God, and *that by believing you may have life* in his name.

65) John 5:39. You diligently study the Scriptures because you think that by them you possess eternal life. These are the Scriptures that *testify about me.*

66) Ephesians 2:20. *[You are] built* on the foundation of the apostles and prophets, with Christ Jesus himself as the *chief cornerstone.*

67) Romans 15:4. For everything that was written in the past was written to teach us, so that through endurance and the *encouragement* of the Scriptures *we might have hope.*

17. The chief purpose of the Bible is to lead all people to know and believe in Jesus as their only hope of salvation.

The Ten
Commandments

THE LAW

The Giving of the Law

18. How does God give his law to all people?

> 68) Romans 2:14,15. When Gentiles, who do not have the law, *do by nature* things required by the law, they are a law for themselves, even though they do not have the law, since they show that the requirements of the law are *written on their hearts.*

18. God gives his law to all people by writing it on their hearts. (natural law)

19. Why does God also give every person a conscience?

> 69) Romans 2:14,15. When Gentiles, who do not have the law, do *by nature* things required by the law . . . they show that the requirements of the law are written on their hearts, their consciences also *bearing witness,* and their thoughts now accusing, now even defending them.

19. God gives every person a conscience as a voice in him which bears witness to God's law.

20. Why isn't a person's conscience completely dependable?

> 70) Romans 1:21. Although they knew God . . . their thinking became futile and their foolish *hearts were darkened.*
>
> 71) Ephesians 4:18,19. They are darkened in their understanding and separated from the life of God because of the ignorance that is in them *due to the hardening of their hearts.* Having *lost all sensitivity,* they have given themselves over to sensuality so as to *indulge in every kind of impurity,* with a continual lust for more.

20a. A person's conscience is not completely dependable because it may be so hardened by sin that it no longer bothers him when he sins.

72) 1 Corinthians 8:7. Some people are still so accustomed to idols that when they eat such food they think of it as having been sacrificed to an idol, and since their *conscience is weak,* it is defiled.

73) Romans 14:2. One man's faith allows him to eat everything, but another man, whose *faith is weak,* eats only vegetables.

20b. A person's conscience is not completely dependable because it may tell him something is a sin which God doesn't say is a sin.

21. Why, then, did God give us his law a second way?

74) Romans 7:7. *I would not have known* what sin was except through the law. For I would not have known what coveting really was if the law had not said, *"Do not covet."*

75) Romans 2:18. *You know his will* and approve of what is superior because you are instructed by the law.

21. God gave us his law a second way so that we would know exactly what his will is.

22. What was the second way God gave us his law?

76) Exodus 20. (God gave the law at Mount Sinai.)

77) Deuteronomy 5:22. These are the commandments *the LORD* proclaimed in a loud voice to your whole assembly there on the mountain from out of the fire, the cloud and the deep darkness; and he added nothing more. Then he *wrote them* on two stone tablets and gave them to me.

78) John 1:17. The law was given through Moses.

79) Romans 13:8-10. (Paul writes about what God wants us to do to fulfill his law.)

22. God gave us his law the second way by having it written in the Bible. (written law)

The Summary of the Law

23. What brief summary of the law did God give us in the Bible?

80) Deuteronomy 5:1-22. (Especially verse 22: These are the commandments *the LORD proclaimed* in a loud voice to your whole

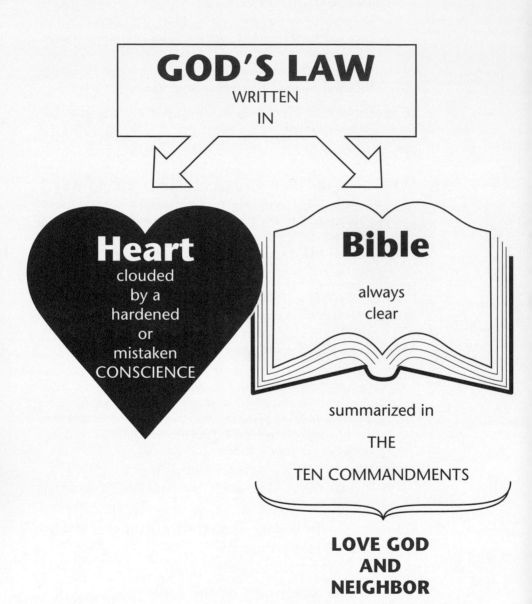

assembly there on the mountain from out of the fire, the cloud and the deep darkness; and *he added nothing more.*)

81) Deuteronomy 10:4. The LORD wrote on these tablets what he had written before, *the Ten Commandments* he had proclaimed to you on the mountain, out of the fire, on the day of the assembly. And the LORD gave them to me.

23. God gave us the Ten Commandments as a summary of his law.

The Law of Moses

On Mt. Sinai God gave three kinds of laws to Moses for the people of Israel. He gave the *civil law* to govern them as a nation. For example, the civil law established the punishment for crimes such as injury to another person or damage to another person's property (see Exodus 21:22).

God also gave Israel the *ceremonial law.* These were the laws that told the people when, where, and how they were to worship God. The laws about priests, the sacrifices, the sabbath days, the tabernacle—all these were the ceremonial laws. The ceremonial laws served as types or pictures that pointed ahead to the promised Savior.

Thirdly, God gave Israel the *moral law.* God had written the moral law in man's heart already at creation because it is God's will for all people of all time. God gave the moral law to the people of Israel in the form of the Ten Commandments. In these Ten Commandments God told the people of Israel how his holy will for all people applied in a special way to them as his chosen people.

In the New Testament God clearly says that the law as he gave it to Moses on Mt. Sinai is no longer in effect (cf. Colossians 2:16,17; Galatians 3:23-25; Galatians 5:1). Why, then, do we use the Ten Commandments? Remember that in the Old Testament the civil and ceremonial laws were special laws made by God *only for Israel* while the Ten Commandments were a special form of God's moral law, his holy will *for all people.* For this reason the basic content of the Ten

Commandments is repeated in the New Testament though not always in the same words or in the same order in which God gave it on Mt. Sinai (cf. Matthew 19:18; Romans 13:8-10; Galatians 5:19).

Luther chose to use the form of the Ten Commandments as given on Mt. Sinai because it is the simplest summary we have in the Bible of God's moral law. He felt this form would be the easiest one to use in teaching God's moral law to children. Therefore, we use Moses' wording of the Ten Commandments, but we need to keep in mind that this wording was the special form in which God gave his summary of the moral law to the Old Testament people. This is especially important to remember in the study of the Third Commandment.

24. What is the simplest summary of God's law?

82) Matthew 22:37-40. Jesus replied: "'Love the Lord your God with all your heart and with all your soul and with all your mind.' This is the *first and greatest* commandment. And the *second is like it:* 'Love your neighbor as yourself.' All the Law and the Prophets hang on these two commandments."

83) Romans 13:9,10. The commandments, "Do not commit adultery," "Do not murder," "Do not steal," "Do not covet," and whatever other commandment there may be, are summed up in this one rule: "Love your neighbor as yourself." Love does no harm to its neighbor. Therefore *love is the fulfillment of the law.*

24. "Love God and your neighbor!" is the simplest summary of God's law.

Obeying the Law

25. Of what does God remind us when he introduces his commandments with the words "I am the LORD your God" (Exodus 20:2)?

84) Psalm 95:6,7. Come, let us bow down in worship, let us kneel before *the LORD our Maker;* for he is our God and we are the people of his pasture.

85) Isaiah 43:11. I, even I, am *the LORD,* and apart from me there is no *savior.*

86) 1 John 4:8,9. *God is love.* This is how God showed his love among us: He sent his one and only Son into the world that we might live through him.

25. When God introduces his commandments with these words, he reminds us that it is our loving Maker and Savior who gave us these commandments.

26. Why does God remind us that our loving Maker and Savior gave us these commandments?

87) 1 John 4:19. We love because *he first loved us.*

88) Ephesians 5:1,2. Be imitators of God, therefore, *as dearly loved children* and live a life of love.

89) 1 John 5:3. This is *love for God: to obey* his commands. And his commands are *not burdensome.*

90) Psalm 119:47. I *delight in your commands* because I love them.

26. God reminds us of this to make us willing and glad to obey his commandments.

27. Why is it wrong to think that obeying God's commandments makes slaves out of us and takes all the fun out of life?

91) Psalm 19:7,8,11. The statutes of the LORD are trustworthy, *making wise the simple.* The precepts of the LORD are right, *giving joy to the heart.* By them is your servant *warned;* in keeping them there is *great reward.*

92) Psalm 119:14,35,45. *I rejoice* in following your statutes as one rejoices in great riches. Direct me in the path of your commands, for there *I find delight.* I will *walk about in freedom,* for I have sought out your precepts.

93) Matthew 5:3-10. (In the Beatitudes Jesus shows how obedience to God's will is the way of true happiness.)

94) Genesis 3:1-6. (The devil deceived Eve into thinking that disobedience to God's command would bring happiness.)

95) John 8:34. Jesus replied, "I tell you the truth, *everyone who sins* is a *slave to sin.*"

27. It is wrong to think that God's commandments make slaves of us because they really show us the way of wisdom, freedom, and happiness in our lives.

Obeying God's Law

Because God is our loving Maker and Savior

GIVE WILLING AND GLAD OBEDIENCE!

Because God seeks our good

OBEDIENCE IS THE WAY TO TRUE FREEDOM AND HAPPINESS!

Because God is holy

OBEY PERFECTLY!

28. How does God want us to obey his commandments?

96) Matthew 5:48. *Be perfect,* therefore, as your heavenly Father is perfect.

97) 1 Peter 1:15,16. Just as he who called you is holy, so *be holy in all you do;* for it is written: "Be holy, because I am holy."

28. God wants us to obey his commandments perfectly.

29. When do we fail to obey God's commandments perfectly?

98) James 4:17. Anyone, then, who knows the good he ought to do and *doesn't do it,* sins.

29a. We fail to obey perfectly when we don't do something that God wants us to do. (sin of omission)

99) Leviticus 5:17. If a person sins and *does what is forbidden* in any of the LORD's commands, even though he does not know it, he is guilty and will be held responsible.

100) 1 John 3:4. Everyone who sins breaks the law.

29b. We fail to obey perfectly when we do something that God forbids. (sin of commission)

30. Who only has obeyed God's commandments perfectly?

101) Romans 3:12. All have turned away, they have together become worthless; there is no one who does good, *not even one.*

102) Hebrews 4:14,15. We have a great high priest who has gone through the heavens, Jesus the Son of God. . . . we have one who has been *tempted in every way,* just as we are—yet *was without sin.*

30. Jesus alone has obeyed God's commandments perfectly.

The Purpose of the Law

31. What purpose does God's law serve in the outward life of all people?

103) 1 Timothy 1:9,10. We also know that law is made not for the righteous but for lawbreakers and rebels, the ungodly and sin-

49

ful, the unholy and irreligious; for those who kill their fathers or mothers, for murderers, for adulterers and perverts, for slave traders and liars and perjurers.

104) Romans 2:14. When Gentiles, who do not have the law, do by nature things required by the law, *they are a law for themselves.*

105) Psalm 119:120. My flesh *trembles in fear of you;* I stand in awe of your laws.

106) Deuteronomy 4:24. The LORD your God is *a consuming fire.*

31. God's law helps to preserve order in the world by keeping the wicked actions of all people within bounds. (the law as a curb)

32. What purpose does God's law serve in the hearts of all people?

107) Romans 3:19,20. Now we know that whatever the law says, it says to those who are under the law, *so that every mouth may be silenced* and the whole world held accountable to God. . . . through the law *we become conscious of sin.*

108) Romans 7:7. I would *not have known what sin was* except through the law. For I would not have known what coveting really was if the law had not said, "Do not covet."

109) Luke 18:13. But the tax collector stood at a distance. He would not even look up to heaven, but beat his breast and said, "God, *have mercy on me, a sinner."*

32. God's law shows all people their sin and their need of a Savior. (the law as a mirror)

33. What purpose does God's law also serve for Christians living in a sinful world?

110) 2 Corinthians 5:15. [Jesus] died for all, that those who live should *no longer live for themselves but for him* who died for them and was raised again.

111) Romans 12:1,2. Therefore, I urge you, brothers, in view of God's mercy, to *offer your bodies as living sacrifices,* holy and pleasing to God—this is your spiritual act of worship. *Do not conform any longer to the pattern of this world,* but be transformed by the renewing of your mind. Then you will be able to *test and approve what God's will is*—his good, pleasing, and perfect will.

The Purpose
of the
LAW

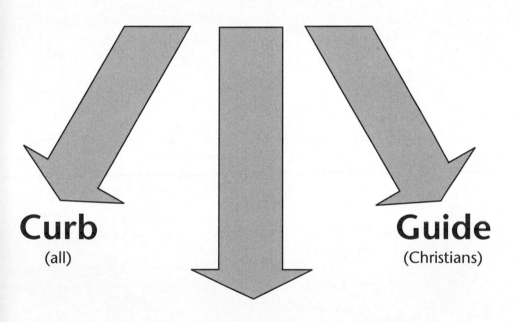

Curb
(all)

Mirror
(all)

Guide
(Christians)

112) Psalm 119:9. How can a young man *keep his way pure?* By living according to your word.

113) Psalm 119:105. *Your word* is a lamp to my feet and a light for my path.

33. God's law tells Christians, surrounded by a sinful world, the way of life that is pleasing to God. (the law as a guide)

THE FIRST COMMANDMENT
(God's Glory)

You shall have no other gods.

What does this mean?

We should fear, love, and trust in God above all things.

34. What does God teach us about his glory in the First Commandment?

114) Isaiah 42:8. I am the LORD; that is my name! I will not give *my glory* to another or my praise to idols.

115) Isaiah 45:21. There is no God apart from me, a righteous God and a Savior; there is *none but me.*

116) Matthew 4:10. Worship the Lord your God, and *serve him only.*

34. God teaches us that he wants us to give glory to him above anyone or anything else.

35. How do we give glory to God above all things?

117) Daniel 3:1-18. (The three men went into the fiery furnace rather than worship the image Nebuchadnezzar set up.)

118) Genesis 39:1-9. (Joseph obeyed God rather than Potiphar's wife. Note especially verse 9, "How then could I do such a wicked thing and sin against God?")

119) Proverbs 8:13. To fear the LORD is *to hate evil.*

120) Psalm 119:11. I have hidden *your word in my heart* that I might not sin against you.

121) Psalm 86:11. Teach me your way, O LORD, and I will walk in your truth; give me *an undivided heart,* that I may fear your name.

35a. We give glory to God above all things by placing his word and command above the word and command of anyone else. (fear God above all things)

122) Hebrews 11:24-26. (God was more important to Moses than the fame or riches of Egypt.)

123) Genesis 22:1-19. (God was dearer to Abraham than his only son, Isaac.)

124) Matthew 22:37. Love the Lord your God with all your heart and with all your soul and with all your mind.

125) Psalm 73:25. Whom have I in heaven but you? And earth has nothing *I desire besides you.*

35b. We give glory to God above all things by considering him more dear to us than anyone or anything else. (love God above all things)

126) Genesis 13,14. (When Abraham gave Lot the first choice of the land and rescued him, Abraham showed his trust in God.)

127) Daniel 6:1-23. (Daniel trusted God to protect him in the lions' den. Note especially verse 23, "No wound was found on him, because he had trusted in his God.")

128) Daniel 3:1-18. (The three men trusted God to protect them in the fiery furnace. Note especially verse 17, "The God we serve is able to save us from it.")

129) 1 Samuel 17:32-50. (David trusted the Lord to give him the victory over Goliath. Note especially verses 37 and 45.)

130) Psalm 37:5,40. *Commit your way* to the LORD; *trust in him.* . . . The LORD helps them and delivers them . . . because they *take refuge in him.*

131) Isaiah 50:10. Let him who walks in the dark, who has no light, trust in the name of the LORD and *rely on his God.*

132) Psalm 124:8. *Our help* is in the name of the LORD, the Maker of heaven and earth.

35c. We give glory to God above all things by relying on him for help more than on anyone or anything else. (trust God above all things)

36. According to the First Commandment, how do people sin openly against God's will?

133) Exodus 32. (Israel worshiped the golden calf. Note especially verse 31, "Oh, what a great sin these people have committed! They have made themselves gods of gold.")

134) 1 Kings 18:17-39. (Ahab led Israel into Baal worship. Note especially verse 18, "You have abandoned the LORD's commands and have followed the Baals.")

135) Exodus 20:4,5. You shall not make for yourself an idol *in the form of anything* in heaven above or on the earth beneath or in the waters below. You shall not bow down to them or worship them.

136) Romans 1:23. *[They] exchanged the glory* of the immortal God for images made to look like mortal man and birds and animals and reptiles.

137) 1 John 5:21. Dear children, keep yourselves from *idols*.

36a. People sin openly against God's will when they give glory to idols as their god. (open idolatry)

138) John 8:42. Jesus said to them, "*If God* were *your Father,* you would *love me,* for I came from God and now am here."

139) John 5:22,23. The Father . . . has entrusted all judgment to the Son, that all may honor the Son *just as* they honor the Father. He who does not honor the Son does not honor the Father, who sent him.

140) 1 John 2:23. No one who *denies the Son* has the Father; whoever acknowledges the Son has the Father also.

36b. People sin openly against God's will when they try to give glory to the Father without also giving equal glory to Jesus. (open idolatry)

37. According to the First Commandment, how do people sin secretly against God's will?

141) Luke 12:15-21. (The rich fool was more concerned about storing up things for himself than about God.)

142) Matthew 19:16-22. (The rich young man loved his possessions more than following Jesus.)

143) 1 John 2:15. Do not love *the world or anything in the world.* If anyone loves the world, the love of the Father is not in him.

144) Psalm 62:10. Though your riches increase, do not *set your heart on them*.

145) Matthew 10:37. Anyone who loves his father or mother *more than me* is not worthy of me; anyone who loves his son or daughter *more than me* is not worthy of me.

God's
GLORY

Do!

— FEAR
— LOVE
— TRUST

} GOD
ABOVE
ALL
THINGS

Don't
Do!

— OPEN
  IDOLATRY
— SECRET
  IDOLATRY

146) Proverbs 3:5. Trust in the LORD with *all your heart* and lean not on *your own understanding.*

147) Jeremiah 17:5. Cursed is the one who *trusts in man,* who depends on flesh for his strength and whose *heart turns away* from the LORD.

37. People sin secretly against God's will when someone or something takes first place in their hearts instead of God. (secret idolatry)

38. How does the First Commandment serve as a mirror for us?

148) Exodus 14:5-12; 16:1-8. (The people of Israel did not always trust God to protect them and to provide for them.)

149) Matthew 26:69-75. (Peter did not always fear God above men.)

150) 1 John 1:8. *If we claim to be without sin,* we deceive ourselves and the truth is not in us.

38. The First Commandment shows us our sins because we have not always given God first place in our lives.

39. How did Jesus save us from our sins against the First Commandment?

151) Matthew 4:1-10. (When he was tempted, Jesus always put God first.)

152) Matthew 17:5. This is my Son, whom I love; *with him I am well pleased.*

153) Romans 5:19. Just as through the disobedience of the one man the many were made sinners, so also *through the obedience of the one* man the many will be made righteous.

39a. Jesus saved us by obeying the First Commandment perfectly for us.

154) 1 Peter 3:18. Christ *died for sins* once for all, the righteous for the unrighteous, to bring you to God.

39b. Jesus saved us by dying to take away all our sins.

40. How does the First Commandment serve as a guideline for us?

155) Colossians 3:17. Whatever you do, whether in word or deed, do it all in the name of the Lord Jesus, *giving thanks* to God the Father through him.

156) 1 Samuel 12:24. Be sure to fear the LORD and serve him faithfully *with all your heart;* consider *what great things he has done for you.*

40. The First Commandment shows us that God wants us to thank him for his goodness by fearing, loving, and trusting in him above all things.

THE SECOND COMMANDMENT
(God's Name)

You shall not misuse the name of the Lord your God.

What does this mean?

We should fear and love God that we do not use his name to curse, swear, lie, or deceive, or use witchcraft, but call upon God's name in every trouble, pray, praise, and give thanks.

41. What is God's name?

157) Genesis 17:1. I am *God Almighty.*

158) Isaiah 42:8. I am *the LORD;* that is my name!

159) Matthew 1:21. You are to give him the name *Jesus.*

160) 2 Corinthians 13:14. May the grace of the *Lord Jesus Christ,* and the love of *God,* and the fellowship of the *Holy Spirit* be with you all.

41a. God's name is every expression that God uses to refer to himself. (God, God the Almighty, Lord, Jesus Christ, Holy Spirit, etc.)

161) Exodus 34:5-7. (Note all the things God wants Moses to remember about him when he hears God's name.)

162) John 17:6-8. I have revealed you [Greek: *your name*] to those whom you gave me out of the world. . . . *Now they know* that everything you have given me comes from you. *For I gave them the words you gave me* and they accepted them.

41b. God's name is everything God has revealed to us about himself in his Word.

42. For what purpose did God reveal his name to us?

163) Psalm 54:6. I will praise your name, O LORD, for *it is good.*

164) Exodus 20:24. Wherever I cause my name to be honored, I will come to you and *bless you.*

165) Romans 10:13. Everyone who calls on the name of the Lord will *be saved.*

166) Proverbs 18:10. The name of the LORD is a strong tower; the righteous run to it and *are safe.*

167) Exodus 20:7. The LORD will not hold *anyone* guiltless who *misuses* his name.

42. God revealed his name to us so that by its use he might bless and save us.

43. Why is cursing, therefore, a sinful misuse of God's name?

168) 2 Samuel 16:5-14. (Shimei cursed David when David fled from Absalom. In verse 11 note how the purpose of Shimei's cursing is compared to Absalom's purpose.)

169) Numbers 22:6-12. (Balak wanted Balaam to curse Israel so that he could defeat God's people.)

170) James 3:10. Out of the same mouth come praise and *cursing.* My brothers, *this should not be.*

171) Romans 12:14. Bless those who persecute you; bless and *do not curse.*

43. Cursing is a sin because it is using God's name to wish evil on someone or something.

44. What is swearing by God's name?

172) Matthew 26:63,64. The high priest said to him, "I charge you *under oath* by the living God: Tell us if you are the Christ, the Son of God." "Yes, it is as you say," Jesus replied.

173) Hebrews 6:16. Men swear *by someone greater than themselves,* and the oath *confirms what is said* and puts an end to all argument.

44. Swearing is using God's name to assure someone that we are telling the truth.

45. When is swearing a sinful misuse of God's name?

174) 1 Kings 21:8-14. (Jezebel murdered Naboth by the lies of two who testified against him.)

175) Matthew 26:69-75. (Note verse 74, where Peter swore to back up his denials of Jesus.)

176) Leviticus 19:12. Do not *swear falsely* by my name and *so profane* the name of your God.

45a. Swearing is a sin when we use God's name to tell a lie. (false swearing)

177) Matthew 5:33-37. (Rather than swearing by all kinds of things, Jesus says, "Simply let your 'Yes' be 'Yes,' and your 'No,' 'No'; *anything beyond this* comes from the evil one.")

178) James 5:12. Above all, my brothers, do not swear—not by heaven or by earth or by anything else. Let your "Yes" be yes, and your "No," no, or you will be condemned.

45b. Swearing is a sin when it is unnecessary. (needless swearing)

179) Mark 6:21-28. (Herod swore to do something even though he did not know what it would be.)

45c. Swearing is a sin when we don't know what we are promising to do. (swearing in uncertain things)

46. How do people use God's name to lie? (See Question 12.)

180) Jeremiah 14:14. The prophets are *prophesying lies in my name.* I have not sent them or appointed them or spoken to them. They are prophesying to you false visions, divinations, idolatries and the *delusions of their own minds.*

181) Jeremiah 23:31. I am against the prophets who *wag their own tongues and yet declare,* "The LORD declares."

182) Matthew 15:9. They worship me in vain; *their teachings* are but *rules taught by men.*

46. People use God's name to lie when they use it to cover up their own false teachings (see Question 12). (false prophets or false teachers)

47. How do people use God's name to deceive?

183) Acts 5:1-11. (Ananias and Sapphira pretended to be giving a gift in love for God's name.)

184) Matthew 23:25-28. (Jesus condemned the hypocrisy of the teachers of the law and the Pharisees.)

185) Matthew 15:7,8. You hypocrites! Isaiah was right when he prophesied about you: "These people *honor me with their lips,* but their *hearts are far from me.*"

47. People use God's name to deceive when they use it to cover up their unbelieving hearts. (hypocrites)

48. How do people misuse God's name in using witchcraft?

186) Acts 13:6-12. (Paul showed that Elymas, the sorcerer, was serving the devil.)

187) Deuteronomy 18:10-12. Let no one be found among you . . . who practices divination or sorcery, interprets omens, engages in witchcraft, or casts spells, or who is a medium or spiritist or who consults the dead. Anyone who does these things is *detestable to the LORD.*

188) Matthew 7:22,23. Many will say to me on that day, "Lord, Lord, did we not prophesy *in your name,* and in your name drive out demons and perform many miracles?" Then I will tell them plainly, "I never knew you. Away from me, you *evildoers!*"

48a. People misuse God's name in using witchcraft because they depend on the power of the devil.

189) 1 Samuel 28:7-25. (King Saul sought the help of the witch of Endor.)

190) Leviticus 19:31. *Do not turn to* mediums *or seek out* spiritists, for you will be defiled by them. I am the LORD your God.

48b. People misuse God's name in using witchcraft because they seek the help of those who do things by the power of the devil.

49. How does God want us to use his name?

191) Psalm 50:15. *Call upon me* in the *day of trouble;* I will deliver you, and you will honor me.

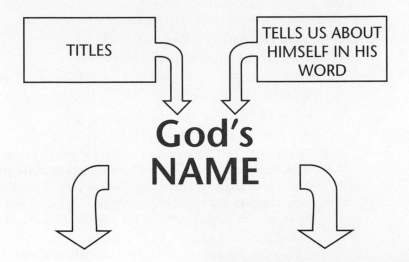

| TITLES | | TELLS US ABOUT HIMSELF IN HIS WORD |

God's NAME

Do!	**Don't Do!**
— Call on it in trouble	— Curse
— Pray regularly	— Swear
— Praise him to others	— Lie by it
— Give him thanks	— Deceive by it
	— Use witchcraft

192) Matthew 8:23-27. (The disciples called on Jesus in time of trouble.)

49a. God wants·us to call on his name in times of trouble.

193) 1 Thessalonians 5:17. Pray *continually.*

194) Daniel 6:10,11. (Daniel prayed regularly.)

195) John 16:23. My Father will give you *whatever* you ask *in my name.*

49b. God wants us to pray in his name regularly.

196) Psalm 145:2,10-12. *Every day* I will praise you and *extol your name* for ever and ever. All you have made will praise you, O LORD; your saints will extol you. *They will tell* of the glory of your kingdom and speak of your might, *so that all men may know* of your mighty acts and the glorious splendor of your kingdom.

197) 1 Peter 2:9. You are a chosen people, a royal priesthood, a holy nation, a people belonging to God, that you may *declare the praises* of him who called you out of darkness into his wonderful light.

198) Acts 4:20. We *cannot help speaking about* what we have seen and heard.

49c. God wants us to use his name in telling others about his blessings. (praise)

199) Luke 17:11-19. (The one leper returned to thank Jesus for healing him.)

200) Psalm 118:1. *Give thanks* to the LORD, for he is good; his love endures forever.

201) Ephesians 5:19,20. *Sing* and make music in your heart to the Lord, *always giving thanks* to God the Father for everything, in the name of our Lord Jesus Christ.

49d. God wants us to use his name in giving thanks to him.

50. How does the Second Commandment serve as a mirror for us?

202) Matthew 26:74,75. (Peter realized he sinned by his cursing and swearing and his denials.)

203) James 3:9. With the tongue we praise our Lord and Father, and with it *we curse men,* who have been made in God's likeness.

204) James 5:12. Do not swear—not by heaven or by earth or by anything else. Let your "Yes" be yes, and your "No," no, or *you will be condemned.*

205) Luke 17:11-19. (Jesus was disappointed with the nine lepers who did not return to thank him.)

206) Matthew 10:32,33. Whoever acknowledges me before men, I will also acknowledge him before my Father in heaven. But whoever *disowns me before men,* I will disown him before my Father in heaven.

50. The Second Commandment shows us our sins because we have not always used God's name as he wants us to use it.

51. How did Jesus save us from our sins against the Second Commandment?

207) John 17:6-8,25,26. (Jesus made God's name known to all who would listen.)

208) Luke 6:12. Jesus went out to a mountainside to pray, and *spent the night praying to God.*

209) John 6:11. Jesus then took the loaves, *gave thanks,* and distributed to those who were seated.

210) 1 John 3:5. [Jesus] appeared so that he might take away our sins. And *in him is no sin.*

51a. Jesus saved us by obeying the Second Commandment perfectly for us.

211) 1 John 1:7. The *blood of Jesus,* his Son, *purifies us* from all sin.

51b. Jesus saved us by dying to purify us from every sin.

52. How does the Second Commandment serve as a guideline for us?

212) 1 Peter 2:9. *You are* a chosen people, a royal priesthood, a holy nation, a people belonging to God, *that you may* declare the praises of him who called you out of darkness into his wonderful light.

213) Philippians 4:6. In everything, by prayer and petition, *with thanksgiving,* present your requests to God.

214) Psalm 39:1. I said, "I will watch my ways and *keep my tongue from sin.*"

215) Psalm 145:1,2. I will exalt you, my God the King; I will praise your name for ever and ever. *Every day* I will praise you and extol your name for ever and ever.

52. The Second Commandment shows us that God wants us to thank him for his goodness by using his name in ways which are pleasing to him.

THE THIRD COMMANDMENT
(God's Word)

Remember the Sabbath day by keeping it holy.

What does this mean?

We should fear and love God that we do not despise preaching and his Word, but regard it as holy and gladly hear and learn it.

53. **According to the Third Commandment, what was God's special will for his Old Testament people?**

   216) Exodus 35:2. For six days, work is to be done, but the *seventh day* shall be your *holy day,* a Sabbath of *rest to the LORD.*

   217) Leviticus 23:3. There are six days when you may work, but the seventh day is a Sabbath of rest, a day of *sacred assembly.*

53. According to the Third Commandment, God wanted his Old Testament people to observe Saturday as a holy day of rest and worship. ("Sabbath" means "rest.")

54. **Why is this special will of God no longer in effect for us today?**

   218) Colossians 2:13,14,16,17. God made you alive with Christ. *He forgave us all our sins,* having *canceled the written code,* with its regulations. . . . Therefore *do not let anyone judge you* by what you eat or drink, or with regard to a religious festival, a New Moon celebration or a *Sabbath day.* These are *a shadow* of the things that were to come; *the reality,* however, is found in Christ.

   219) Matthew 11:28,29. Come to me, all you who are weary and burdened, and *I will give you rest.* Take my yoke upon you and learn from me, for I am gentle and humble in heart, and *you will find rest for your souls.*

54. This special will of God is no longer in effect since Christ fulfilled the Old Testament Sabbath by giving us the true rest, the forgiveness of sins.

55. According to the Third Commandment, what is the will of God that is still in effect for all people?

220) Acts 13:42-48. (Note especially verse 48. The Gentiles at Antioch accepted and honored God's Word.)

221) Acts 17:10-12. (The Bereans received God's Word with eagerness.)

222) Luke 8:4-15. (Note especially verse 15. By a parable Jesus teaches how God wants us to receive his Word in our hearts.)

223) Colossians 3:16. Let the word of Christ dwell in you.

224) John 5:24. Whoever *hears my word and believes* him who sent me has eternal life and will not be condemned; he has crossed over from death to life.

225) Hebrews 4:2,9-11. We also have had the gospel preached to us, just as they did. . . . There remains, then, a *Sabbath-rest* for the people of God; for anyone who enters *God's rest* also rests from his own work, just as God did from his. Let us, therefore, *make every effort* to enter that rest.

55. God wants all people to receive his Word eagerly because it tells about Jesus, who gives us God's true rest.

56. When are we guilty of despising God's Word?

226) Acts 13:42-50. (Note especially verses 45 and 50. The Jews at Antioch mocked and refused to hear the Word.)

227) Luke 10:16. He who listens to you listens to me; he who *rejects you rejects me.*

228) Hebrews 10:25. Let us not *give up meeting together,* as some are in the habit of doing.

229) John 8:47. He who belongs to God hears what God says. The reason you *do not hear* is that you do not belong to God.

56a. We are guilty of despising God's Word if we refuse to hear it.

230) Luke 14:16-24. (By the parable of the great banquet, Jesus warns against letting the things of the world keep us from accepting his invitation.)

231) Luke 8:14. (The cares and pleasures of the world like thorns can choke God's Word out of our lives.)

232) 1 John 2:15. Do not love the world or *anything in the world.* If anyone loves the world, the love of the Father is not in him.

56b. We are guilty of despising God's Word if we let anything in the world crowd it out of our lives.

233) Ecclesiastes 5:1. Guard your steps when you go to the house of God. Go near *to listen* rather than *to offer the sacrifice of fools,* who do not know that they do wrong.

234) Hebrews 4:2. The message *they heard* was of no value to them, because those who heard *did not combine it with faith.*

235) James 1:22-24. Do not *merely listen to the word,* and so deceive yourselves. Do what it says. Anyone who listens to the word but *does not do what it says* is like a man who looks at his face in a mirror and, after looking at himself, goes away and immediately forgets what he looks like.

236) 1 Samuel 15:1-23. (God rejected Saul as king because he did not do what God told him.)

56c. We are guilty of despising God's Word if we listen to it but don't believe it or don't do what it says.

57. How does God want us to regard his Word?

237) Romans 1:2. He promised . . . through his prophets in the *Holy* Scriptures.

238) Proverbs 30:5. *Every word* of God is *flawless.*

239) John 17:17. Your word is *truth.*

57. God wants us to regard his Word as holy and true.

58. How does God want us to use his Word?

240) 1 Samuel 3:1-18. (Eli taught Samuel to say, "Speak, LORD, for your servant is listening.")

241) Luke 10:38-42. (Jesus said Mary chose the one and only thing that was needed when she sat and listened to his Word.)

242) Acts 2:42,46. They *devoted themselves* to the apostles' teaching and to the fellowship, to the breaking of bread and to prayer. *Every day* they continued to meet together in the temple courts.

243) Acts 17:11. The Bereans . . . received the message *with great eagerness* and examined the Scriptures *every day* to see if what Paul said was true.

244) Psalm 119:72. The law from your mouth is *more precious* to me than thousands of pieces of silver and gold.

245) John 6:45. Everyone who *listens* to the Father *and learns* from him comes to me.

246) Psalm 122:1. I *rejoiced* with those who said to me, "Let us *go to the house of the LORD.*"

58a. God wants us to hear and learn his Word gladly every day.

247) John 20:31. These are written *that you may believe* that Jesus is the Christ, the Son of God, and *that by believing* you may have life in his name.

248) John 2:22. After he was raised from the dead, his disciples recalled what he had said. Then *they believed* the Scripture and the words that Jesus had spoken.

249) Acts 4:4. Many who heard the message *believed,* and the number of men grew to about five thousand.

250) Luke 11:28. Blessed . . . are those who hear the word of God *and obey it.*

251) Psalm 119:133. *Direct my footsteps* according to your word; let no sin rule over me.

58b. God wants us to believe and obey his Word.

252) Mark 16:15. Go into *all the world* and *preach the good news* to all creation.

253) Acts 8:4. Those who had been scattered *preached the word wherever they went.*

58c. God wants us to share his Word with all people.

59. Why do we observe special days, such as Sundays and festivals?

254) Galatians 4:9-11. (Paul warned the Galatians not to fall into a slavish observing of days.)

255) Psalm 26:8. *I love* the house where you live, O LORD, the place where your glory dwells.

256) Psalm 84:10. *Better* is *one day* in your courts *than a thousand* elsewhere.

257) Psalm 122:1. *I rejoiced* with those who said to me, "Let us go to the house of the LORD."

59a. We observe these special days not because we have to but because we want to.

258) 1 Peter 5:2. *Be shepherds* of God's flock that is under your care, *serving as overseers.*

259) Acts 20:28. Keep watch over yourselves and all the flock of which *the Holy Spirit has made you overseers.* Be shepherds of the church of God, which he bought with his own blood.

260) John 21:17. Jesus said, "*Feed* my sheep."

261) 2 Timothy 4:2. *Preach the Word;* . . . correct, rebuke and encourage—with great patience and *careful instruction.*

262) 1 Peter 1:25; 2:2. This is the word that was preached to you. Like newborn babies, *crave pure spiritual milk,* so that by it *you may grow up* in your salvation.

263) Ephesians 4:11-13. It was he [Jesus] who gave . . . some to be pastors and teachers, *to prepare* God's people for works of service, so that the body of Christ *may be built up* until we all reach unity in the faith and in the knowledge of the Son of God and become mature.

59b. We observe these special days to be fed with the Word by our God-given shepherd (pastor).

264) Psalm 145:3-5. Great is the LORD and *most worthy of praise;* his greatness no one can fathom. *One generation will commend your works to another;* they will tell of your mighty acts. They will speak of the glorious splendor of your majesty, and *I will meditate* on your *wonderful works.*

265) Colossians 3:16. Let the word of Christ dwell in you richly as you *teach and admonish one another* with all wisdom, and as you sing psalms, hymns and spiritual songs with gratitude in your hearts to God.

266) Hebrews 10:25. *Let us not give up meeting together,* as some are in the habit of doing, *but let us encourage one another—* and all the more as you see the Day approaching.

71

⌐ 59c. We observe these special days to praise God for his wonderful works and to encourage one another in our faith and lives.

SUNDAY AND THE CHURCH YEAR

It became a practice in the early Christian church to observe Sunday as the day for public worship (cf. John 20:19,26; Acts 20:7; 1 Corinthians 16:2; Revelation 1:10). Sunday was chosen because it marked several great events: The beginning of creation, Jesus' resurrection from the dead (Easter), and the sending of the Holy Spirit (Pentecost). We have continued this practice because it helps us do everything "in a fitting and orderly way" as God's Word urges us to do in 1 Corinthians 14:40. Since we know when the public worship service will be each week, we can plan our week so that we can attend worship regularly.

The Sundays of each "church year" are arranged in two groups. Each group makes up about one-half of the year. The first group of Sundays is called the "Festival Half." The themes for all the Sundays in this half of the church year are arranged according to the events of Christ's life. Those parts of our order of service which change (the propers: introit, gradual, prayers, Scripture readings, hymns, and sermon) focus each Sunday on the part of Christ's life which is being highlighted at that time in the church year. The following chart gives a brief outline of the main festivals:

The Festival Half of the Church Year
General theme: The Life of Christ

Time: December to May

1. *Advent*	(Coming)	four Sundays
2. *Christmas*	(Birth)	December 25
3. *Epiphany*	(Appearing)	January 6 and four to nine Sundays (The last

		three Sundays are sometimes considered a transition to Lent.)
4. *Lent*	(Suffering and Death)	six Sundays including Palm Sunday, Maundy Thursday (Institution of the Lord's Supper), and Good Friday (Death and Burial)
5. *Easter*	(Resurrection)	six Sundays
6. *Ascension*	(Return to Heaven)	forty days after Easter
7. *Pentecost*	(Sending of the Holy Spirit)	fifty days after Easter

The Non-Festival Half of the Church Year

The non-festival half of the church year extends from June to November. It may include 22 to 27 Sundays. It begins with Trinity Sunday, and the Sundays that follow are called the Trinity season. Some prefer to call these Sundays the Sundays after Pentecost. There is no special theme that runs through all these Sundays. Rather, the theme for each Sunday and for the parts of the service which change will usually correspond to the sermon text the pastor has chosen for that Sunday.

There are several special days that we observe during the non-festival half of the church year. They are Reformation Day (October 31) and Thanksgiving Day (the fourth Thursday of November in the United States, the second Monday of October in Canada). Many of our congregations also celebrate a special Mission Sunday either during this non-festival half of the church year, or during the festival half, or both.

```
            ┌─────────────────┐
            │   OT SABBATH    │
            │    pictured     │
            │  REST IN CHRIST │
            │                 │
            │    told us in   │
            └────────┐ ┌──────┘
                     ▼ ▼
```

God's WORD

Do!	Don't Do!
— Hear ⎫	— Refuse to hear
— Learn ⎬ every	— Let world crowd
— Believe ⎮ day	it from our lives
— Obey ⎭	— Refuse to believe
	— Refuse to obey

60. How does the Third Commandment serve as a mirror for us?

267) Luke 10:38-42. (Martha was distracted from Jesus' word by other concerns.)

268) Hebrews 2:1. We must *pay more careful attention,* therefore, to what we have heard, so that we do not *drift away.*

269) James 1:22. *Do not merely listen* to the word, and so deceive yourselves. *Do what it says.*

270) Hebrews 4:12,13. The word of God is living and active. Sharper than any double-edged sword, it penetrates even to dividing soul and spirit, joints and marrow; it *judges the thoughts and attitudes of the heart.* Nothing in all creation is hidden from God's sight. Everything is uncovered and laid bare before the eyes of him to whom *we must give account.*

60. The Third Commandment shows us our sins because we have not always received God's Word in the way he wants us to receive it.

61. How did Jesus save us from our sins against the Third Commandment?

271) Luke 2:41-47. (As a 12-year-old boy, Jesus gladly heard and learned God's Word.)

272) Luke 4:16. On the Sabbath day he [Jesus] went into the synagogue, *as was his custom.*

273) John 8:46,47. Can any of you *prove me guilty of sin?* If I am telling the truth, why don't you believe me? He who belongs to God hears what God says.

61a. Jesus saved us by keeping the Third Commandment perfectly for us.

274) Isaiah 53:6. We all, like sheep, have gone astray, each of us has turned to his own way; and the LORD *has laid on him* the iniquity of us all.

61b. Jesus saved us by dying for all our sins.

62. How does the Third Commandment serve as a guideline for us?

275) Psalm 119:16. *I delight* in your decrees; *I will not neglect* your word.

276) Psalm 119:103. *How sweet* are your words to my taste, sweeter than honey to my mouth!

277) Psalm 119:161,162. My *heart trembles* at your word. I rejoice in your promise like one who finds great spoil.

278) Psalm 107:21. Let them *give thanks* to the LORD for his unfailing love and his wonderful deeds for men.

62. **The Third Commandment shows us that God wants us to thank him for his goodness by regarding his Word as holy and gladly hearing and learning it.**

THE FOURTH COMMANDMENT

(God's Representatives)

Honor your father and mother, that it may go well with you and that you may enjoy long life on the earth.

What does this mean?

We should fear and love God that we do not dishonor or anger our parents and others in authority, but honor, serve, and obey them, and give them love and respect.

63. Who are the people whom God wants us to honor?

279) Ephesians 6:1,2. Children, obey your *parents* in the Lord, for this is right. "Honor your father and mother."

280) Hebrews 13:7,17. Remember your *leaders, who spoke the word of God to you.* . . . Obey your leaders and submit to their authority. They keep watch over you as men who must give an account.

281) 1 Peter 2:13,14. Submit yourselves for the Lord's sake to *every authority instituted among men:* whether to the *king,* as the supreme authority, or to *governors.*

63. God wants us to honor those in authority, especially those in our homes, our churches, and our government.

64. Why do these people have authority over us?

282) Colossians 3:20. Children, obey your parents in everything, for this *pleases the Lord.*

283) Ephesians 6:1. Children, obey your parents *in the Lord,* for this is right.

284) Acts 20:28. Keep watch over yourselves and all the flock of which the *Holy Spirit has made you overseers.*

285) 2 Corinthians 5:19,20. [God] has committed to us the message of reconciliation. *We are therefore Christ's ambassadors,* as though God were making his appeal through us. We implore you *on Christ's behalf:* Be reconciled to God.

286) Romans 13:1. Everyone must submit himself to the governing authorities, for there is *no authority except that which God has established.* The authorities that exist have been established by God.

287) Romans 13:4. For he is God's servant to do you good. . . . He is *God's servant,* an agent of wrath to bring punishment on the wrongdoer.

64. They have this authority because God placed them over us as his representatives.

65. What blessing does God give us through his representatives in our churches?

288) Hebrews 13:7. Remember your leaders, who spoke the *word of God* to you.

289) 1 Timothy 4:16. Watch your life and *doctrine* closely. Persevere in them, because if you do, you will *save* both yourself and *your hearers.*

65. Through his representatives in our churches, God gives us the blessing of instruction in his saving Word. (care of our souls)

66. What blessing does God give us through his representatives in our government?

290) Hosea 4:1-3. (Israel suffered greatly because the governing authorities kept no law and order.)

291) Romans 13:3. Rulers hold no terror for those who do right, but for *those who do wrong.*

292) Romans 13:6. The authorities are God's servants, who give their *full time* to governing.

66. Through his representatives in our government, God gives us the blessing of law and order. (care of our bodies)

67. Why does God call special attention in this commandment to our parents as his representatives?

293) 1 Timothy 5:8. If anyone does not *provide* for his relatives, and *especially for his immediate family,* he has denied the faith and is worse than an unbeliever.

294) Ephesians 6:4. Fathers, do not exasperate your children; instead, bring them up in the training and *instruction of the Lord.*

295) Proverbs 1:3,5,8,9. *For acquiring a disciplined and prudent life,* doing what is right and just and fair; . . . let the wise listen. . . . Listen, my son, to your *father's instruction* and do not forsake your *mother's teaching.* They will be a garland to grace your head and a chain to adorn your neck.

296) Psalm 103:13. As *a father has compassion* on his children, so the LORD has compassion on those who fear him.

297) 1 Thessalonians 2:7. We were gentle among you, like *a mother caring for* her little children.

67. God calls special attention to our parents because through them he gives us many blessings: our daily needs such as food, clothing, and shelter; instruction in his Word; guidance for life; and loving concern. (care of body and soul)

68. How does God emphasize that he wants to bless us through his representatives?

298) Ephesians 6:2,3. "Honor your father and mother"—which is *the first commandment with a promise*—"that it may go well with you and that you may enjoy long life on the earth."

68. God emphasizes that he wants to bless us through his representatives by adding a promise to the Fourth Commandment.

69. How does God want us to honor his representatives?

299) Ruth 1:15-18; 2:11,12. (Ruth faithfully served her mother-in-law, Naomi.)

300) 1 Samuel 3:1-6. (Samuel faithfully served Eli the priest.)

301) 1 Samuel 19:4-6; 24:1-7. (David faithfully served and respected Saul the king.)

302) Colossians 3:20. Children, *obey* your parents *in everything,* for this pleases the Lord.

303) Hebrews 13:7,17. *Remember* your leaders, who spoke the word of God to you. Consider the outcome of their way of life and *imitate their faith. . . . Obey* them so that their work will be a joy, not a burden.

304) Titus 3:1. Remind the people to *be subject* to rulers and authorities, to *be obedient,* to be ready to *do whatever is good.*

305) Galatians 5:13. Serve one another *in love.*

306) 1 Thessalonians 5:12,13. We ask you . . . to *respect* those who work hard among you, who are over you in the Lord and who admonish you. Hold them in the highest regard *in love* because of their work.

307) Romans 13:7. Give everyone what you owe him: If you owe taxes, pay taxes; if revenue, then revenue; if *respect,* then respect; if honor, then *honor.*

69. God wants us to honor his representatives by serving and obeying them in a spirit of love and respect.

70. How long does God want us to honor his representatives?

308) 1 Kings 2:19. (When Solomon became king, he honored his mother.)

309) 1 Timothy 5:4. Children or grandchildren . . . should learn . . . to put their religion into practice by *caring for their own family* and so repaying their *parents and grandparents,* for this is pleasing to God.

310) Proverbs 23:22. Listen to your father who gave you life, and do not despise your mother *when she is old.*

311) Leviticus 19:32. Rise in the presence of *the aged, show respect for the elderly* and revere your God.

70. God wants us to honor his representatives also when they grow old.

71. What does God forbid in this commandment?

312) 1 Samuel 2:22-25. (Eli's sons did not listen to their father.)

313) 2 Kings 2:23,24. (Some young people called Elisha the prophet a "baldhead" and were punished by God.)

314) 2 Samuel 15:1-12; 18:14-17. (Absalom said and did things to turn the people against his father, the king. His rebellion ended in a shameful death.)

315) Deuteronomy 21:18,21. If a man has a stubborn and rebellious son who *does not obey* his father and mother and *will not listen* to them when they discipline him, . . . Then all the men of his town shall stone him to death.

316) Proverbs 30:11,17. There are those who *curse their fathers* and *do not bless* their mothers. The eye that *mocks* a father, that *scorns obedience to a mother,* will be pecked out by the ravens of the valley, will be eaten by the vultures.

317) 2 Timothy 3:1,2. Mark this: There will be terrible times in the last days. People will be . . . abusive, *disobedient to their parents,* ungrateful.

318a) Exodus 32:19-24. (The people of Israel made Moses angry by their wickedness.)

318b) Numbers 16:12-15. (Dathan and Abiram angered Moses by refusing to obey him.)

319) Proverbs 14:35. A king delights in a wise servant, but a shameful servant *incurs his wrath.*

71. God forbids us to disobey, dishonor, or anger our parents or others in authority.

72. What does God want his representatives to do with those who sin against this commandment?

320) 1 Samuel 2:29; 3:13. (God held Eli responsible for correcting his sons when they sinned.)

321) Proverbs 13:24. He who spares the rod *hates his son,* but he who *loves him* is careful to *discipline* him.

322) Colossians 3:21. Fathers, *do not embitter* your children, or they will become discouraged.

323) 2 Timothy 4:2. Preach the Word; . . . *correct, rebuke* and encourage—with great *patience* and careful *instruction.*

324) Romans 13:2-4. He who rebels against the authority is rebelling against what God has instituted, and those who do so will bring judgment on themselves. For rulers hold no terror for those who do right, but for those who do wrong. . . . But if you do wrong, be afraid, for he does not bear the sword for nothing. He is God's servant, an agent of wrath to *bring punishment* on the wrongdoer.

72. God wants his representatives patiently to rebuke and instruct those who sin against this commandment and to punish them when necessary. (discipline)

73. How can such discipline be a blessing?

> 325) 1 Samuel 2:30-32; 3:11-14; 4:10,11. (Because Eli did not correct his sons, they died under God's judgment.)
>
> 326) Proverbs 19:18. Discipline your son, for in that there is hope; *do not be a willing party to his death.*
>
> 327) Proverbs 23:13. Do not withhold discipline from a child; if you punish him with the rod, *he will not die.*
>
> 328) Hebrews 10:31. It is a *dreadful thing* to fall into the hands of the living God.

73. Such discipline can be a blessing because it might prevent a person from falling under God's terrible judgment.

74. Why, then, will a Christian honor God's representatives also when they discipline him?

> 329) Proverbs 6:23. The *corrections* of discipline are *the way to life.*
>
> 330) Hebrews 12:11. No discipline seems pleasant at the time, but *painful.* Later on, however, it produces *a harvest* of righteousness and peace for those who have been *trained by it.*

74. A Christian will honor God's representatives also when they discipline him because he knows this is an important training in his life.

75. When is the only time that God does not want us to obey those in authority over us?

> 331) Acts 5:29. We must obey God *rather than* men!
>
> 332) Matthew 10:37. Anyone who loves his father or mother *more than me is* not worthy of me.

75. God does not want us to obey those in authority over us if they tell us to do something contrary to his Word.

76. How does the Fourth Commandment serve as a mirror for us?

GOD BLESSES US BY

Church
Soul

Home
Soul and Body

Government
Body

HIS
REPRESENTATIVES

Do!

HONOR
by
serving and obeying
in
love and respect
always

also

old
age

when
disciplined

Don't
Do!

— Disobey

— Dishonor

— Anger

333) Genesis 27:1-35. (Jacob deceived his father.)

334) Luke 15:11-32. (Note especially verse 21. The lost son sinned against heaven and his father.)

335) Psalm 25:7. Remember not the sins of my youth and *my rebellious ways.*

76. The Fourth Commandment shows us our sins because we have not always honored God's representatives as he wants us to honor them.

77. How did Jesus save us from our sins against the Fourth Commandment?

336) Luke 2:51. [Jesus] went down to Nazareth with them [his parents] and was obedient to them.

337) John 19:26,27. (Jesus provided for the care of his mother.)

338) Matthew 22:19-21. (Jesus honored the government.)

339) 1 Peter 2:22. He [Jesus] committed *no sin,* and no deceit was found in his mouth.

77a. Jesus saved us by keeping the Fourth Commandment perfectly for us.

340) Hebrews 10:10. We have been made holy *through the sacrifice* of the body of Jesus Christ once for all.

77b. Jesus saved us by dying as a sacrifice for all our sins.

78. How does the Fourth Commandment serve as a guideline for us?

341) Colossians 3:20. Children, obey your parents in everything, for *this pleases the Lord.*

342) Ephesians 6:7. Serve wholeheartedly, as *if you were serving the Lord* not men.

343) Ephesians 5:20,21. *Giving thanks* to God the Father for everything, in the name of our Lord Jesus Christ. *Submit* to one another *out of reverence for Christ.*

78. The Fourth Commandment shows us that God wants us to thank him for his goodness by honoring, serving, and obeying his representatives.

THE FIFTH COMMANDMENT
(God's Gift of Life)

You shall not murder.

What does this mean?

We should fear and love God that we do not hurt or harm our neighbor in his body, but help and befriend him in every bodily need.

79. What is God protecting by the Fifth Commandment?

344) Genesis 2:7. The LORD God *formed the man* from the dust of the ground and *breathed into his nostrils the breath of life,* and the man became a living being.

345) Acts 17:25,28. He himself *[God] gives* all men *life* and breath. . . . *in him* we live and move and have our being.

346) Genesis 9:5,6. For your lifeblood *I will surely demand an accounting.* I will demand an accounting from every animal. And from each man, too, I will demand an accounting for the life of his fellow man. Whoever sheds the blood of man, by man shall his blood be shed; for in the image of God has God made man.

79. By the Fifth Commandment, God is protecting his gift to man of body and life.

80. Why is the time of a person's life so important?

347) Luke 16:19-24. (Lazarus died and went to heaven. The rich man died and went to hell.)

348) Matthew 25:1-13. (The five foolish virgins were given no second chance.)

349) Isaiah 55:6. Seek the LORD *while he may be found.*

350) 2 Corinthians 6:1,2. We urge you not to receive God's grace in vain. . . . I tell you, *now is the time* of God's favor, now is *the day of salvation.*

351) Hebrews 9:27. Man is destined to die once, and *after that* to face judgment.

80. Man's time of life is so important because once a person dies he is either saved or lost forever. (time of grace)

81. Who only has the right to end a person's life?

352) Deuteronomy 32:39. There is no god besides me. *I put to death and I bring to life.*

353) Psalm 31:15. My times are *in your hands.*

354) Psalm 90:3. *You* turn men back to dust, saying, "Return to dust, O sons of men."

355) Genesis 9:5,6. From each man, too, *I will demand an accounting* for the life of his fellow man. Whoever sheds the blood of man, *by man* shall his blood be shed.

356) Romans 13:4. He [the governing authority] does not bear the sword for nothing. *He is God's servant,* an agent of wrath *to bring punishment* on the wrongdoer.

81. Only God or his appointed representatives in government have the right to end a person's life.

82. What does God forbid regarding his gift of body and life?

357) Proverbs 23:20,31-33. Do not join those who *drink too much wine* or *gorge themselves* on meat. . . . Do not gaze at wine when it is red, when it sparkles in the cup, when it goes down smoothly! In the end it bites like a snake and *poisons like a viper.* Your eyes will see strange sights and your *mind imagine confusing things.*

82a. God forbids anyone to harm his own body in any way. (overeating, overdrinking, poisoning one's body or losing control of one's senses by the abuse of alcohol or drugs)

358) 1 Samuel 31:4; Matthew 27:5. (Saul and Judas committed suicide.)

359) Acts 1:25. Judas left [his ministry] to go *where he belongs.*

360) Psalm 31:15. My times are *in your hands.*

82b. God forbids suicide.

361) Genesis 4:2-15. (Cain killed Abel.)

362) 2 Samuel 11:2-17. (David killed Uriah through others.)

363) Exodus 21:29; Deuteronomy 22:8. (People caused the death of others through their carelessness.)

364) Exodus 21:22-24. (Note in verse 23 "life for life"; God considered life in the womb equal to any other life.)

82c. God forbids anyone to cause the loss of another person's life in any way. (directly or indirectly or as a result of carelessness, abortion, "mercy death")

365) Exodus 21:18,19,23,26,27. (God forbade harming another person's body in any way.)

366) Numbers 35:16-18. (Harm done to another can result in death.)

367) Genesis 37:11-35. (The brothers by their deeds made Joseph's life miserable. By their words they made their father's life miserable.)

368) Romans 12:18-21. (God forbids revenge.)

369) 1 Peter 3:9. Do not repay *evil with evil* or *insult with insult.*

82d. God forbids all words or deeds that harm another person's body, shorten his life, or make his life miserable.

370) Matthew 5:21,22. You have heard that it was said to the people long ago, "Do not murder, and anyone who murders will be subject to judgment." But I tell you that *anyone who is angry* with his brother will be subject to judgment. . . . But *anyone who says,* "You fool!" will be in danger of the fire of hell.

371) 1 John 3:15. Anyone who hates his brother is a *murderer,* and you know that no murderer has eternal life in him.

372) Genesis 4:5-7. (God warned Cain not to let anger continue in his heart.)

82e. God forbids every hateful thought or word.

83. According to the Fifth Commandment, what does God want us to do?

373) 1 John 4:7,20. Let us *love one another,* for love comes from God. . . . anyone who does not love his brother, whom he has seen, cannot love God, whom he has not seen.

374) 1 Thessalonians 5:14,15. *Be patient* with everyone. Make sure that nobody pays back wrong for wrong, but always try to *be kind* to each other and to everyone else.

375) Ephesians 4:31,32. Get rid of all bitterness, rage and anger. . . . *Be kind and compassionate* to one another, *forgiving each other,* just as in Christ God forgave you.

376) Genesis 45:3-15; 50:15-21. (Joseph forgave his brothers from his heart.)

377) Matthew 18:35. This is how my heavenly Father will treat each of you unless you forgive your brother *from your heart.*

83a. God wants us to be patient, kind, and forgiving from our hearts toward everyone.

378) Genesis 45:8-11,16-23. (Joseph provided for the bodily needs of his father and brothers.)

379) Luke 10:33-35. (The Good Samaritan helped the man who was robbed and beaten.)

380) Romans 12:20. If your enemy is hungry, *feed him;* if he is thirsty, *give him something to drink.*

381) Matthew 25:35,36. I was *hungry* and you gave me something to eat, I was *thirsty* and you gave me something to drink, I was a *stranger* and you invited me in, I *needed clothes* and you clothed me, I was *sick* and you looked after me, I was *in prison* and you came to visit me.

83b. God wants us to help and befriend everyone in every bodily need.

84. How does the Fifth Commandment serve as a mirror for us?

382) Luke 9:51-55. (James and John wanted to destroy a Samaritan village in their anger.)

383) 1 Samuel 25:32-34. (David lost his temper and intended to kill Nabal.)

384) Galatians 5:19-21. The acts of the sinful nature are obvious: . . . *hatred, discord,* jealousy, *fits of rage,* selfish ambition, dissensions, factions and envy; *drunkenness, orgies,* and the like. I warn you, as I did before, that those who live like this will not inherit the kingdom of God.

God's
Gift of
LIFE

Do!

— Be patient

— Be kind

— Be forgiving

— Be helpful

— Be a friend

**TIME
OF
GRACE**

Don't
Do!

— Harm my own body

— Suicide

— Harm another's body

— Murder

— Hateful thoughts
and words

**Ended only
by God
or
his representative**

84. The Fifth Commandment shows us our sins because we have not always respected God's gift of body and life the way he wants us to respect it.

85. How did Jesus save us from our sins against the Fifth Commandment?

385) Matthew 4:24. People brought to him all who were ill with various diseases, those suffering severe pain, the demon-possessed, those having seizures, and the paralyzed, and *he healed them.*

386) Luke 23:34. Jesus said, "Father, *forgive them,* for they do not know what they are doing."

387) 1 Peter 2:22,23. *He committed no sin,* and no deceit was found in his mouth. When they hurled their insults at him, *he did not retaliate;* when he suffered, *he made no threats.*

85a. Jesus saved us by keeping the Fifth Commandment perfectly for us.

388) 1 Peter 2:24. He himself *bore our sins* in his body on the tree . . . ; *by his wounds* you have been healed.

85b. Jesus saved us by dying for all our sins.

86. How does the Fifth Commandment serve as a guideline?

389) 1 John 3:23. This is his command: to believe in the name of his Son, Jesus Christ, and to *love one another as he commanded us.*

390) Colossians 3:12,13. Therefore, *as God's chosen people, holy and dearly loved,* clothe yourselves with compassion, kindness, humility, gentleness and patience. Bear with each other and forgive whatever grievances you may have against one another. Forgive *as the Lord forgave you.*

86. The Fifth Commandment shows us that God wants us to thank him for his goodness by treating his gift of body and life in ways which are pleasing to him.

THE SIXTH COMMANDMENT
(God's Gift of Marriage)

You shall not commit adultery.

What does this mean?

We should fear and love God that we lead a pure and decent life in words and actions, and that husband and wife love and honor each other.

87. What is God protecting by the Sixth Commandment?

> 391) Genesis 2:19-24. (God gave marriage when he brought Eve to Adam.)
>
> 392) Proverbs 18:22. He who finds a wife finds what is good and receives *favor from the LORD.*
>
> 393) Hebrews 13:4. *Marriage should be honored by all,* and the marriage bed kept pure, for *God will judge* the adulterer and all the sexually immoral.

87. By the Sixth Commandment, God is protecting his gift of marriage.

88. According to God's Word, what is marriage?

> 394) Genesis 2:24. A man will leave his father and mother and *be united* to his wife, and they will become *one flesh.*
>
> 395) Matthew 19:5,6. A man will leave his father and mother and be united to his wife, and *the two* will become one flesh. So they are no longer two, but one. Therefore what God has joined together, let man *not separate.*
>
> 396) Romans 7:2. A married woman is bound to her husband *as long as he is alive,* but if her husband dies, she is released from the law of marriage.

88. According to God's Word, marriage is a lifelong union of one man and one woman.

Entering Marriage

The marriage union is established when a man and a woman freely choose to leave father and mother and enter a lifelong union as husband and wife (Matthew 19:5,6; Genesis 24:57). Usually there is a period of time between the day when a man and woman make the promise to one another that they will be united for life and the day that they actually begin living together as husband and wife (cf. Joseph and Mary, Matthew 1:18-20,24). This is not a time for the couple to reconsider their promise to one another, but a time in which they can publicly announce their promise and make whatever preparations are necessary for their marriage and their life together. No Christian will ever want to break any promise he or she makes (Ephesians 4:25). This is especially true of the promise to unite oneself with another person for life because this promise involves the deepest feelings and the entire life of the other person. To break such a promise is not only a sin in itself, but it will also surely make the other person's life miserable, which is also a sin (see Answer 82d).

According to the Fourth Commandment, a Christian man and woman will not promise one another that they will be united for life without seeking the counsel and consent of their parents, nor will they begin living together as husband and wife before they have fulfilled the legal requirements that the government has set down for entering marriage.

89. How does God bless us in marriage?

397) Genesis 2:18. The LORD God said, "It is not good for the man to be alone. I will make *a helper suitable for him.*"

398) Ephesians 5:24,25. Now *as the church submits* to Christ, *so also wives should submit* to their husbands in everything. *Husbands, love* your wives, just *as Christ loved* the church and gave himself up for her.

399) 1 Corinthians 11:3. The head of every man is Christ, and *the head* of the woman *is man,* and the head of Christ is God.

89a. God blesses us in marriage with a loving companionship in which the man is the head and the woman is his helper.

400) Genesis 2:24. They will become *one flesh.*

401) 1 Corinthians 7:2-5. (God provides for sexual happiness in marriage.)

402) Song of Songs 1:15,16; 4:1-7; 5:10-16. (The physical attraction of husband and wife is natural and beautiful.)

89b. God blesses us in marriage with sexual happiness.

403) Psalm 127:3. Sons are a heritage *from the LORD, children a reward from him.*

404) Genesis 33:5. Jacob answered, "They are the children *God has graciously given your servant."*

405) 1 Samuel 1:9-20. (God gave Hannah a son in answer to her fervent prayer for a child.)

406) Psalm 113:9. He settles the barren woman in her home as a *happy mother of children.*

407) Genesis 1:27,28. Male and female he created them. *God blessed them* and said to them, "Be fruitful and increase in number; fill the earth and subdue it."

408) Proverbs 17:6. Children's children are *a crown* to the aged.

89c. God blesses us in marriage with his precious gift of children.

90. How does a married person sin against God's will in regard to his gift of marriage?

409) Colossians 3:19. *Husbands,* love your wives and *do not be harsh* with them.

410) Proverbs 21:19. Better to live in a desert than with a *quarrelsome and ill-tempered wife.*

90a. A married person sins if he or she destroys the loving companionship of the marriage.

411) 2 Samuel 11:1-4. (David sinned when he lusted for Uriah's wife, Bathsheba, and had her come to his house, so that he could have sexual intercourse with her.)

412) Hebrews 13:4. Marriage should be honored by all, and the *marriage bed kept pure,* for God will judge the *adulterer* and all the sexually immoral.

93

90b. A married person sins if he or she has sexual intercourse with anyone other than the marriage partner.

413) Matthew 19:9. I tell you that anyone who divorces his wife, *except for marital unfaithfulness,* and marries another woman commits adultery.

414) 1 Corinthians 7:15. If the unbeliever *leaves,* let him do so. A believing man or woman is *not bound in such circumstances.*

90c. A married person sins if he or she divorces the marriage partner for any reason except marital unfaithfulness or desertion.

91. How does an unmarried person sin against God's will in regard to his gift of marriage?

415) Genesis 39:6-12. (Joseph refused to have sexual intercourse with Potiphar's wife saying, "How could I do *such a wicked thing and sin against God?*")

416) 1 Thessalonians 4:3-5. It is God's will that you should be sanctified; that you should *avoid sexual immorality;* that each of you should learn to *control his own body* in a way that is holy and honorable, *not in passionate lust* like the heathen, who do not know God.

417) Ephesians 5:5. Of this you can be sure: No *immoral, impure* or greedy *person* . . . has any inheritance in the kingdom of Christ and of God.

91. An unmarried person sins if he or she has sexual intercourse before marriage.

92. What does God also forbid in this commandment for both married and unmarried?

418) Ephesians 5:3,4. Among you there must not be *even a hint* of sexual immorality, or of any kind of impurity. . . . Nor should there be *obscenity, foolish talk* or *coarse joking,* which are out of place.

419) Ephesians 5:12. It is *shameful* even to mention what the disobedient do in secret.

420) Matthew 5:27,28. You have heard that it was said, "Do not commit adultery." But I tell you that anyone who *looks at a*

woman lustfully has already committed adultery with her in his heart.

92. God forbids all impure words and lustful thoughts.

93. What does God say about homosexuality?

421) 1 Corinthians 6:9,10. Do you not know that *the wicked* will not inherit the kingdom of God? Do not be deceived: Neither the sexually immoral nor idolaters nor adulterers nor male prostitutes nor *homosexual offenders* nor thieves nor the greedy nor drunkards nor slanderers nor swindlers will inherit the kingdom of God.

422) Romans 1:26,27. God gave them over to *shameful lusts.* Even their women exchanged natural relations for unnatural ones. In the same way the men also abandoned natural relations with women and were inflamed with lust for one another. Men committed *indecent acts* with other men, and received in themselves the due penalty for their perversion.

93. God condemns homosexuality as sin.

94. According to the Sixth Commandment, what does God want us to do?

423) 1 Timothy 5:22. Do not share in the sins of others. *Keep yourself pure.*

424) Romans 13:13,14. Let us *behave decently,* . . . not in sexual immorality and debauchery. . . . Rather, *clothe yourselves with the Lord Jesus Christ,* and *do not think* about how to gratify the desires of the sinful nature.

425) Psalm 51:10. Create in me a *pure heart,* O God, and renew a *steadfast spirit* within me.

426) Philippians 4:8. Whatever is *pure,* whatever is lovely, whatever is admirable . . . *think about* such things.

94a. God wants us to be pure and decent in our thoughts, words, and actions.

427) Ephesians 5:33. Each one of you . . . must *love his wife* as he loves himself, and the wife must *respect her husband.*

428) 1 Corinthians 11:11. In the Lord . . . woman is *not independent* of man, *nor* is man *independent* of woman.

429) 1 Peter 3:1,3,4,7. Wives, . . . be submissive to your husbands. . . . Your beauty should not come from outward adornment, such as braided hair and the wearing of gold jewelry and fine clothes. Instead, it should be that of your inner self, the unfading beauty of a *gentle and quiet spirit,* which is of great worth in God's sight. . . . Husbands, *in the same way be considerate* as you live with your wives, *and treat them with respect.*

94b. God wants us as husband and wife to honor and love each other.

95. Of what does God remind us to encourage us to keep this commandment?

430) 1 Corinthians 6:18,19. *Flee from* sexual immorality. All other sins a man commits are outside his body, but he who sins sexually sins against his own body. Do you not know that *your body is a temple of the Holy Spirit,* who is in you, whom you have received from God? You are not your own; you were bought at a price. Therefore *honor God with your body.*

431) Proverbs 1:10. My son, if sinners entice you, *do not give in* to them.

432) 2 Timothy 2:22. *Flee* the evil desires of youth.

433) 1 Corinthians 15:33. Do not be misled: "*Bad company* corrupts good character."

95. God reminds us that our bodies are the dwelling-place of the Holy Spirit so that we flee from people and places which tempt us to sin against this commandment.

96. How does the Sixth Commandment serve as a mirror for us?

434) Psalm 51:1-12. (David confesses his failure to be pure in his heart and in his life.)

435) Colossians 3:5,6. Put to death . . . whatever belongs to your earthly nature: sexual immorality, impurity, lust, evil desires. . . . Because of these, *the wrath of God* is coming.

96. The Sixth Commandment shows us our sins because we have not always been pure in thought, word, and action.

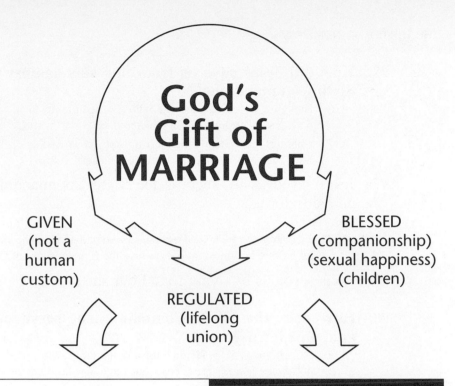

God's Gift of MARRIAGE

GIVEN
(not a human custom)

REGULATED
(lifelong union)

BLESSED
(companionship)
(sexual happiness)
(children)

Do!

— Be pure in thought, word, and deed

— Honor and love marriage partner

— Flee temptation

Don't Do!

— Destroy companionship

— Be unfaithful

— Divorce

— Have premarital sex

— Have impure words and thoughts

— Be a homosexual

97. How did Jesus save us from our sins against the Sixth Commandment?

436) Hebrews 4:15. We have one who has been tempted in every way, just as we are—yet was *without sin.*

437) Hebrews 7:26. Such a high priest *meets our need*—one who is holy, blameless, *pure,* set apart from sinners.

97a. Jesus saved us by keeping the Sixth Commandment perfectly for us.

438) 2 Corinthians 5:21. God made him who had no sin to be sin *for us,* so that in him *we might become* the righteousness of God.

97b. Jesus saved us by dying for all our sins.

98. How does the Sixth Commandment serve as a guideline for us?

439) 2 Corinthians 5:15. He died for all, that those who live should *no longer live for themselves* but for him who died for them and was raised again.

440) 1 Thessalonians 4:1,7. We instructed you how to live in order *to please God. . . .* For God did *not* call us to be *impure, but* to live *a holy life.*

441) Ephesians 5:1-4. Be imitators of God . . . as dearly loved children and *live a life of love,* just as Christ loved us and gave himself up for us as a fragrant offering and sacrifice to God. But among you there must not be even a hint of sexual immorality. . . . Nor should there be obscenity, foolish talk or coarse joking, which are out of place, but rather *thanksgiving.*

98. The Sixth Commandment shows us that God wants us to thank him for all his goodness by honoring his gift of marriage in ways which are pleasing to him.

THE SEVENTH COMMANDMENT
(God's Gift of Possessions)

You shall not steal.

What does this mean?

We should fear and love God that we do not take our neighbor's money or property, or get it by dishonest dealing, but help him to improve and protect his property and means of income.

99. What is God protecting by the Seventh Commandment?

442) Job 1:13-22. (Job recognized that all his possessions came from God. Note especially verse 21, "The LORD gave and the LORD has taken away; may the name of the LORD be praised.")

443) James 1:17. Every good and perfect gift *is from above,* coming down from the Father of the heavenly lights.

99. By the Seventh Commandment, God is protecting his gift of possessions.

100. How does God give us our possessions?

444) Deuteronomy 8:17,18. You may say to yourself, "My power and the strength of my hands have produced this wealth for me." But remember the LORD your God, for it is he who *gives you the ability to produce wealth.*

445) Genesis 32:9,10; 33:10,11. (Jacob knew that what he had was the result of God blessing his 20 years of work.)

446) 2 Thessalonians 3:10-12. If a man will not *work,* he shall not eat. We hear that some among you are idle. . . . Such people we command and urge in the Lord Jesus Christ to settle down and *earn* the bread they eat.

447) Genesis 23:16-19. (Abraham purchased the field and cave of Machpelah.)

100a. God blesses us with the ability to work so that we can purchase possessions or trade for them.

> 448) 1 Kings 21:3. (Naboth inherited his vineyard.)
>
> 449) Matthew 7:11. If you, then, though you are evil, know how to *give good gifts* to your children, how much more will your Father in heaven give good gifts to those who ask him!

100b. God blesses us with possessions through inheritance and gifts.

101. How does God want us to use our possessions?

> 450) 1 Timothy 5:8. If anyone does not *provide for his relatives,* and especially for his immediate *family,* he has denied the faith and is worse than an unbeliever.

101a. God wants us to use our possessions to provide for our families.

> 451) 1 John 3:17. If anyone has material possessions and sees *his brother in need* but has no pity on him, how can the love of God be in him?
>
> 452) Matthew 5:42. *Give* to the one *who asks* you, and do not turn away from the one *who wants to borrow* from you.
>
> 453) Luke 19:8. Zacchaeus stood up and said to the Lord, "Look, Lord! Here and now I give half of my possessions *to the poor.*"

101b. God wants us to use our possessions to give or to lend to those in need.

> 454) Romans 13:6,7. This is also why you pay taxes, for the authorities are God's servants, who give their full time to governing. Give everyone what you owe him: *If you owe taxes, pay taxes;* if revenue, then revenue.

101c. God wants us to use our possessions to pay the taxes we owe to the government.

> 455) Mark 12:41-44. (Jesus rejoiced in the widow's generous offering.)
>
> 456) Malachi 3:8-10. (God said the people were robbing him and challenged them to test how he would bless their offerings.)

457) 1 Corinthians 16:2. On the first day of *every week,* each one of you should set aside a sum of money *in keeping with his income, saving it up.*

458) 2 Corinthians 9:7. Each man should give what he has *decided in his heart* to give, not reluctantly or under compulsion, for God loves a *cheerful giver.*

101d. God wants us to use our possessions to make regular and planned offerings for the work of the church.

102. What reminder does God give us to encourage the faithful use of our possessions?

459) Psalm 24:1. The earth is the LORD's, and *everything in it.*

460) Matthew 25:14-30. (Jesus teaches that everyone is responsible to God for how he manages God's gifts.)

461) 1 Corinthians 4:2. It is *required* that those who have been given a trust *must prove faithful.*

102. God reminds us that we are responsible to him for how faithfully we use our possessions.

103. What does God forbid regarding his gift of possessions?

462) Luke 15:11-20. (The lost son wasted his possessions.)

463) Matthew 14:20; 15:37. (Jesus had the disciples pick up the leftovers so that none would be wasted.)

103a. God forbids us to waste the possessions he gives us.

464) Luke 10:30-37. (The man on the road to Jericho was beaten and robbed.)

465) Proverbs 22:16,22. (God warns against using one's power to exploit others.)

103b. God forbids us to take the possessions of others by force. (robbery)

466) John 12:6. [Judas] was a *thief;* as keeper of the money bag, he used to help himself to what was put into it.

467) Matthew 24:43. If the owner of the house had known at what time of night the *thief* was coming, he would have kept watch and would not have let his house be broken into.

Ability to work		Gift or inheritance

God's Gift of POSSESSIONS

provide for family   help the needy   pay taxes   support work of the church

Do!	Don't Do!
— Be content	— Waste
— Do faithful work	— Robbery
— Help others	— Theft
	— Fraud
	— Greedy thoughts

103c. God forbids us to take the possessions of others secretly. (theft)

468) Leviticus 19:35. Do not use *dishonest standards* when measuring length, weight or quantity.

469) Psalm 37:21. The wicked borrow and *do not repay.*

470) James 5:4. The wages you *failed to pay* the workmen who mowed your fields are crying out against you.

471) Proverbs 16:8. Better a little with righteousness than much gain *with injustice.*

472) Proverbs 21:6. A fortune made by a *lying tongue* is a fleeting vapor and a deadly snare.

103d. God forbids us to get the possessions of others by dishonest dealing. (fraud)

473) 1 Kings 21:4-16. (Ahab's greed led him to take Naboth's vineyard.)

474) 1 Timothy 6:9,10. People who want to get rich fall into temptation and a trap and into many *foolish and harmful desires* that plunge men into ruin and destruction. For the love of money is a root of all kinds of evil. Some people, eager for money, have wandered from the faith and pierced themselves with many griefs.

475) Luke 12:15. Watch out! Be on your guard against *all kinds of greed;* a man's life does not consist in the abundance of his possessions.

103e. God forbids us to have greedy thoughts about the possessions of others.

104. According to the Seventh Commandment, what does God want us to do?

476) 1 Timothy 6:6-8. Godliness with contentment is great gain. For we brought nothing into the world, and we can take nothing out of it. But if we have food and clothing, *we will be content* with that.

477) Hebrews 13:5. Keep your lives free from the love of money and *be content* with what you have, because God has said, "Never will I leave you; never will I forsake you."

104a. God wants us to be content with the possessions he gives us.

> 478) Genesis 39:2-6,20-23; Daniel 6:1-4. (Joseph and Daniel were faithful in their work.)
>
> 479) Colossians 3:22,23. Slaves, obey your earthly masters in everything; and do it, *not only when their eye is on you* and to win their favor, but with sincerity of heart and reverence for the Lord. Whatever you do, *work at it with all your heart,* as working for the Lord, not for men.

104b. God wants us to help our employer with his money and property by faithful work.

> 480) 1 Corinthians 10:24. Nobody should *seek* his own good, but *the good of others.*
>
> 481) Genesis 13:5-12; 14:12-16. (Abraham generously gave Lot the first choice of land and recovered his property for him at the risk of his [Abraham's] own life.)
>
> 482) Proverbs 11:25. A *generous man* will prosper; he who *refreshes others* will himself be refreshed.

104c. God wants us to be as concerned about helping others with their money and property as we are about our own.

105. How does the Seventh Commandment serve as a mirror for us?

> 483) Genesis 25:29-33. (Jacob took advantage of Esau to get him to sell his birthright.)
>
> 484) James 2:14-17. (Failure to help the needy is a sin.)
>
> 485) 2 Corinthians 9:7. Each man should give what he has decided in his heart to give, *not reluctantly or under compulsion,* for God loves a cheerful giver.
>
> 486) Colossians 3:5. Put to death . . . whatever belongs to your earthly nature: . . . *desires and greed,* which is idolatry.

105. The Seventh Commandment shows us our sins because we have not always been content with our possessions or used them as God wants us to.

106. How did Jesus save us from our sins against the Seventh Commandment?

487) 2 Corinthians 8:9. You know the grace of our Lord Jesus Christ, that though he was rich, yet *for your sakes he became poor,* so that you through his poverty might become rich.

488) Romans 5:19. Just as through the disobedience of the one man the many were made sinners, so also *through the obedience of the one* man the many will be made righteous.

106a. Jesus saved us by keeping the Seventh Commandment perfectly for us.

489) Galatians 3:13. Christ redeemed us from the curse of the law by *becoming a curse for us,* for it is written: "Cursed is everyone who is hung on a tree."

106b. Jesus saved us by dying to take away the curse of our sins.

107. How does the Seventh Commandment serve as a guideline for us?

490) Ephesians 4:28. He who has been stealing must *steal no longer, but* must *work,* doing something useful with his own hands, that he may have something *to share with those in need.*

491) Hebrews 11:24-26. (Moses rejected the treasures of Egypt to belong to God's people.)

492) Hebrews 13:15,16. Through Jesus . . . let us continually offer to God a *sacrifice of praise*—the fruit of lips that confess his name. And do not forget to *do good and to share with others,* for with such sacrifices *God is pleased.*

107. The Seventh Commandment shows us that God wants us to thank him for his goodness by using his gift of possessions in ways which are pleasing to him.

THE EIGHTH COMMANDMENT
(God's Gift of a Good Name)

You shall not give false testimony against your neighbor.

What does this mean?

We should fear and love God that we do not tell lies about our neighbor, betray him, or give him a bad name, but defend him, speak well of him, and take his words and actions in the kindest possible way.

108. What is God protecting by the Eighth Commandment?

493) Proverbs 22:1. A good name is *more desirable* than great riches; to be esteemed is *better* than silver or gold.

494) Proverbs 11:9. With his mouth the godless *destroys* his neighbor.

495) Matthew 12:36. I tell you that *men will have to give account* on the day of judgment for every careless word they have spoken.

108. By the Eighth Commandment, God is protecting the gift of a good name.

109. Why is God's gift of a good name important?

496) Leviticus 19:16. Do not go about spreading *slander* among your people.

497) Proverbs 16:28. A perverse man *stirs up dissension,* and a gossip *separates close friends.*

498) Genesis 39:16-20. (Potiphar threw Joseph into prison because of a lie.)

109. A good name is important because it determines whether or not other people will respect us or trust us.

110. What does God forbid regarding his gift of a good name?

499) Colossians 3:9. Do not lie *to each other.*

500) Proverbs 19:5. A false witness will *not go unpunished,* and he who pours out lies will *not go free.*

501) John 8:44. [The devil] is a liar and the *father of lies.*

502) Genesis 39:16-20. (Potiphar's wife told a lie about Joseph.)

503) Psalm 109:2. They have spoken *against me* with lying tongues.

110a. God forbids us to lie to another person or about him.

504) John 13:2. The devil had already prompted Judas Iscariot, son of Simon, to *betray* Jesus.

505) Proverbs 25:9. Do not *betray* another man's confidence.

506) Proverbs 11:13. A gossip *betrays a confidence,* but a trustworthy man *keeps a secret.*

110b. God forbids us to betray another person's secrets.

507) 2 Samuel 15:1-6. (Absalom criticized his father to give him a bad name.)

508) James 4:11. Do not *slander* one another.

509) Proverbs 17:9. He who covers over an offense promotes love, but whoever *repeats the matter* separates close friends.

510) 1 Timothy 5:13. They get into the habit of being idle and *going about from house to house.* And not only do they become idlers, but also *gossips* and busybodies, *saying things they ought not to.*

110c. God forbids us to say anything that will give another person a bad name.

111. What, then, does God mean when he forbids false testimony?

511) Genesis 3:1-5. (The devil spoke from a heart that intended to hurt God's good name and to hurt Adam and Eve.)

512) Matthew 22:15-18. (The Pharisees spoke from hearts that intended to trap Jesus.)

513) John 12:1-6. (Judas spoke against Mary from a heart that had evil intentions.)

514) Proverbs 6:16-19. The Lord hates . . . a *heart that devises wicked schemes,* . . . a false witness who pours out lies and a man who stirs up dissension among brothers.

111. When God forbids false testimony, he means all talk, whether true or untrue, that comes from a heart with evil intentions.

112. What does God want us to do according to the Eighth Commandment?

515) 1 Samuel 20:30-32. (Jonathan defended David.)

516) Proverbs 31:8,9. *Speak up* for those who cannot speak for themselves, . . . *defend* the rights of the poor and needy.

112a. God wants us to defend the good name of others.

517) 1 Samuel 19:1-6. (Jonathan spoke well of David.)

518) Luke 7:1-5. (The Jews spoke well of the centurion.)

112b. God wants us to speak well of others.

519) 1 Corinthians 13:5-7. [Love] *keeps no record* of wrongs. *Love does not delight in evil* but rejoices with the truth. It *always protects,* always trusts, always hopes, always perseveres.

520) Luke 6:37. *Do not judge,* and you will not be judged. *Do not condemn,* and you will not be condemned. *Forgive,* and you will be forgiven.

521) Proverbs 10:12. Hatred stirs up dissension, but *love covers over all wrongs.*

522) 1 Peter 4:8. Above all, love each other deeply, because *love covers over a multitude of sins.*

112c. God wants us to take the words and actions of others in the kindest possible way.

113. What does God want us to do when we know about another person's sin?

523) 2 Samuel 12:1-14. (Nathan pointed out David's sin to him.)

524) Matthew 14:1-4. (John pointed out Herod's sin to him.)

525) Matthew 18:15. If your brother sins against you, go and *show him his* fault, just *between the two of you.* If he listens to you, you have *won your brother over.*

God's
Gift of a
GOOD NAME

Do!

— Defend others

— Speak well
of others

— Take words and
actions in the
kindest possible
way

— Lead to
repentance

Don't
Do!

— Lie

— Betray

— Give anyone
a bad name

**OTHERS RESPECT
AND
TRUST US**

526) Luke 17:3. If your brother sins, *rebuke him,* and if he repents, *forgive him.*

113. God wants us to go to him and show him his sin in order to lead him to repent.

114. How does the Eighth Commandment serve as a mirror for us?

527) James 3:2,6. We all stumble in many ways. If anyone is *never at fault in what he says,* he is a perfect man, able to keep his whole body in check. The *tongue. . . is a fire,* a world of evil among the parts of the body. *It corrupts the whole person,* sets the whole course of his life on fire, and is itself *set on fire by hell.*

528) Romans 1:29-32. They have become filled with *every kind of wickedness. . . .* They are *gossips, slanderers. . . .* they know God's righteous decree that those who do such things *deserve death.*

114. The Eighth Commandment shows us our sins because we have not always honored God's gift of a good name as he wants us to.

115. How did Jesus save us from our sins against the Eighth Commandment?

529) Matthew 12:1-7. (Jesus defended his disciples.)

530) Matthew 26:6-13. (Jesus spoke well of Mary.)

531) Luke 23:34. (Jesus took the words and actions of those who crucified him in the kindest possible way.)

532) 1 Peter 2:22,23. He committed no sin, and no deceit was found in his mouth. When they hurled their insults at him, *he did not retaliate;* when he suffered, *he made no threats.* Instead, he entrusted himself to him who judges justly.

115a. Jesus saved us by keeping the Eighth Commandment perfectly for us.

533) Romans 5:8,10. While we were still sinners, *Christ died for us.* . . . when we were God's enemies, *we were reconciled* to him through the death of his Son.

115b. Jesus saved us by dying for all our sins.

116. How does the Eighth Commandment serve as a guideline for us?

> 534) Ephesians 4:25. Each of you must *put off falsehood* and *speak truthfully* to his neighbor.
>
> 535) Colossians 3:12,13. As *God's chosen people,* holy and dearly loved, *clothe yourselves* with compassion, *kindness,* humility, gentleness and *patience. Bear with* each other and *forgive* whatever grievances you may have against one another. Forgive *as the Lord forgave you.*
>
> 536) 1 Peter 3:8-10. *Live in harmony* with one another; be sympathetic, love as brothers, be compassionate and humble. *Do not repay* evil with evil or *insult with insult,* but with *blessing, because* to this you were called so that you may inherit a blessing. For, "Whoever would love life and see good days must keep *his tongue* from evil and *his lips* from deceitful speech."

116. The Eighth Commandment shows us that God wants us to thank him for his goodness by the way we speak about the good name of other people.

THE NINTH COMMANDMENT
(Holy Desires)

You shall not covet your neighbor's house.

What does this mean?

We should fear and love God that we do not scheme to get our neighbor's inheritance or house, or obtain it by a show of right, but do all we can to help him keep it.

THE TENTH COMMANDMENT

You shall not covet your neighbor's wife, workers, animals, or anything that belongs to your neighbor.

What does this mean?

We should fear and love God that we do not force or entice away our neighbor's spouse, workers, or animals, but urge them to stay and do their duty.

117. What does God mean when he forbids us to covet?

537) Romans 7:7,8. *I would not have known what coveting really was* if the law had not said, "Do not covet." But sin, seizing the opportunity afforded by the commandment, produced in me every kind of covetous *desire.*

538) Joshua 7:20,21. (Achan had a sinful desire for the forbidden plunder.)

539) Psalm 10:2,3. The wicked man . . . boasts of the *cravings of his heart;* he blesses the greedy and reviles the LORD.

540) James 4:2. You . . . covet, but you *cannot have what you want.*

117. When God forbids us to covet, he is forbidding us to have a sinful desire or craving in our hearts for something we should not want to have.

118. What is God deeply impressing on us, then, by the two commands, "You shall not covet"?

541) Psalm 94:11. *The LORD knows the thoughts* of man.

542) Proverbs 15:26. *The LORD detests the thoughts* of the wicked, but those of the pure are pleasing to him.

543) Hebrews 4:12,13. The word of God . . . judges the *thoughts and attitudes of the heart.* Nothing in all creation is hidden from God's sight. Everything is uncovered and laid bare before the eyes of him to whom *we must give account.*

118. God is impressing on us that he knows and condemns not only our sinful words and actions but also our sinful thoughts.

119. What will sinful desires tempt us to do?

544) James 1:14,15. Each one is tempted when, by his own evil desire, he is dragged away and enticed. Then, after desire has conceived, *it gives birth to sin.*

545) 1 Timothy 6:10. The love of money is *a root* of all kinds of evil.

119a. Sinful desires will tempt us to sin also in word or action.

546) 1 Kings 21:1-16. (Ahab's coveting of Naboth's inheritance led to scheming that included false witness and murder.)

547) Isaiah 5:8. Woe to you who add house to house and join field to field.

548) James 5:5,6. You have lived on earth in luxury and self-indulgence. You have *fattened yourselves* in the day of slaughter. *You have condemned* and murdered *innocent men,* who were not opposing you.

119b. Sinful desires will tempt us to scheme to get another person's property or house or obtain it by a show of right.

549) Matthew 14:3,4. (Herod took his brother Philip's wife away from him.)

550) 2 Samuel 15:2-6. (Absalom turned the hearts of the people away from King David to himself.)

551) 2 Samuel 12:1-5. (Nathan pictures a rich man who forced the poor man to give up his pet lamb.)

119c. Sinful desires will tempt us to force or entice away another person's spouse, workers, or animals.

120. What does God teach us by adding the words "or anything that belongs to your neighbor"?

552) 1 Corinthians 7:17. Each one should retain *the place in life* that the Lord assigned to him and to which God has called him.

553) Philippians 4:11-13. I have learned to be *content whatever the circumstances.* I know what it is to be in need, and I know what it is to have plenty. I have learned the secret of being *content in any and every situation,* whether well fed or hungry, whether living in plenty or in want. I can do everything *through him who gives me strength.*

554) Hebrews 13:5. Be content with what you have, *because God has said, "Never* will I leave you; *never* will I forsake you."

120. By adding these words, God teaches us always to be content with everything in our lives so that we do not covet anything that belongs to our neighbor.

121. What kind of desires does God want us to have in our hearts?

555) Leviticus 19:2. *Be holy* because I, the LORD your God, am holy.

556) Matthew 5:8. Blessed are the *pure in heart,* for they will see God.

557) Philippians 4:8. Whatever is pure, whatever is lovely, whatever is admirable—if anything is excellent or praiseworthy—*think about such things.*

121. God wants us to have only pure and holy desires in our hearts.

122. What will such holy desires lead us to do?

558) Galatians 5:13. *Serve one another* in love.

559) Philippians 2:4. Each of you should *look* not only to your own interests, but also *to the interests of others.*

560) Genesis 14:13-24. (Abraham helped Lot and the king of Sodom recover their property.)

122a. Holy desires lead us to do all we can to help another person keep his property and house.

561) Genesis 39:8-10. (By resisting her advances Joseph urged Potiphar's wife to be faithful to her husband.)

562) Philemon 12. (Paul urged the slave Onesimus to go back to his master.)

563) Exodus 23:4. If you come across your enemy's ox or donkey wandering off, be sure to *take it back to him.*

122b. Holy desires will lead us to urge another person's spouse, workers, or animals to stay and do their duty.

123. How do the Ninth and Tenth Commandments serve as a mirror for us?

564) Romans 7:7,8. *I would not have known* what coveting really was if the law had not said, "Do not covet." But sin, seizing the opportunity afforded by the commandment, *produced in me every kind of covetous desire.*

565) Proverbs 20:9. *Who can say,* "I have kept my heart pure; I am clean and without sin"?

566) James 4:1,2. What causes fights and quarrels among you? Don't they come *from your desires* that battle within you? *You want* something but don't get it. You kill and covet, *but you cannot have* what you want.

123. The Ninth and Tenth Commandments show us our sins because we have sinful desires or cravings for something we should not want to have.

124. How did Jesus save us from our sins against these commandments?

567) Hebrews 4:15. We have one who has been *tempted in every way,* just as we are—yet was *without sin.*

568) 1 John 3:5. In him [Jesus] is no sin.

124a. Jesus saved us by keeping the Ninth and Tenth Commandments perfectly for us.

569) 1 Corinthians 15:3. Christ *died for our sins* according to the Scriptures.

570) Hebrews 9:26. He has appeared once for all at the end of the ages to *do away with sin by the sacrifice of himself.*

124b. Jesus saved us by dying as a sacrifice for all our sins.

125. How do the Ninth and Tenth Commandments serve as a guideline for us?

571) Galatians 5:24. Those who *belong to Christ Jesus* have *crucified* the sinful nature with its *passions and desires.*

572) Ephesians 4:22-24. *You were taught,* with regard to your former way of life, to *put off* your old self, which is being corrupted by its *deceitful desires; to be made new in the attitude of your minds; and to put on the new self, created to be like God in true righteousness and holiness.*

573) 1 Peter 1:14-16. As obedient children, do not conform to the evil desires you had when you lived in ignorance. But just as he who called you is holy, so be holy in all you do; for it is written: *"Be holy,* because I am holy."

574) 1 Peter 4:1,2. *Since Christ suffered* in his body, arm yourselves . . . with the same attitude, because he who has suffered in his body is done with sin. As a result, he does *not live* the rest of his earthly life *for evil human desires, but* rather *for the will of God.*

575) 1 John 3:2,3. We know that when he appears, we shall be like him, for we shall see him as he is. *Everyone who has this hope* in him *purifies himself,* just as he is pure.

125. The Ninth and Tenth Commandments show us that God wants us to thank him for his goodness by having only holy desires in our hearts.

The Old Adam and the New Man or New Person

126. Why do we have so many sinful desires?

576) Romans 7:18. I know that *nothing good* lives in me, that is, in my *sinful nature.*

577) Genesis 6:5. The LORD saw how great man's wickedness on the earth had become, and that *every inclination* of the thoughts *of his heart* was *only evil all the time.* (See also Genesis 8:21.)

578) Mark 7:21,22. From within, *out of men's hearts,* come evil thoughts, sexual immorality, theft, murder, adultery, greed, malice, deceit, lewdness, envy, slander, arrogance and folly.

579) Romans 8:7. The *sinful mind is hostile to God.* It does not submit to God's law, *nor can it do so.*

126. We have so many sinful desires because by nature we have a heart and a mind that are inclined only toward evil. (sinful nature, flesh, old Adam, old man, or old self)

127. Why do we have by nature a heart and a mind that are inclined only toward evil?

580) Genesis 2:16,17; 3:6. (Adam and Eve disobeyed God's command and so brought sin and death into the world.)

581) Romans 5:12. Just as sin entered the world through one man, and death through sin, and *in this way death came to all men, because all sinned.*

582) John 3:6. Flesh *gives birth* to flesh.

583) Psalm 51:5. Surely I was *sinful at birth,* sinful *from the time my mother conceived me.*

584) Ephesians 2:3. Like the rest, we were *by nature* objects of wrath.

127. We have such a heart and mind by nature because all people are conceived and born in sin as a result of Adam's fall into sin. (inherited or original sin)

128. What punishment do we deserve because of our sinful nature and the sinful desires it produces in us?

585) Genesis 6:4-7. (God brought the judgment of the flood on men both because of their evil deeds and their sinful desires.)

586) Matthew 5:28,29. Anyone who looks at a woman lustfully has already *committed adultery* with her in his heart. If your right eye causes you to sin, gouge it out and throw it away. It is better for you to lose one part of your body than for your whole body to *be thrown into hell.*

587) 1 John 3:15. Anyone who hates his brother is a *murderer,* and you know that *no murderer has eternal life* in him.

588) Romans 6:23. The wages of sin is *death.*

128. We deserve the same punishment of death and hell for sinful thoughts as we do for sinful words and actions.

129. How are we saved from the punishment we deserve because of our sinful nature and the sinful desires it produces in us?

589) Ephesians 2:1,3-5. As for you, you were *dead in* your transgressions and sins. . . . All of us . . . lived among them at one time, gratifying the *cravings of our sinful nature* and following its desires and thoughts. Like the rest, we were *by nature objects of wrath.* But because of his great love for us, *God,* who is rich in mercy, *made us alive with Christ* even when we were dead in transgressions—it is *by grace* you have been saved.

590) Romans 5:17. If, *by the trespass of the one man,* death reigned through that one man, how much more will those who receive God's abundant provision of *grace* and of the *gift of righteousness* reign in life *through the one man, Jesus Christ.*

129. It is only by God's grace to us in Christ that we are saved from the punishment we deserve because of our sinful nature.

130. What is the only reason that we have pure and holy desires in our hearts?

591) Ezekiel 11:19,20. *I will give them* an *undivided heart* and put a *new spirit* in them; I will remove from them their heart of stone and give them a heart of flesh. *Then they will follow my decrees* and be careful to *keep my laws.*

592) 2 Corinthians 5:17,18. If anyone is *in Christ,* he is a *new creation;* the old has gone, the new has come! *All this is from God,* who reconciled us to himself through Christ.

593) Ephesians 4:21-24. You heard of him [Christ] and were taught in him in accordance with the truth that is in Jesus. You were taught . . . to put off your old self, which is being corrupted by its deceitful desires; to be *made new in the attitude of your minds;* and to put on the *new self,* created to be like God in true righteousness and *holiness.*

594) Romans 7:22. In my inner being *I delight* in God's law.

COVETING

(sinful desires)

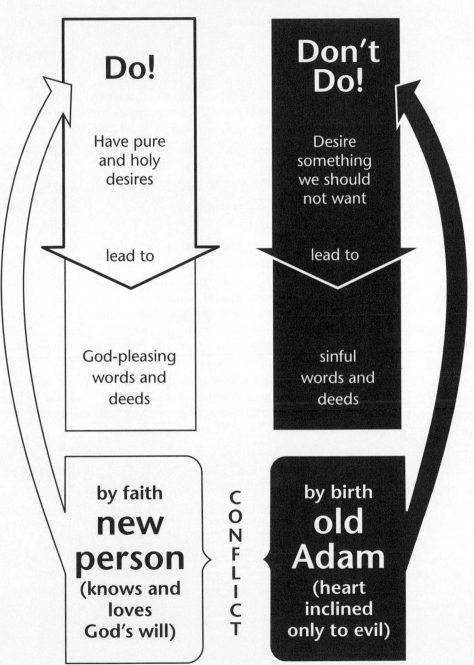

Do!

Have pure and holy desires

lead to

God-pleasing words and deeds

by faith
new person
(knows and loves God's will)

Don't Do!

Desire something we should not want

lead to

sinful words and deeds

by birth
old Adam
(heart inclined only to evil)

CONFLICT

130. We have pure and holy desires only because of the new heart and mind that God creates in us by faith in Jesus. (new man, new person, new self, inner being, spirit)

131. What is the result of our having both an old Adam and a new man in us?

595) Romans 7:25. So then, I myself in my mind am *a slave to God's law,* but in the sinful nature *a slave to the law of sin.*

596) Galatians 5:17. The sinful nature desires what is *contrary* to the Spirit, and the Spirit what is *contrary* to the sinful nature. They are in *conflict* with each other.

131. The result is a constant conflict in us between our old Adam and our new man.

132. How are we strengthened in this conflict to fight the old Adam and to follow the new man?

597) Romans 7:22-25. In my inner being I delight in God's law; but I see another law at work in the members of my body, waging war against the law of my mind and making me a prisoner of the law of sin at work within my members. What a wretched man I am! Who will rescue me from this body of death? Thanks be to God—*through Jesus Christ our Lord!*

598) Galatians 2:20. I have been crucified with Christ and I no longer live, but *Christ lives in me.* The life I live in the body, *I live by faith in the Son of God,* who loved me and gave himself for me.

132. God strengthens us by faith in Jesus to fight the old Adam and to follow the new man. (See "Belonging to Christ" under The Second Article, "Sanctified to Do Good Works" under The Third Article, and the fourth part of Baptism.)

THE CONCLUSION

*What does God say about all
these commandments?*

He says, "I, the LORD your God, am a jealous God, punishing the children for the sin of the fathers to the third and fourth generation of those who hate me, but showing love to a thousand generations of those who love me and keep my commandments."

What does this mean?

God threatens to punish all who transgress these commandments. Therefore we should fear his anger and not disobey what he commands.

But he promises grace and every blessing to all who keep these commandments. Therefore we should love and trust in him and gladly obey what he commands.

133. How does God want his commandments to be kept?

    599) Leviticus 19:2. *Be holy* because I, the LORD your God, am holy.

    600) Matthew 5:48. *Be perfect,* therefore, as your heavenly Father is perfect.

    601) James 2:10. Whoever keeps the whole law and yet *stumbles at just one point* is guilty of breaking all of it.

133. God wants his commandments to be kept perfectly.

134. What does God call any breaking of his commandments?

    602) 1 John 3:4. Everyone who sins breaks the law; in fact, *sin* is lawlessness.

603) Isaiah 53:5. He was pierced for our *transgressions,* he was crushed for our *iniquities.*

134. God calls any breaking of his commandments sin (missing the mark), transgression (crossing the forbidden line), and iniquity (failing to measure up perfectly).

135. With what does God threaten to punish all who break his commandments?

604) Genesis 3:17,18. (God cursed the ground as a constant reminder of his anger with sin.)

605) Genesis 4:1-16. (God was angry with Cain and punished him for his sin of killing his brother Abel.)

606) Psalm 38:1-8. (David felt the anger of God resting on him.)

607) Isaiah 57:21. "There is no peace," says my God, "for the wicked."

608) Romans 1:18. *The wrath of God* is being revealed from heaven against all the godlessness and wickedness of men.

609) 1 Samuel 15:22,23. (God rejected Saul as king because of his disobedience.)

610) 1 Kings 17:1; 18:16-18. (God brought a famine on the people of Israel because Ahab led them to worship Baal.)

135a. God threatens to punish all who break his commandments with his anger and with trouble during their lives on earth.

611) Genesis 2:17; 3:17,19. (The result of sin is death.)

612) Ezekiel 18:4. The soul who *sins* is the one who will *die.*

613) Romans 6:23. The *wages of sin* is *death.*

614) Romans 5:12. *Death* came to all men, *because all sinned.*

615) Luke 16:22-24. (After death the rich man was in the torment of hell.)

616) Matthew 10:28. Be afraid of the One who can *destroy both soul and body* in hell.

617) Matthew 25:41,46. Then he will say to those on his left, "Depart from me, you who are cursed, into the eternal fire prepared for the devil and his angels." Then they will go away to *eternal punishment.*

135b. God threatens to punish all who break his commandments with death and the eternal fire of hell.

136. What does God want to impress on us by his threat to punish to the third and fourth generation of those that hate him?

618) Deuteronomy 5:9. I, the LORD your God, am *a jealous God,* punishing the children for the sin of the fathers to the third and fourth generation of those who hate me.

619) Deuteronomy 6:13,15. Fear the LORD your God, *serve him only* . . . for the LORD your God, who is among you, is a jealous God.

620) Deuteronomy 4:24. The LORD your God is *a consuming fire,* a jealous God.

621) Galatians 3:10. Cursed is everyone who does *not continue* to *do everything* written in the Book of the Law.

136. By this threat God wants to impress on us that he is a jealous God, that is, he is serious about wanting us to keep every one of his commandments.

137. Why do we need God's threat to punish sinners?

622) Romans 8:7,8. The sinful mind is *hostile to God.* It does not submit to God's law. . . . Those controlled by the sinful nature cannot please God.

623) Genesis 8:21. *Every inclination* of his heart *is evil* from childhood.

137. We need God's threat to punish sinners because our sinful nature opposes God's will and is inclined to do only evil.

138. What should God's threat to punish sinners lead us to do?

624) Psalm 119:120. My *flesh trembles* in fear of you; I *stand in awe of your laws.*

625) Psalm 119:80. May my heart be *blameless toward your decrees,* that I may not be put to shame.

138. God's threat to punish sinners should lead us to fear God's anger and not disobey what he commands.

139. What does God promise to those who love him and keep his commandments?

626) Deuteronomy 7:9. Know therefore that the LORD your God is God; he is the faithful God, *keeping his covenant of love to a thousand generations* of those who love him and keep his commands.

627) Psalm 103:11. As high as the heavens are above the earth, *so great is his love* for those who fear him.

628) Luke 1:50. His *mercy* extends to those who fear him.

629) Genesis 22:1-18. (Note especially verses 16-18. God promises blessings to obedient Abraham.)

630) Matthew 5:3-10. (God promises many blessings to those who love and obey his commands.)

139. God promises grace and every blessing to those who love him and keep his commandments.

140. What does God want to impress on us with his promise to bless those who love him and keep his commandments?

631) Deuteronomy 5:9,10. I, the LORD your God, am a *jealous God* . . . showing love to a thousand generations of those who love me and keep my commandments.

632) 1 John 2:5. If anyone *obeys his word,* God's love is truly made complete in him.

633) James 1:25. The man who looks intently into the perfect law that gives freedom, and *continues to do this,* not forgetting what he has heard, but doing it—he will be blessed in what he does.

634) Deuteronomy 5:29. Oh, that their hearts would be inclined to fear me and keep *all my commands always,* so that it might go well with them and their children forever!

140. By this promise God wants to impress on us that he is a jealous God, that is, he is serious about wanting us to keep every one of his commandments.

141. How does God's promise to bless our obedience also reveal his grace to us?

635) Romans 11:35. Who has ever given to God, that God should *repay* him?

636) Luke 17:10. So you also, when you have done everything you were told to do, should say, "We are unworthy servants; we have *only done our duty.*"

JEALOUS GOD

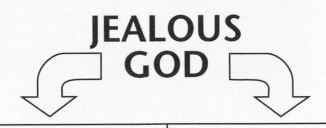

Threat

Anger
and
Trouble

Death
and
Hell

FEAR
AND
NOT DISOBEY

Promise

Mercy

Grace

Every
Blessing

LOVE AND TRUST
AND
GLADLY OBEY

**OBEY EVERY ONE
OF GOD'S COMMANDS**

141. Since it is our duty to obey God's commandments, his promise to bless our obedience is really an undeserved gift.

142. What should God's gracious promise lead us to do?

637) Psalm 119:58-60. I have sought your face with all my heart; be gracious to me according to your promise. *I have considered my ways* and have *turned my steps* to your statutes. I will hasten and not delay *to obey your commands.*

638) Deuteronomy 10:12. What does the LORD your God ask of you but *to fear* the LORD your God, *to walk* in all his ways, *to love* him, *to serve* the LORD your God with *all your heart* and with *all your soul?*

142. God's gracious promise should lead us to love and trust in him and gladly obey what he commands.

143. In summary, then, what is the Lord our God urging us to do by the combination of his threat and his promise?

639) Deuteronomy 11:26-28,32. See, I am setting before you today *a blessing and a curse*—the *blessing if you obey* the commands of the LORD your God that I am giving you today; the *curse if you disobey* the commands of the LORD your God. . . . *be sure that you obey all the decrees and laws* I am setting before you today.

143. By the combination of his threat and his promise, God is urging us to obey every one of his commandments.

144. What, however, must we all confess in spite of God's threat and promise?

640) Isaiah 64:6. *All of us* have become like one who is *unclean,* and all our righteous acts are like filthy rags.

641) Romans 3:23. All have sinned and *fall short* of the glory of God.

642) Psalm 143:2. [O LORD], do not bring your servant into judgment, for *no one living is righteous* before you.

643) Luke 18:13. God, have mercy on me, *a sinner.*

144. In spite of God's threat and promise, we must all confess that we are sinners who have fallen far short of the perfection which God demands.

The Creed

THE GOSPEL

The Differences between Law and Gospel

145. Why is the gospel so comforting to us sinners, who stand condemned by God's law?

644) Luke 2:8-12. (The angel brought good news of great joy at the birth of the Savior.)

645) Romans 1:16. I am not ashamed of the *gospel*, because it is the power of God for the *salvation* of everyone who believes.

646) John 3:16. *God so loved the world* that he *gave his one and only Son,* that whoever believes in him shall not perish but have *eternal life.*

145. The gospel is so comforting to us because it tells us that God in his love for us sinners sent Jesus to save us.

146. In what ways is the gospel different from the law?

647) Romans 2:14,15. When Gentiles, who do not have the law, do by nature things required by the law . . . they show that the requirements of the *law* are *written on their hearts.*

648) 1 Corinthians 2:9,10. *"No eye* has seen, *no ear* has heard, *no mind* has conceived what God has prepared for those who love him"—but *God has revealed it* to us by his Spirit.

649) 2 Timothy 3:15. From infancy you have known *the holy Scriptures,* which are able to *make you wise for salvation* through faith in Christ Jesus.

146a. The law is written in our hearts and in the Bible (see Question 18), but the gospel is revealed to us only in the Bible.

650) Galatians 3:12. The *law* is not based on faith; on the *contrary,* "The man who *does these things* will live by them."

651) John 3:16. *God so loved* the world that *he gave* his one and only Son, that whoever believes in him shall not perish but have eternal life.

652) 1 John 4:10. This is love: *not that we* loved God, *but that he* loved us and sent his Son as an atoning sacrifice for our sins.

146b. The law teaches us what we are to do and not to do (see Question 14), but the gospel teaches us what God has done to save us.

653) Galatians 3:8,10. The Scripture foresaw that God would justify the Gentiles by faith, and announced the *gospel* in advance to Abraham: *"All nations* will be *blessed* through you." All who rely on observing the *law* are under a curse, for it is written: *"Cursed is everyone* who does not continue to do everything written in the Book of the Law."

654) John 3:16. God so loved the world that he gave his one and only Son, that whoever believes in him shall *not perish but have eternal life.*

655) Colossians 2:13,14. When you were dead in *your sins* and in the uncircumcision of your sinful nature, God made you alive with Christ. *He forgave us all our sins,* having canceled the written code, with its regulations, that was against us and that stood opposed to us; *he took it away,* nailing it to the cross.

146c. The law teaches us about sin and God's punishment of sin (see Question 15), but the gospel teaches us about our Savior from sin and God's gift of eternal life.

147. How does the gospel change our attitude toward obeying the law?

656) Romans 3:28. A man is justified by faith *apart from observing the law.*

657) Colossians 3:17. Whatever you do, whether in word or deed, do it all in the name of the Lord Jesus, *giving thanks* to God the Father through him.

658) Romans 12:1. *In view of God's mercy* . . . offer your bodies as living sacrifices, holy and pleasing to God—this is your *spiritual act of worship.*

659) 2 Corinthians 5:14,15. Christ's love compels us. . . . he died for all, that those who *live* should no longer live for themselves but *for him* who died for them and was raised again.

147. The gospel leads us to obey the law out of thanks to God for our completed salvation instead of obeying it to try to save ourselves.

Differences
between

LAW GOSPEL

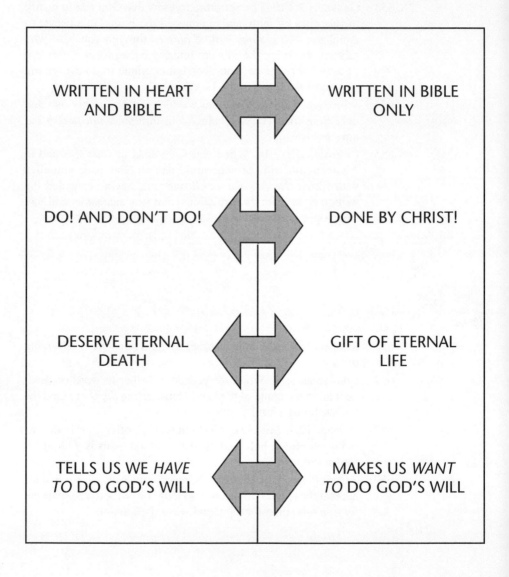

WRITTEN IN HEART AND BIBLE ⟷ WRITTEN IN BIBLE ONLY

DO! AND DON'T DO! ⟷ DONE BY CHRIST!

DESERVE ETERNAL DEATH ⟷ GIFT OF ETERNAL LIFE

TELLS US WE *HAVE TO* DO GOD'S WILL ⟷ MAKES US *WANT TO* DO GOD'S WILL

The Creeds

A creed is a statement of what a person or a group of people believes and teaches. The creed that we will be studying is called the Apostles' Creed because it is a brief statement of the gospel truths which were taught by the apostles.

The Apostles' Creed developed in the early Christian church because people felt a need to have a brief summary of what they believed and taught as Christians. The wording of the Apostles' Creed developed gradually, but it soon was used wherever the Christian church had spread. Christians used it to tell others what they believed and also to confess their faith with one another when they met for worship. The Apostles' Creed also was used in the early church to teach children the basic gospel truths of the Bible.

The gospel is summarized by the Apostles' Creed in three parts because the true God is three persons: Father, Son, and Holy Spirit. Each part of the Apostles' Creed is called an article, and each article tells us what one of the divine persons has done and is still doing to bless us and to save us. Thus the gospel message of the Apostles' Creed is the good news that our God has made us, that he has redeemed us, and that he sanctifies us.

There also are two other Christian creeds that are similar to the Apostles' Creed. They are the Nicene Creed (see page 15) and the Athanasian Creed. When some false doctrines about God arose in the early Christian church, these two creeds were written to confess the Bible truth about God and to reject the errors. We will not be studying either of these two creeds, but they are also good to know because we use them at times in our worship services to confess our faith.

The Nature and Characteristics of God

148. Why do we refer to God with the word "triune"?

660) Matthew 3:16,17. (God reveals himself as three persons at Jesus' baptism.)

661) John 15:26. When the *Counselor* comes, whom *I* will send to you from the *Father, the Spirit of truth who goes out from the Father,* he will testify about *me.*

662) Matthew 28:19. Go and make disciples of all nations, baptizing them in the name of the *Father* and of the *Son* and of the *Holy Spirit.*

663) Genesis 1:26. Then God said, "Let *us* make man in *our* image, in *our* likeness."

664) 2 Corinthians 13:14. May the grace of the *Lord Jesus Christ,* and the love of *God,* and the fellowship of the *Holy Spirit* be with you all.

665) Deuteronomy 6:4. Hear, O Israel: The LORD our God, the LORD is *one.*

666) John 10:30. I and the Father are *one.*

667) 1 Corinthians 8:4. There is no God but *one.*

148. We refer to God as triune because he reveals himself as three persons yet one God. (Trinity)

149. Why do we believe that God is triune even though this truth is impossible to understand or explain?

668) Numbers 23:19. God is not a man, that he should *lie.*

669) John 17:17. Your word is *truth.*

670) John 16:13. When he, the Spirit of truth, comes, he will *guide you into all truth.*

149. We believe that God is triune because God reveals this truth to us in his Word.

150. What does God reveal to us in his Word about his characteristics?

671) Psalm 42:2. My soul thirsts for God, for the *living* God.

672) John 4:24. God is *spirit.*

673) Luke 24:39. (Jesus proved to his disciples that he was not a spirit because he had flesh and bones.)

150a. In his Word God reveals that he is a spirit, that is, a living being without flesh and bones.

674) Deuteronomy 33:27. The *eternal* God is your refuge, and underneath are the *everlasting* arms.

GOD
is
TRIUNE

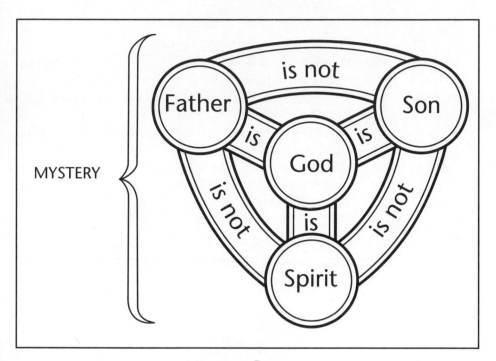

and a
SPIRIT

A REAL PERSON   WITHOUT A BODY

675) Genesis 17:1. I am God *Almighty.*

676) John 21:17. Lord, you *know all things.*

677) Jeremiah 23:24. "Do not I *fill heaven and earth?*" declares the LORD.

150b. In his Word God reveals that he is eternal, almighty (omnipotent), all-knowing (omniscient), and present everywhere (omnipresent).

678) Leviticus 19:2. I, the LORD your God, am *holy.*

679) Deuteronomy 32:4. A faithful God who does no wrong, upright and *just* is he.

680) 2 Timothy 2:13. If we are faithless, he will remain *faithful,* for he cannot disown himself.

681) Psalm 145:9. The LORD is *good* to all; he has compassion on all he has made.

682) Exodus 34:6,7. The LORD, the *compassionate* and *gracious* God, *slow to anger, abounding in love* and faithfulness, maintaining love to thousands, and *forgiving* wickedness, rebellion and sin. Yet he does *not leave the guilty unpunished.*

150c. In his Word God reveals that he is holy, just, faithful, good, compassionate, gracious, loving, and forgiving.

THE FIRST ARTICLE
(Creation)

I believe in God the Father almighty, maker of heaven and earth.

What does this mean?

I believe that God created me and all that exists, that he gave me my body and soul, eyes, ears, and all my members, my mind and all my abilities.

And I believe that God still preserves me by richly and daily providing clothing and shoes, food and drink, property and home, spouse and children, land, cattle, and all I own, and all I need to keep my body and life. God also preserves me by defending me against all danger, guarding and protecting me from all evil. All this God does only because he is my good and merciful Father in heaven, and not because I have earned or deserved it. For all this I ought to thank and praise, to serve and obey him.

This is most certainly true.

Faith

151. What does it mean when a Christian says, "I believe in God"?

> 683) Romans 10:14. *How can they believe* in the one of whom they have *not heard?*
>
> 684) Romans 10:17. *Faith comes from hearing* the message, and the message is heard *through the word* of Christ.

> 685) John 17:3. Now this is eternal life: that they may *know* you, the only *true God,* and Jesus Christ, whom you have sent.
>
> 686) 1 Thessalonians 2:13. You *accepted* it not as the word of men, but as it actually is, the *word of God.*

151a. When a Christian says, "I believe in God," it means he has learned to know the true God and accepts the Bible as God's Word.

> 687) Psalm 31:14. But I *trust in you,* O LORD; I say, "You are my God."
>
> 688) Matthew 8:5-13. (Jesus called the centurion's trust in him a great faith.)
>
> 689) Matthew 15:21-28. (Jesus called the Canaanite woman's trust in him a great faith.)
>
> 690) 1 Samuel 17, especially verses 37 and 45-47. (David put his trust in the Lord.)
>
> 691) Romans 4:20,21. [Abraham] *did not waver* through unbelief regarding the promise of God, but was strengthened in his faith and gave glory to God, being *fully persuaded* that God had power to do what he had promised.
>
> 692) John 20:24-29. (Jesus rebuked Thomas for insisting that he had to see before he would believe.)
>
> 693) Hebrews 11:1. Faith is *being sure* of what we *hope for* and *certain* of what we *do not see.*
>
> 694) 2 Timothy 1:12. I know whom I have believed, and am *convinced* that he is able to guard what I have *entrusted* to him for that day.

151b. When a Christian says, "I believe in God," it means he trusts in God and is certain that all of God's promises will be fulfilled.

152. Why do we as believers call the first person of the triune God "the Father"?

> 695) Malachi 2:10. Have we not all one *Father?* Did not one God *create us?*

152a. As believers we call the first person of the triune God "the Father" because he created us.

DIFFERENCES
BETWEEN

FAITH   UNBELIEF

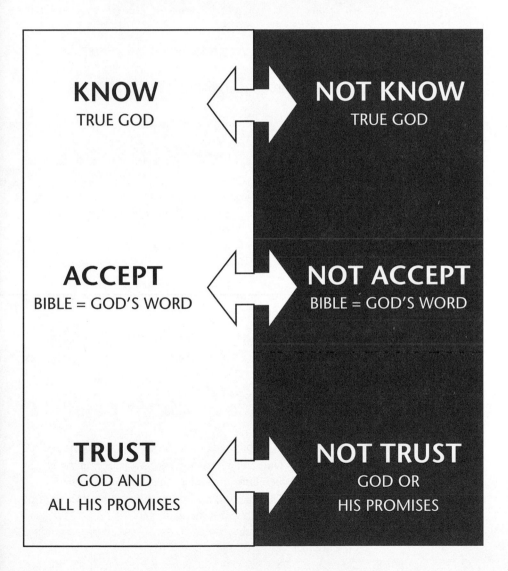

KNOW
TRUE GOD

NOT KNOW
TRUE GOD

ACCEPT
BIBLE = GOD'S WORD

NOT ACCEPT
BIBLE = GOD'S WORD

TRUST
GOD AND
ALL HIS PROMISES

NOT TRUST
GOD OR
HIS PROMISES

696) John 20:17. I am returning to *my Father* and *your Father,* to my God and your God.

697) Galatians 4:4,5. When the time had fully come, God sent *his Son,* born of a woman, born under law, to redeem those under law, that we might *receive the full rights of sons.*

698) Galatians 3:26. You are all sons of God *through faith* in Christ Jesus.

152b. As believers we call the first person of the triune God "the Father" because he is the Father of our Lord Jesus and also our Father through faith in Jesus.

Creation

153. Why do we confess that God the Father is the "almighty, maker of heaven and earth"?

699) Genesis 1:1–2:3. (God created heaven and earth out of nothing.)

700) Exodus 20:11. *In six days* the LORD made the heavens and the earth, the sea, and *all that is in them.*

701) Psalm 33:6,9. *By the word of the LORD* were the heavens made. . . . *he spoke,* and it came to be; *he commanded,* and it stood firm.

702) Psalm 124:8. Our help is in the name of the LORD, *the Maker* of heaven and earth.

153. We confess this because the Bible teaches that God the Father made all things in six days out of nothing by his almighty word.

154. What does the Bible teach us about the origin of mankind?

703) Genesis 1:26-31. (God made man and woman on the sixth day.)

704) Genesis 1:27. God created man *in his own image,* in the image of God he created him; male and female he created them.

705) Genesis 1:28. God blessed them and said to them, "Be fruitful and increase in number; fill the earth and *subdue it. Rule over* the fish of the sea and the birds of the air and over every living creature that moves on the ground."

706) Genesis 2:7. The LORD God *formed the man* from the dust of the ground and *breathed into his nostrils* the breath of life, and the man became a living being.

707) Isaiah 45:12. *It is I* who made the earth and *created mankind* upon it.

708) Mark 10:6. *At the beginning* of creation *God made* them male and female.

154. The Bible teaches us that on the sixth day God made man and woman in his own image as special creatures to rule over everything God had created.

155. **What does the Bible mean when it says that God created man and woman "in his own image"?**

709) Ephesians 4:24. Put on the new self, created to be like God in *true righteousness and holiness.*

710) Colossians 3:10. Put on the new self, which is being renewed in *knowledge* in the image of its Creator.

155. When the Bible says that God created man and woman "in his own image," it means that they were created holy and with the knowledge of God's holy will.

156. **Why don't we accept as fact any man-made theories about the origin of the world and of man?**

711) Job 38,39. (Note especially 38:4. No man was present to witness the origin of all things.)

712) 2 Peter 3:5,6. They *deliberately forget* that long ago by God's word the heavens existed and the earth was formed out of water and by water. By these waters also the *world of that time* was deluged and *destroyed.*

713) 1 Timothy 6:20,21. Turn away from *godless chatter* and the *opposing ideas* of what is *falsely called knowledge,* which *some* have professed and in so doing have *wandered from the faith.*

714) Hebrews 11:3. *By faith we understand* that the universe was formed at God's command, so that what is seen was not made out of what was visible.

156. We do not accept these man-made theories as fact because they are attempts by men to explain what we can know only by faith.

157. **How did God the Father show his goodness in my creation?**

715) Job 31:15. Did not *he* who *made me* in the womb make them? Did not the same one form us both within our mothers?

716) Job 10:11,12. [Did you not] clothe me with skin and flesh and knit me together with bones and sinews? You gave me life and *showed* me *kindness.*

717) Matthew 10:28. Do not be afraid of those who kill the *body* but cannot kill the *soul.*

718) Ecclesiastes 12:7. The dust returns to the ground it came from, and the *spirit* returns to *God* who *gave it.*

719) Job 38:36. Who endowed the heart with wisdom or *gave understanding to the mind?*

720) Exodus 4:11. Who *gave* man his mouth? Who *makes* him deaf or mute? Who *gives* him sight or *makes* him blind? Is it not I, the LORD?

721) 1 Corinthians 12:12,14-26. (God gave all the parts of the body an ability with which each part could help the whole body.)

722) Psalm 139:14. I praise you because I am *fearfully* and *wonderfully* made.

157. God the Father showed his goodness in my creation by giving me my body and soul, eyes, ears, and all my members, my mind and all my abilities.

Preservation

158. How does my heavenly Father show his goodness in my preservation?

723) Psalm 36:6,7. O LORD, you *preserve* both man and beast. How priceless is your *unfailing love!*

724) Matthew 6:25-34. (God provides our daily food and clothing.)

725) Psalm 145:15,16. The eyes of all look to you, and you *give them their food* at the proper time. You open your hand and *satisfy the desires* of every living thing.

726) 1 Peter 5:7. Cast all your anxiety on him because *he cares for you.*

158. My heavenly Father shows his goodness in my preservation by providing all that I need to keep my body and life.

DIFFERENCES
BETWEEN

CREATION   EVOLUTION

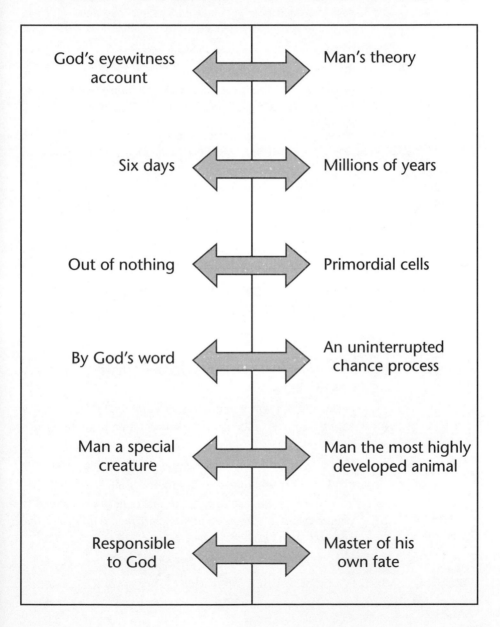

CREATION	EVOLUTION
God's eyewitness account	Man's theory
Six days	Millions of years
Out of nothing	Primordial cells
By God's word	An uninterrupted chance process
Man a special creature	Man the most highly developed animal
Responsible to God	Master of his own fate

159. How does my heavenly Father preserve me?

727) Psalm 104:14. He makes grass grow for the cattle, and plants for man to cultivate—bringing forth food *from the earth.*

728) Genesis 8:22. As long as the earth endures, seedtime and harvest, cold and heat, summer and winter, day and night *will never cease.*

729) Genesis 3:17-19. (Man has to work hard to get the food that the ground is able to produce.)

730) Genesis 9:3. Everything that lives and moves will be food for you. Just as I gave you the green plants, *I now give you everything.*

159a. My heavenly Father usually preserves me by natural means.

731) Exodus 16:1–17:7. (God provided food and water for Israel in the wilderness by miracles.)

732) 1 Kings 17:1-16. (God provided for Elijah through miracles.)

733) John 6:3-13. (Jesus fed 5,000 by a miracle.)

734) Matthew 19:26. With God all things are possible.

159b. My heavenly Father can also preserve me by miracles.

160. How well does my heavenly Father provide for my bodily needs?

735) Psalm 37:25. I was young and now I am old, yet I have *never seen* the righteous forsaken or their children begging bread.

736) Acts 14:17. He has shown kindness by giving you rain from heaven and crops in their seasons; he provides you with *plenty of food* and fills your hearts with joy.

737) 2 Corinthians 9:8. God is able to make all grace abound to you, so that in all things at *all times, having all that you need,* you will abound in every good work.

738) Luke 11:3. Give us each day our *daily* bread.

160. My heavenly Father provides for my bodily needs richly and daily.

GOD'S PROVIDENCE

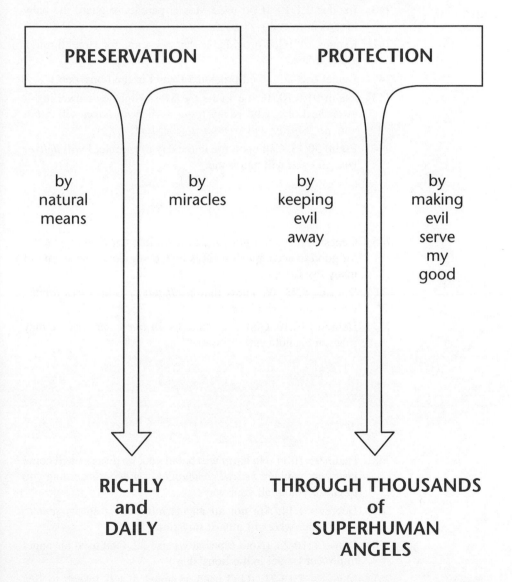

PRESERVATION

PROTECTION

by
natural
means

by
miracles

by
keeping
evil
away

by
making
evil
serve
my
good

RICHLY
and
DAILY

THROUGH THOUSANDS
of
SUPERHUMAN
ANGELS

Protection

161. In what ways does my heavenly Father protect me?

739) Genesis 19:1-29. (Through Abraham God rescued Lot from the destruction of Sodom and Gomorrah.)

740) Exodus 2:1-10. (God used Moses' parents to guard the baby Moses from evil.)

741) Exodus 14. (God provided a way of escape for Israel through the Red Sea.)

742) Daniel 6:16-23. (God protected Daniel in the lions' den.)

743) Psalm 91:9,10. If you make the Most High your dwelling— even the LORD, who is my refuge—then *no harm* will *befall* you, *no disaster* will *come near* your tent.

744) Psalm 50:15. Call upon me in the day of trouble; I will *deliver you,* and you will honor me.

161a. My heavenly Father protects me by keeping evil from me or by delivering me from its harm.

745) Genesis 50:20. *You intended* to harm me, *but God intended* it for good to accomplish what is now being done, the saving of many lives.

746) Romans 8:28. We know that *in all things* God works *for the good* of those who love him.

747) Hebrews 12:10. God disciplines us *for our good,* that we may share in his holiness.

161b. My heavenly Father protects me by making everything in my life serve for my good.

162. Who are the special creatures my heavenly Father sends to protect me?

748) Psalm 91:10,11. No harm will befall you, no disaster will come near your tent. For *he will command his angels* concerning you *to guard* you in all your ways.

749) Hebrews 1:14. Are not all angels ministering spirits *sent to serve* those who will inherit salvation?

750) Daniel 6:16-23. (Note especially verse 22. God used his angel to protect Daniel in the lions' den.)

751) Matthew 2:13-21. (God used an angel to tell Joseph to flee from Herod's slaughter.)

752) Acts 12:5-11. (An angel delivered Peter from prison.)

162. The special creatures my heavenly Father sends to protect me are his angels.

163. Why is it comforting to know that God's angels protect me?

753) Revelation 5:11. I looked and heard the voice of *many angels,* numbering thousands upon thousands, and ten thousand times ten thousand.

754) Psalm 103:20. Praise the LORD, you his angels, you *mighty ones* who *do his bidding,* who obey his word.

755) 2 Peter 2:10,11. These men are not afraid to slander celestial beings; yet even *angels,* although they are *stronger* and *more powerful,* do not bring slanderous accusations.

756) Psalm 91:11. He will command his angels concerning you to guard you *in all your ways.*

757) Hebrews 1:14. Are not all angels ministering *spirits* sent to *serve those who will inherit salvation?*

163. It is comforting to know that God's angels protect me because they are a very large number of powerful spirits who constantly watch over me.

My Thanks

164. Why does my heavenly Father preserve and protect me?

758) Psalm 118:1. Give thanks to the LORD, for he is *good;* his *love endures* forever.

759) Romans 9:16. It does *not . . .* depend on *man's desire or effort, but* on God's *mercy.*

760) Romans 8:32. He who did not spare his own Son, but gave him up for us all—how will he not also, along with him, *graciously* give us *all things?*

761) Genesis 32:10. I am *unworthy* of all the kindness and faithfulness you have shown your servant.

762) Romans 11:35. Who has *ever* given to God, that God should *repay* him?

164. My heavenly Father preserves and protects me because he is good and merciful, not because I have earned or deserved it.

165. How does my heavenly Father want me to show that I appreciate his goodness and mercy to me?

763) Psalm 106:1. *Give thanks* to the LORD, for he is good; his love endures forever.

764) Psalm 103:1,2. *Praise* the LORD, O my soul; all my inmost being, *praise* his holy name. *Praise* the LORD, O my soul, and *forget not* all his benefits.

765) 1 Samuel 12:24. Be sure to fear the LORD and *serve him faithfully* with all your heart; *consider* what great things he has done for you.

766) Deuteronomy 10:12. What does the LORD your God *ask of you* but to fear the LORD your God, to *walk in all his ways,* to love him, to *serve the LORD* your God with all your heart and with all your soul?

767) 1 Corinthians 10:31. Whether you eat or drink or whatever you do, *do it all* for the glory of God.

165. My heavenly Father wants me to show that I appreciate his goodness and mercy by thanking and praising, serving and obeying him.

The Ruin of God's Creation

166. How was God's creation ruined?

768) Genesis 3:1-19. (Adam and Eve fell into sin and brought death upon themselves.)

769) Romans 5:12. Sin entered the world through one man, and *death through sin.*

770) Romans 8:22. We know that the *whole creation* has been *groaning* as in the pains of childbirth right up to the present time.

166. God's creation was ruined when sin and death entered the world by Adam and Eve's sin. (the fall)

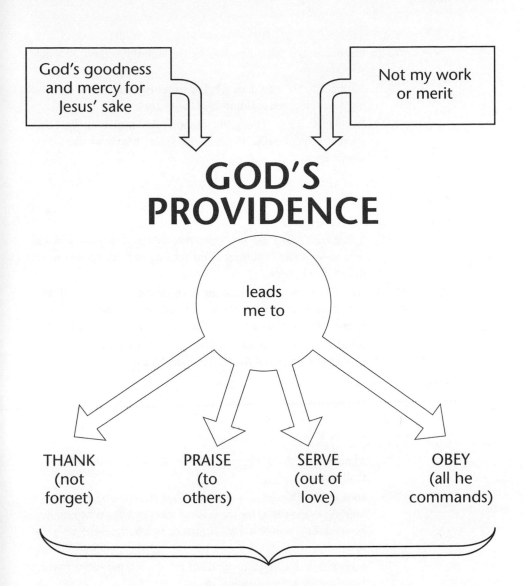

God's goodness and mercy for Jesus' sake

Not my work or merit

GOD'S PROVIDENCE

leads me to

THANK (not forget)

PRAISE (to others)

SERVE (out of love)

OBEY (all he commands)

GIVE GLORY TO HIM ALL MY LIFE

167. Who tempted and led Adam and Eve into sin?

771) Genesis 3:1-6. (The devil spoke through the serpent to tempt Eve.)

772) 1 John 3:8. He who does what is sinful is of the devil, because the *devil* has been sinning *from the beginning.*

773) Revelation 12:9. The great dragon was hurled down—that ancient *serpent called the devil, or Satan,* who leads the *whole world* astray.

167. The devil tempted and led Adam and Eve into sin.

168. Who is the devil?

774) 2 Peter 2:4. God did not spare *angels* when they *sinned,* but sent them to *hell,* putting them into gloomy dungeons to be held for judgment.

775) Jude 6. The *angels* who *did not keep* their positions of authority but *abandoned* their own home—these he has kept in darkness, *bound with everlasting chains* for judgment on the great Day.

776) Matthew 25:41. Depart from me, you who are cursed, into *the eternal fire prepared for the devil and his angels.*

168. The devil is the leader of the angels who sinned and were condemned to the eternal fire of hell.

169. Why did the devil ruin God's creation?

777) Matthew 13:36-43. (Jesus describes the devil as the enemy of God's work.)

778) John 8:44. [The devil] was *a murderer* from the beginning, not holding to the truth, for there is *no truth in him.* When he lies, he speaks *his native language,* for he is a liar and the *father of lies.*

779) 1 Peter 5:8. *Your enemy* the devil prowls around like a roaring lion *looking for someone to devour.*

780) Revelation 12:12. Woe to the earth and the sea, because the devil has gone down to you! He is *filled with fury,* because he knows that *his time is short.*

781) 2 Timothy 2:25,26. Those who oppose him he must gently instruct, in the hope . . . that they will come to their senses and escape from the *trap of the devil,* who has taken them captive *to do his will.*

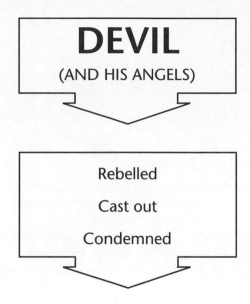

DEVIL
(AND HIS ANGELS)

Rebelled

Cast out

Condemned

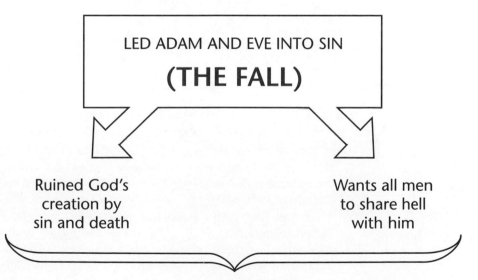

LED ADAM AND EVE INTO SIN
(THE FALL)

Ruined God's
creation by
sin and death

Wants all men
to share hell
with him

GOD SENDS
THE
SAVIOR

169. The devil ruined God's creation because he is an enemy of God who opposes the truth and wants to trap all people into sharing hell with him.

170. Why didn't God destroy the ruined world and start over again?

782) Lamentations 3:22. Because of the LORD's *great love* we are not consumed.

783) Ezekiel 33:11. As surely as I live, declares the Sovereign LORD, I take *no pleasure* in the death of the wicked, but *rather that they turn* from their ways *and live.*

784) Matthew 25:34. Take your inheritance, the kingdom *prepared* for you *since the creation* of the world.

785) 1 John 3:8. The reason the Son of God appeared was *to destroy the devil's work.*

786) 2 Timothy 1:9. [God] *saved us* . . . not because of anything we have done but because of *his own purpose and grace.* This grace was given us in Christ Jesus *before the beginning of time.*

170. God didn't destroy the ruined world because in his gracious love he chose to send his Son to save the world from the results of Satan's work.

171. What, then, has God my heavenly Father also done for me in his goodness and mercy besides creating, preserving, and protecting me?

787) Genesis 3:15. I will put enmity between you and the woman, and between your offspring and hers; *he will crush your head,* and you will strike his heel.

788) 2 Timothy 1:9,10. This *grace* was given us in Christ Jesus before the beginning of time, but it has *now been revealed* through the appearing of our Savior, Christ Jesus, who has *destroyed death* and has *brought* life and immortality to light *through the gospel.*

789) John 3:16,17. God so loved the world that *he gave his one and only Son,* that whoever believes in him shall not perish but have eternal life. For God did *not* send his Son into the world *to condemn* the world, *but to save* the world through him.

171. God, my heavenly Father, in his goodness and mercy has sent his one and only Son to save me.

THE SECOND ARTICLE

(Redemption)

I believe in Jesus Christ, his only Son, our Lord, who was conceived by the Holy Spirit, born of the virgin Mary, suffered under Pontius Pilate, was crucified, died, and was buried. He descended into hell. The third day he rose again from the dead. He ascended into heaven and is seated at the right hand of God the Father almighty. From there he will come to judge the living and the dead.

What does this mean?

I believe that Jesus Christ, true God, begotten of the Father from eternity, and also true man, born of the virgin Mary, is my Lord.

He has redeemed me, a lost and condemned creature, purchased and won me from all sins, from death, and from the power of the devil, not with gold or silver but with his holy, precious blood and with his innocent suffering and death.

All this he did that I should be his own, and live under him in his kingdom, and serve him in everlasting righteousness, innocence, and blessedness, just as he has risen from death and lives and rules eternally.

This is most certainly true.

Christ's Person

172. Why do I believe that Jesus Christ is true God?

790) 1 John 5:20. We are in him who is true—even in his Son Jesus Christ. His is the *true God* and eternal life.

791) Romans 9:5. Christ . . . is *God* over all, forever praised!

792) Matthew 1:23. "The virgin will be with child and will give birth to a son, and they will call him Immanuel"—which means *"God* with us."

793) Luke 2:11. Today in the town of David a Savior has been born to you; he is Christ *the Lord.*

794) 2 Peter 1:17. He received honor and glory from God the Father when the voice came to him from the Majestic Glory, saying, "This is *my Son,* whom I love; with him I am well pleased."

795) John 3:16. God so loved the world that he gave his *one and only Son.*

796) John 20:28. Thomas said to him, "My *Lord* and my *God!"*

797) Matthew 16:16. Simon Peter answered, "You are the Christ, the *Son of the living God."*

172a. I believe that Jesus is true God because the Bible calls him God. (divine names)

798) John 1:2. He was *with God in the beginning.*

799) Hebrews 13:8. Jesus Christ is *the same* yesterday and today and *forever.*

800) Matthew 28:20. Surely I am *with you always.*

801) Matthew 28:18. *All authority* in heaven and on earth has been given to me.

802) John 21:17. Lord, you *know all things.*

172b. I believe that Jesus is true God because he has characteristics which only God has. (divine attributes)

803) John 1:3. Through him *all things were made.*

804) Hebrews 1:3. The Son is the radiance of God's glory and the exact representation of his being, *sustaining all things* by his powerful word.

805) John 2:1-11. (Jesus changed water into wine.)

806) Luke 5:17-26. (Jesus healed the paralytic.)

807) Matthew 8:23-27. (Jesus calmed the furious storm.)

808) Mark 5:1-20. (Jesus had power over devils.)

809) John 11:38-44. (Jesus raised Lazarus from the dead.)

810) Matthew 28:6,7. (Jesus himself rose from the dead.)

811) Romans 1:4. [Jesus] was declared with power *to be the Son of God by his resurrection* from the dead.

812) Matthew 9:6. The Son of Man has *authority* on earth *to forgive sins.*

813) John 5:22. The Father judges no one, but has entrusted *all judgment* to the Son.

172c. I believe that Jesus is true God because he does things which only God can do. (divine works)

814) John 5:22,23. The Father . . . has entrusted all judgment to the Son, that all may honor the Son *just as* they honor the Father. He who does not honor the Son does not honor the Father, who sent him.

172d. I believe that Jesus is true God because the Bible tells me to honor him as God. (divine honor)

173. Why do I believe that Jesus Christ is true man?

815) 1 Timothy 2:5. There is one God and one mediator between God and men, *the man* Christ Jesus.

816) Romans 1:3. His Son . . . as to his *human nature* was a descendant of David.

817) Acts 17:31. [God] has set a day when he will judge the world with justice by *the man* he has appointed. He has given proof of this to all men by raising him from the dead.

818) Hebrews 2:14. Since the children have flesh and blood, he too *shared in their humanity.*

819) Matthew 26:2. As you know, the Passover is two days away—and the *Son of Man* will be handed over to be crucified.

173a. I believe that Jesus is true man because the Bible calls him man.

820) Galatians 4:4. God sent his Son, *born of a woman.*

821) Luke 2:12. You will find *a baby* wrapped in cloths and lying in a manger.

153

JESUS' PERSON

TRUE MAN

— called man
— human body
  and soul
— human actions

TRUE GOD

— divine names
— divine attributes
— divine works
— divine glory

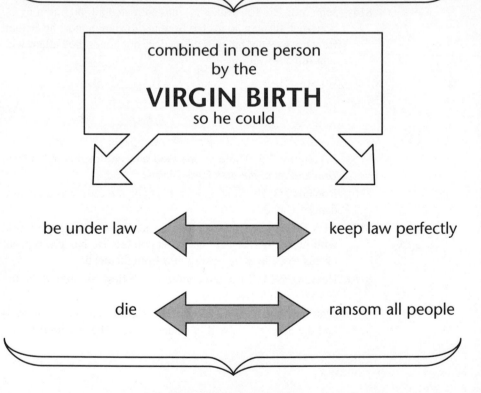

combined in one person
by the

VIRGIN BIRTH

so he could

be under law ⟷ keep law perfectly

die ⟷ ransom all people

SAVIOR

822) Luke 2:40. The child *grew and became strong.*

823) Luke 24:39. Look at my *hands and my feet.* It is I myself! Touch me and see; a ghost does not have *flesh and bones,* as you see I have.

824) Matthew 26:38. *My soul* is overwhelmed with sorrow to the point of death.

173b. I believe that Jesus is true man because he has a human body and soul.

825) Matthew 4:2. After fasting forty days and forty nights, *he was hungry.*

826) Mark 4:38. Jesus was in the stern, *sleeping* on a cushion.

827) John 11:35. Jesus *wept.*

828) John 19:28. Jesus said, "I am *thirsty.*"

829) Psalm 22:1,2,14-17,24. (Jesus suffered.)

830) Mark 15:37,44-46. (Jesus died and his body was given to Joseph of Arimathea for burial.)

173c. I believe that Jesus is true man because he did things which are normal actions for human beings.

174. How did God's Son become true man?

831) Luke 1:26-38. (The angel Gabriel told the virgin Mary that the child she would give birth to is God's Son. Note especially verse 35, *"The Holy Spirit* will come upon you, and *the power of the Most High* will overshadow you. So the holy one to be *born* will be called the Son of God.")

832) Matthew 1:20. Joseph son of David, do not be afraid to take Mary home as your wife, because what is *conceived* in her is *from the Holy Spirit.*

833) Matthew 1:22,23. All this took place to fulfill what the Lord had said through the prophet: *"The virgin* will be with child and will *give birth to a son."*

834) Galatians 4:4. When the time had fully come, God sent *his Son, born of a woman.*

174. God's Son became true man when he was conceived by the Holy Spirit and born of the virgin Mary. (the miracle of the virgin birth, the incarnation)

175. What, then, do I believe about Jesus' person?

835) Colossians 2:9. In Christ all *the fullness* of the *Deity* lives in *bodily form.*

836) 1 Timothy 2:5. There is *one God* and one mediator between God and men, *the man* Christ Jesus.

175. I believe that Jesus is true man and true God in one person.

176. Why was it necessary that Jesus be both true man and true God in one person?

837) Galatians 4:4,5. God sent his Son, born of a woman, *born under law, to redeem those under law.*

838) Romans 3:23. *All have sinned* and fall *short of the glory of God.*

839) John 8:46. Can any of you *prove me guilty of sin?*

840) Hebrews 4:15. We have one who has been tempted in every way, just as we are—yet was *without sin.*

841) Romans 5:19. *Through the obedience* of the one man the many will be made righteous.

176a. It was necessary that Jesus be both true man and true God in one person so that he could be under God's law and also keep it perfectly for me. (active obedience)

842) Hebrews 2:14. Since the children have flesh and blood, he too shared in their humanity *so that by his death* he might destroy him who holds the power of death—that is, the devil.

843) Psalm 49:7,8. *No man* can redeem the life of another or give to God a ransom for him—the ransom for a life is costly, *no payment is ever enough.*

844) John 1:29. Look, the Lamb of God, who *takes away the sin of the world!*

845) Mark 10:45. The Son of Man did not come to be served, but to serve, and to *give his life as a ransom for many.*

176b. It was necessary that Jesus be both true man and true God in one person so that he could die and also ransom me by his death. (passive obedience)

Christ's Office

177. To what office did God anoint Christ?

846) Acts 10:38. *God anointed Jesus* of Nazareth with the Holy Spirit and power.

847) Deuteronomy 18:15. The LORD your God will raise up for you *a prophet* like me from among your own brothers.

848) Hebrews 3:1. Fix your thoughts on Jesus, the apostle and *high priest* whom we confess.

849) John 18:37. Jesus answered, "You are right in saying I am *a king.*"

177. God anointed Christ to the office of prophet, high priest, and king. ("Christ" means "The Anointed.")

178. What were the Old Testament prophets anointed to do?

850) 1 Kings 19:16. *Anoint* Elisha . . . to succeed you *as prophet.*

851) Jeremiah 1:7. You must *go* to everyone I send you to *and say* whatever I command you.

852) Acts 3:18. God fulfilled what he had *foretold through all the prophets,* saying that *his Christ* would suffer.

178. The Old Testament prophets were anointed to tell people God's Word, especially the good news about the coming Savior.

179. What did Christ do as the Prophet while he was on earth?

853) Isaiah 61:1. The Spirit of the Sovereign LORD is on me, because the LORD has *anointed me to preach good news* to the poor.

854) Luke 8:1. Jesus traveled about from one town and village to another, *proclaiming the good news* of the kingdom of God.

855) Matthew 17:5. This is my Son, whom I love; with him I am well pleased. *Listen to him!*

856) John 6:68. Lord, to whom shall we go? You have *the words of eternal life.*

179. As the Prophet, Christ preached God's Word, especially the good news of eternal life.

180. What were the Old Testament high priests anointed to do?

857) Exodus 30:30. *Anoint* Aaron and his sons and consecrate them so they may serve me *as priests.*

858) Hebrews 5:1. Every high priest is selected from among men and is appointed *to represent* them in matters related to God, *to offer gifts and sacrifices for sins.*

859) Leviticus 16. (The high priest entered God's presence with blood to remind Israel that the promised Savior's blood would be shed for their sins. See also Hebrews 10:4.)

860) Hebrews 9:7. *Only the high priest* entered the inner room, and that only once a year, and *never without blood,* which he *offered for himself and for the sins the people* had committed in ignorance.

180. The Old Testament high priests were anointed to represent the people before God and to offer sacrifices for the people's sins.

181. What did Christ do as the High Priest while he was on earth?

861) Hebrews 7:26,27. Such a high priest meets our need—one who is *holy, blameless, pure, set apart from sinners,* exalted above the heavens. Unlike the other high priests, he does not need to offer sacrifices day after day, first for his own sins, and then for the sins of the people. *He sacrificed for their sins once for all* when he *offered himself.*

862) Hebrews 9:24,26. Christ did not enter a man-made sanctuary that was only a copy of the true one; he *entered heaven itself,* now to appear for us in God's presence. . . . he has appeared once for all at the end of the ages *to do away with sin by the sacrifice of himself.*

863) Ephesians 5:2. Christ loved us and gave himself up for us as a fragrant *offering and sacrifice to God.*

864) John 1:29. Look, the Lamb of God, who *takes away the sin of the world!*

865) 1 John 2:2. He is *the atoning sacrifice* for our sins, and not only for ours but also *for the sins of the whole world.*

181. As the High Priest, Christ represented the whole world before God and sacrificed himself for the sins of all. (vicarious atonement)

CHRIST'S OFFICE

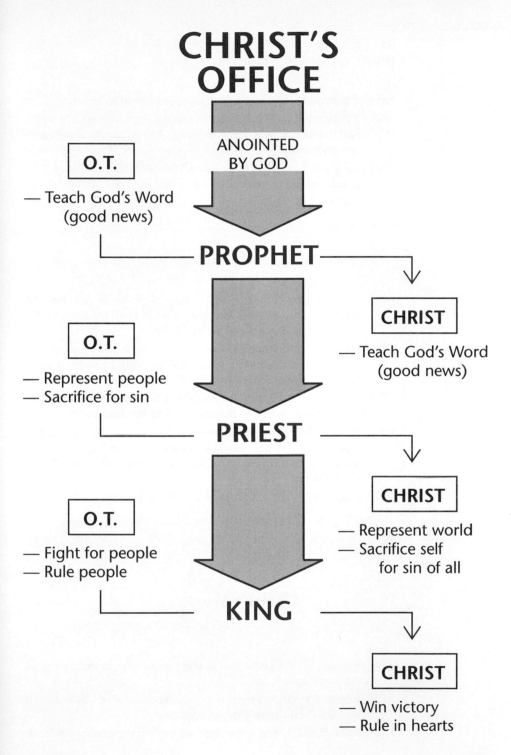

ANOINTED BY GOD

O.T.
— Teach God's Word (good news)

PROPHET

CHRIST
— Teach God's Word (good news)

O.T.
— Represent people
— Sacrifice for sin

PRIEST

CHRIST
— Represent world
— Sacrifice self for sin of all

O.T.
— Fight for people
— Rule people

KING

CHRIST
— Win victory
— Rule in hearts

182. What were the Old Testament kings anointed to do?

866) 1 Samuel 16:12,13. (Samuel anointed David to be king.)

867) 1 Samuel 9:17. When Samuel caught sight of Saul, the LORD said to him, "This is the man I spoke to you about; he will *govern* my people."

868) 1 Samuel 8:20. We will be like all the other nations, with a king *to lead us* and to go out before us and *fight our battles.*

182. The Old Testament kings were anointed to rule the people and to protect them.

183. What did Christ do as the King while he was on earth?

869) 1 Corinthians 15:56,57. The sting of *death* is *sin,* and the power of sin is the law. But thanks be to God! He gives us *the victory through our Lord Jesus Christ.*

870) Hebrews 2:14. Since the children have flesh and blood, he too shared in their humanity so that by his death he might *destroy* him who holds the *power of death*—that is, *the devil.*

871) Romans 14:9. For this very reason, Christ died and returned to life *so that he might be the Lord* of both the dead and the living.

872) John 18:36,37. My kingdom is *not of this world.* . . . I am a king. In fact, for this reason I was born, and for this I came into the world, to *testify to the truth.* Everyone on the side of truth *listens to me.*

873) Luke 17:21. The kingdom of God is *within you.*

183. As the King, Christ won the victory over sin, death, and the devil so that he might rule in the hearts of believers by his Word.

Christ's Work

184. Why are we all lost and condemned creatures by nature?

874) Romans 7:18. I know that *nothing good* lives in me, that is, *in my sinful nature.*

875) Romans 3:22,23. There is no difference, for *all have sinned* and fall short of the glory of God.

876) Ephesians 2:1. You were *dead in your transgressions and sins.*

877) John 8:34. Everyone who sins is *a slave to sin.*

878) Romans 5:12. *Death came to all men,* because all sinned.

879) 1 John 3:8. He who does what is sinful is *of the devil.*

184. We are all lost and condemned creatures because by nature we are slaves of sin, death, and the devil.

185. **What is Christ's work called by which he ransomed us from the slavery of sin, death, and the devil?**

880) Hebrews 9:15. He has died as a *ransom to set them free* from the sins committed under the first covenant.

881) Hebrews 9:12. He entered the Most Holy Place once for all by his own blood, having obtained eternal *redemption.*

185. Christ's work, by which he ransomed us from this slavery, is called redemption.

186. **What ransom price did God require Christ to pay in order to redeem us from this slavery?**

882) Leviticus 17:10-14. (God required blood to pay for sin because the life of a body is its blood.)

883) Revelation 1:5,6. To him who loves us and has *freed us* from our sins *by his blood* . . . be glory and power for ever and ever!

884) Ephesians 1:7. We have *redemption through his blood,* the forgiveness of sins.

885) Isaiah 53:5. *He was pierced* for our transgression, *he was crushed* for our iniquities; the *punishment* that brought us peace was *upon him,* and *by his wounds* we are healed.

886) Matthew 20:28. The Son of Man did not come to be served, but to serve, and to *give his life as a ransom* for many.

186. God required Christ to pay the ransom price of his blood and his suffering and death in order to redeem us from this slavery.

187. **Why do we call Christ's blood holy?**

887) 1 John 1:7. The *blood of Jesus, his Son,* purifies us from all sin.

888) 1 Peter 1:18,19. You know that it was not with perishable things such as silver or gold that you were redeemed . . . but with the precious *blood of Christ,* a lamb *without blemish or defect.*

└── 187. We call Christ's blood holy because it is the blood of God's perfect Son.

┌── **188. Why do we call Christ's blood precious?**

889) Psalm 49:7,8. No man can redeem the life of another or give to God a ransom for him—*the ransom for a life is costly,* no payment is ever enough.

890) Matthew 16:26. What good will it be for a man if he gains *the whole world,* yet forfeits his soul? Or what can a man give in exchange for his soul?

891) 1 Peter 1:18,19. You know that it was *not with* perishable things such as *silver or gold* that you were redeemed . . . *but with* the *precious blood of Christ,* a lamb without blemish or defect.

└── 188. We call Christ's blood precious because it paid the ransom price for us that all the world's gold and silver could never have paid.

┌── **189. Why do we call Christ's suffering and death innocent?**

892) 2 Corinthians 5:21. God made him *who had no sin* to be sin *for us,* so that in him we might become the righteousness of God.

893) Hebrews 4:15. We have one who has been tempted in every way, just as we are—yet was *without sin.*

894) Hebrews 7:26,27. Such a high priest meets our need—one who is *holy, blameless, pure, set apart from sinners,* exalted above the heavens. Unlike the other high priests, *he does not need to offer* sacrifices day after day, *first for his own sins,* and then for the sins of the people. He sacrificed *for their sins* once for all when he offered himself.

895) Isaiah 53:5,6. He was pierced *for our transgressions,* he was crushed *for our iniquities;* the punishment that brought us peace was upon him, and *by his wounds* we are healed. We all, like sheep, have gone astray, each of us has turned to his own way; and the LORD laid *on him* the iniquity *of us all.*

└── 189. We call Christ's suffering and death innocent because Jesus was paying the price for all people's sins, not his own. (our substitute)

CHRIST'S WORK

REDEMPTION
(pay ransom to free)

PRICE

holy precious blood
(God-man)

innocent suffering
and death
(Substitute)

RESULT

SIN = no curse
or
condemnation

DEATH = no
punishment
in hell
and
enter eternal
life

DEVIL = power
over his
temptations
and
free from
his accusations

190. In what sense did Christ's redemption free me from the slavery of sin?

896) John 8:34,36. Everyone who sins is a slave to sin. So if the Son *sets you free,* you will be free indeed.

897) 1 John 1:7. The blood of Jesus, his Son, *purifies us from all sin.*

898) Galatians 3:13. Christ redeemed us *from the curse* of the law by becoming a curse for us.

899) Colossians 2:13. When you were dead in your sins . . . God made you alive with Christ. He *forgave us all our sins.*

900) Romans 8:1. There is now *no condemnation* for those who are in Christ Jesus.

901) Psalm 103:10. He does not treat us *as our sins deserve.*

190. Christ's redemption freed me from the punishment that I deserve for all my sins.

191. In what sense did Christ's redemption free me from the slavery of death?

902) Matthew 10:28. Be afraid of the One who can *destroy both soul and body in hell.*

903) 1 Corinthians 15:54,57. *"Death has been swallowed up in victory."* . . . thanks be to God! He gives us the victory through our Lord Jesus Christ.

904) John 11:25,26. I am the resurrection and the life. He who believes in me *will live, even though he dies;* and whoever lives and believes in me *will never die.*

905) 2 Timothy 1:10. Our Savior, Christ Jesus . . . has *destroyed death* and has *brought life and immortality* to light through the gospel.

191. Christ's redemption freed me from the punishment of eternal death in hell.

192. What assurance does Christ's redemption also give me about the end of my earthly life?

906) Luke 8:49-56; John 11:11-14. (Jesus spoke of the death of Jairus' daughter and of Lazarus as a sleep.)

907) Acts 7:57-60. (Stephen's death is described as falling asleep.)

908) Acts 13:36. When David had served God's purpose in his own generation, *he fell asleep;* he was buried with his fathers and his body decayed.

909) 1 Thessalonians 4:13-18. (Paul assures believers that death is only a sleep from which Jesus will awaken us to be with him forever. Note especially verse 14: "We believe that Jesus died and rose again and so we believe that God will bring with Jesus those who have *fallen asleep in him.*")

910) Daniel 12:2. Multitudes who *sleep* in the dust of the earth *will awake;* some *to everlasting life,* others to shame and everlasting contempt.

192. Christ's redemption assures me that the end of my earthly life is a sleep from which I will awake to everlasting life.

193. **In what sense did Christ's redemption free me from the slavery of the devil?**

911) Genesis 3:15. I will put enmity between you and the woman, and between your offspring and hers; *he will crush your head,* and you will strike his heel.

912) 1 John 3:8. The reason the Son of God appeared was to *destroy the devil's work.*

913) Hebrews 2:14. Since the children have flesh and blood, he too shared in their humanity so that by his death *he might destroy him who holds the power of death*—that is, *the devil.*

914) James 4:7. Resist the devil, and he will *flee from you.*

915) Revelation 12:10,11. *The accuser of our brothers,* who accuses them before our God day and night, has been hurled down. They *overcame him* by the blood of the Lamb.

916) Romans 8:34. *Who is he that condemns?* Christ Jesus, who died—more than that, who was raised to life—is at the right hand of God and is also interceding for us.

193. Christ's redemption freed me from the power of the devil's temptations and accusations.

Christ's Humiliation

194. **What do we mean when we speak of Christ's humiliation?**

917) Philippians 2:6-8. [Christ Jesus], *being in very nature God,* did not consider equality with God something to be grasped, but

DIFFERENCES
BETWEEN
CHRIST'S

HUMILIATION EXALTATION

Gave up the full use of
his heavenly
glory

Again took up the
full use of his
heavenly glory

To live in a humble
way on earth

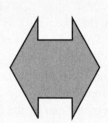

To live in an exalted
way filling heaven
and earth

Done to redeem us

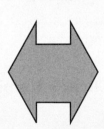

Done to assure us
that we are
redeemed

made himself nothing, taking the very *nature of a servant,* being made in human likeness. And being found in appearance as a man, *he humbled himself* and became obedient to death— even death on the cross!

918) 2 Corinthians 8:9. You know the grace of our Lord Jesus Christ, that *though he was rich,* yet for your sakes *he became poor,* so that you through his poverty might become rich.

919) John 18:3-6; Matthew 26:47-56. (Although Jesus had the power to knock the soldiers down and to call on the help of many angels, he allowed himself to be arrested.)

194) Christ's humiliation means that Christ chose not to make full use of his heavenly power and glory so that he might live and die in a lowly way.

195. How did Christ humble himself?

920) Matthew 1:18-20. (Christ came to earth in a lowly manner when he was conceived in the womb of Mary as a human child.)

921) Luke 2:1-14. (Jesus was born as a child of poor parents in some very lowly circumstances.)

922) Luke 9:58. Jesus replied, "Foxes have holes and birds of the air have nests, but the Son of Man has *no place to lay his head.*"

923) Mark 15:15. Wanting to satisfy the crowd, *Pilate* released Barabbas to them. He *had Jesus flogged,* and *handed him over to be crucified.*

924) Mark 15:22,24. They brought Jesus to the place called Golgotha (which means The Place of the Skull). And they *crucified* him.

925) Mark 15:37. With a loud cry, Jesus *breathed his last.*

926) Mark 15:46. Joseph bought some linen cloth, *took down the body,* wrapped it in the linen, and *placed it in a tomb* cut out of rock.

195. Christ humbled himself by the lowly manner of his conception; his lowly birth and life; his suffering under Pontius Pilate; his crucifixion, death, and burial.

196. Why did Christ humble himself?

927) 2 Corinthians 8:9. He became poor, *so that you* through his poverty *might become rich.*

928) Mark 10:45. The Son of Man did not come to be served, but *to serve,* and to give his life *as a ransom* for many.

196. Christ humbled himself to serve as our Redeemer.

Christ's Exaltation

197. What do we mean when we speak of Christ's exaltation?

929) Philippians 2:9. *God exalted him* to the highest place and gave him the name that is above every name.

930) John 17:5. Father, glorify me in your presence *with the glory I had* with you before the world began.

931) Ephesians 4:10. He who descended is *the very one* who ascended higher than all the heavens, in order to fill the whole universe.

932) Hebrews 2:9. We see Jesus, who was made a little lower than the angels, *now crowned with glory and honor* because he suffered death.

197. When we speak of Christ's exaltation, we mean that as the God-man he again made full use of his heavenly power and glory.

198. How was Christ exalted?

933) 1 Peter 3:19. He went and preached *to the spirits in prison.*

934) Romans 6:4. Christ was *raised from the dead* through the glory of the Father.

935) Mark 16:19. After the Lord Jesus had spoken to them, he was *taken up* into heaven and he *sat at the right hand of God.*

936) Acts 10:42. He is the one whom God appointed as *judge of the living and the dead.*

198. Christ was exalted by descending into hell, rising from the dead, ascending into heaven, sitting at the right hand of God, and becoming the judge of the living and the dead.

199. Why did God exalt Christ?

937) Acts 2:32,33,36. God has *raised this Jesus to life.* . . . *Exalted to the right hand of God,* he has . . . poured out what you now

see and hear. Therefore let all Israel *be assured* of this: God has made this Jesus, whom you crucified, *both Lord and Christ.*

938) Philippians 2:9-11. *God exalted him* to the highest place and gave him the name that is above every name, that at the name of Jesus every knee should bow, in heaven and on earth and under the earth, and every tongue confess *that Jesus Christ is Lord,* to the glory of God the Father.

939) Acts 5:31. *God exalted him* to his own right hand *as Prince and Savior.*

199. God exalted Christ to assure us that he is our Redeemer.

200. Of what does Christ's descent into hell assure us?

940) 1 Peter 3:19. He went and *preached* to the spirits in prison.

941) Colossians 2:15. Having disarmed the powers and authorities, *he made a public spectacle* of them, *triumphing over them* by the cross.

200. Christ's descent into hell assures us of his victory over the devil and all the evil angels.

201. Of what does Christ's resurrection assure us?

942) Romans 1:4. [Jesus] was *declared* with power *to be the Son of God* by his resurrection from the dead.

201a. Christ's resurrection assures us that he is God's Son.

943) Romans 4:25. He was delivered over to death for our sins and was raised to life *for our justification.*

944) 1 Corinthians 15:17. *If Christ has not been raised,* your faith is futile; you are *still in your sins.*

945) 1 Peter 1:3. In his great mercy he [God] has given us *new birth into a living hope* through the resurrection of Jesus Christ from the dead.

201b. Christ's resurrection assures us that he is our Redeemer.

946) John 14:19. Because I live, you also *will live.*

947) 1 Corinthians 15:22,23. In Christ all will be made alive. But each in his own turn: *Christ, the firstfruits; then,* when he comes, *those who belong to him.*

169

948) John 11:25. *I am the resurrection* and the life. He who believes in me *will live,* even though he dies.

201c. Christ's resurrection assures us that he will raise us from the dead.

202. Of what does Christ's ascension assure us?

949) Mark 16:19. After the Lord Jesus had spoken to them, he was *taken up into heaven* and he sat at the right hand of God.

950) Ephesians 4:7-10. (Christ's ascension as a conquering hero assures us that he accomplished what God had sent him to do.)

202a. Since Christ returned to heaven as a conquering hero, his ascension assures us that he is our Redeemer.

951) John 14:2,3. In my *Father's house* are many rooms; if it were not so, I would have told you. I am going there *to prepare a place for you.* And if I go and prepare a place for you, I will come back and take you to be with me that *you also may be where I am.*

202b. Christ's ascension assures us that there is a place where we will be with him forever.

203. Of what does Christ's sitting at the right hand of God assure us?

952) Ephesians 1:20-22. [God] seated him at his right hand in the heavenly realms, *far above all rule and authority,* power and dominion. . . . And God *placed all things under his feet* and appointed him to be head over everything *for the church.*

953) Matthew 28:18. *All authority in heaven and on earth* has been given to me.

203. Christ's sitting at the right hand of God assures us that he rules over all things for the good of his church.

204. How does Christ carry out his office of Prophet, Priest, and King now while he is at God's right hand?

954) Matthew 28:19,20. *Go and make disciples* of all nations, *baptizing* them in the name of the Father and of the Son and of the

Descent into Hell	
(victory march)	
Resurrection	
(God's Son, Savior, raise us)	
Ascension	**CHRIST'S EXALTATION** is our **ASSURANCE OF REDEMPTION**
(conquering hero, place in heaven)	
At God's Right Hand	
(Prophet, Priest, King)	
Judgment	
(glorious return, believer or unbeliever)	

Holy Spirit, *and teaching* them to obey everything I have commanded you. And surely I am with you always, to the very end of the age.

955) Mark 16:15. Go into all the world and *preach the good news* to all creation.

956) Ephesians 4:10,11. *The very one who ascended . . . gave* some to be apostles, some to be prophets, some to be evangelists, and *some to be pastors and teachers.*

204a. Christ carries out his office of Prophet now by sending believers to share his good news with everyone.

957) Hebrews 10:12. When this *priest* had offered for all time one sacrifice for sins, he sat down *at the right hand of God.*

958) Romans 8:34. Christ . . . is at the right hand of God and is also *interceding for us.*

959) 1 John 2:1. If anybody does sin, we have one who *speaks to the Father in our defense*—Jesus Christ, the Righteous One.

204b. Christ carries out his office of High Priest now by pleading our case before God.

960) 1 Corinthians 15:25. He must reign until he has *put all his enemies under his feet.*

961) Romans 8:38,39. I am convinced that neither death nor life, neither angels nor demons, neither the present nor the future, nor any powers, neither height nor depth, nor anything else in all creation, *will be able to separate us from the love of God* that is in Christ Jesus our Lord.

962) 2 Timothy 4:18. The Lord will *rescue me* from every evil attack and will *bring me safely* to his heavenly kingdom.

204c. Christ carries out his office of King now by protecting us from all our enemies in order to bring us safely to his heavenly kingdom.

205. Why is Christ's judgment of the living and the dead also part of his exaltation?

963) Matthew 25:31,32. When the Son of Man comes *in his glory,* and all the angels with him, he will sit on his throne *in heavenly glory. All the nations* will be gathered *before him.*

964) Acts 17:31. [God] has set a day when he will *judge the world* with justice by the man he has appointed. He has given proof of this to all men by raising him from the dead.

965) Revelation 1:7. Look, he is coming with the clouds, and *every eye will see him,* even those who pierced him.

205. Christ's judgment is also part of his exaltation because he will appear in his heavenly glory to judge all people.

206. When will Christ come to judge the living and the dead?

966) Matthew 24:36. *No one knows about that day or hour,* not even the angels in heaven, nor the Son, but only the Father.

206. No one knows when Christ will come to judge the living and the dead.

207. When does God want us to be ready for Christ's second coming?

967) Matthew 24:42,44. Therefore *keep watch,* because *you do not know on what day* your Lord will come. So you also must *be ready,* because the Son of Man will come at *an hour when you do not expect him.*

968) Matthew 25:1-13. (Like the five wise virgins, we should always be ready to meet Christ.)

207. God wants us always to be ready for Christ's second coming.

208. On what basis will Christ judge all people?

969) Mark 16:15,16. Go into all the world and preach the good news to all creation. *Whoever believes* and is baptized will be saved, but *whoever does not believe* will be condemned.

970) John 3:18. Whoever believes in him is not condemned, but whoever does not believe stands condemned already *because he has not believed in the name of God's one and only Son.*

971) John 12:48. *There is a judge* for the one who rejects me and does not accept my words; *that very word which I spoke* will condemn him at the last day.

972) Matthew 25:31-46. (Jesus will use the deeds of faith done by believers as evidence of their faith, and the lack of deeds of faith as evidence of the unbeliever's lack of faith.)

208. Christ will judge all people on the basis of whether they believed in him and his Word or not.

Belonging to Christ

209. Why did Christ redeem me?

973) 1 Corinthians 6:19,20. You are *not your own; you were bought at a price.* Therefore *honor* God with your body.

974) Romans 6:22. Now that you have been *set free from sin* and have *become slaves to God,* the benefit you reap leads to *holiness,* and the result is *eternal life.*

975) Titus 2:14. [Christ] gave himself for us to *redeem us from all wickedness* and to purify for himself *a people that are his very own,* eager to do what is good.

976) 2 Corinthians 5:15. He died for all, that those who live should no longer *live* for themselves but *for him* who died for them and was raised again.

977) Luke 1:68,74,75. Praise be to the Lord, the God of Israel, because he has come and has redeemed his people. . . . *to rescue us* from the hand of our enemies, and to enable us *to serve him* without fear in holiness and righteousness before him *all our days.*

978) Colossians 1:10,13. And we pray this in order that you may *live a life worthy of the Lord* and may please him in every way. . . . For he has *rescued us* from the dominion of darkness and *brought us into the kingdom* of the Son he loves.

209. Christ redeemed me so that I might be his own and use my whole life to serve him in his kingdom.

210. Why is this life of service to my Redeemer one of righteousness, innocence, and blessedness?

979) Isaiah 61:10. I delight greatly in the LORD; my soul rejoices in my God. For he has *clothed me* with garments of salvation and arrayed me *in a robe of righteousness.*

980) Revelation 7:14. They have *washed their robes* and made them white *in the blood of the Lamb.*

210a. My life of service to my Redeemer is one of righteousness because he covers all my sins with the robe of his righteousness.

981) Luke 19:1-10. (Zacchaeus' life was changed when he came to faith in Jesus.)

982) Psalm 26:5-7. *I abhor* the assembly of evildoers *and refuse* to sit with the wicked. I wash my hands *in innocence* and go about your altar, O LORD, *proclaiming* aloud your praise *and telling* of all your wonderful deeds.

983) Titus 2:11-13. For the grace of God that brings salvation has appeared to all men. It teaches us *to say "No"* to ungodliness and worldly passions, and *to live self-controlled, upright and godly lives* in this present age, *while we wait* for the blessed hope—the glorious appearing of our great God and Savior, Jesus Christ.

984) Ephesians 4:24. Put on the *new self,* created to be like God in true righteousness and holiness.

210b. My life of service to my Redeemer is one of innocence because in my new man I hate sin and desire to live a godly life.

985) John 12:1-8. (Mary anointed Jesus with expensive perfume to express her love and thanks.)

986) Psalm 100:2,4,5. *Worship the LORD with gladness; . . . give thanks to him* and praise his name. For the LORD is good and his love endures forever.

987) Ephesians 5:2. *Live a life of love,* just as Christ loved us and gave himself up for us as a fragrant offering and sacrifice to God.

988) Colossians 3:17. Whatever you do, whether in word or deed, do it all in the name of the Lord Jesus, *giving thanks* to God the Father through him.

210c. My life of service to my Redeemer is one of blessedness because I gladly serve him in thankful love.

211. When only will I be able to serve my Redeemer in perfect and everlasting righteousness, innocence, and blessedness?

989) Revelation 7:14,15. These are they who have *come out of the great tribulation;* they have washed their robes and made them white in the blood of the Lamb. Therefore, they *are before the throne of God and serve him* day and night in his temple.

PURPOSE
of
REDEMPTION

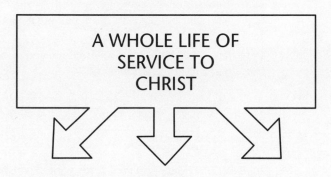

A WHOLE LIFE OF
SERVICE TO
CHRIST

**in
RIGHTEOUSNESS**
(covered
by
his holiness)

**in
INNOCENCE**
(hate sin,
do his
will)

**in
BLESSEDNESS**
(gladly in
faith-born
love)

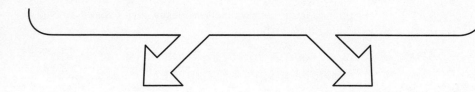

**Imperfectly
now**

**Perfectly
in heaven**

990) Colossians 3:4. When Christ, who is your life, appears, then you also will appear *with him in glory.*

991) 2 Peter 3:13. In keeping with his promise we are looking forward to a new heaven and a new earth, *the home of righteousness.*

992) Revelation 14:4,5. They were purchased from among men and offered as firstfruits to God and the Lamb. No lie was found in their mouths; they are *blameless.*

993) Psalm 16:11. You will *fill me with joy* in your presence, *with eternal pleasures* at your right hand.

211. I will be able to serve my Redeemer in perfect and everlasting righteousness, innocence, and blessedness only when he takes me to be with him in heaven.

212. Why am I sure that I will be with Christ in heaven?

994) Romans 1:4. [Jesus] was *declared* with power to be the Son of God *by his resurrection* from the dead.

995) Job 19:25-27. *I know that my Redeemer lives,* and that in the end he will stand upon the earth. And after my skin has been destroyed, yet *in my flesh I will see God;* I myself will see him with my own eyes—I, and not another. How my heart yearns within me!

996) 1 Corinthians 6:14. By his power God *raised the Lord* from the dead, and he *will raise us also.*

997) Philippians 3:20,21. The Lord Jesus Christ, who, by the power that enables him to bring *everything under his control,* will transform our lowly bodies so that they will be like his glorious body.

998) Revelation 11:15. The kingdom of the world has become the kingdom of our Lord and *of his Christ,* and he will *reign forever and ever.*

212. I am sure that I will be with Christ in heaven because he has risen from death and lives and rules eternally.

Faith and the Holy Spirit

213. How does the redemption that Christ won for me become my own?

CHRIST'S REDEMPTION

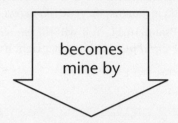

becomes
mine by

FAITH

impossible
by
nature

possible
only by
the work
of the
HOLY SPIRIT

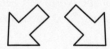

dead
in
sins

enemy
of
God

999) Luke 14:15-24. (By the parable of the great banquet, Jesus teaches that those who do not accept the invitation to the banquet lose all its blessings.)

1000) Acts 16:30,31. "Sirs, what must I do to be saved?" They replied, "*Believe* in the Lord Jesus, and you will be saved."

1001) Mark 1:15. The kingdom of God is near. Repent and *believe* the good news!

1002) Romans 10:4. Christ is the end of the law so that there may be righteousness for everyone *who believes.*

1003) John 3:16. God so loved the world that he gave his one and only Son, that *whoever believes* in him shall not perish but have eternal life.

213. The redemption that Christ won for me becomes my own by faith in Jesus Christ.

214. What is my natural spiritual condition?

1004) Ephesians 2:1. As for you, you were *dead* in your transgressions and sins.

1005) Acts 26:17,18. I am sending you to them to *open their eyes* and turn them from *darkness* to light, and from the *power of Satan* to God.

1006) Romans 8:6,7. The mind of sinful man is death . . . , the *sinful mind is hostile to God.*

214. By nature I am spiritually dead in sins, spiritually blind, under the power of Satan, and an enemy of God.

215. What is impossible for me to do because of my natural spiritual condition?

1007) 1 Corinthians 1:18. The message of the cross is *foolishness* to those who are perishing.

1008) 1 Corinthians 2:14. The man without the Spirit *does not accept* the things that come from the Spirit of God, for they are *foolishness* to him, and he *cannot understand them,* because they are spiritually discerned.

1009) Psalm 82:5. [The wicked] *know nothing,* they *understand nothing.* They walk about in darkness.

1010) Matthew 13:14. You will be ever *hearing* but *never understanding;* you will be ever *seeing* but *never perceiving.*

1011) Ephesians 4:17,18. You must no longer live as the Gentiles do, in the *futility of their thinking.* They are darkened in their understanding and separated from the life of God.

1012) John 15:16. *You did not choose me,* but I chose you.

1013) Psalm 65:3,4. When we were overwhelmed by sins, you forgave our transgressions. Blessed are those *you choose and bring near* to live in your courts!

215. My natural spiritual condition makes it impossible for me by my own thinking or choosing to believe in Jesus or come to him.

216. How only can I come to believe in Jesus?

1014) Matthew 16:16,17. Simon Peter answered, "You are the Christ, the Son of the living God." Jesus replied, "Blessed are you, Simon son of Jonah, for this was *not* revealed to you *by man,* but by my Father in heaven."

1015) 1 Corinthians 12:3. No one can say, "Jesus is Lord," *except by the Holy Spirit.*

1016) Romans 5:5. God has poured out his love into our hearts *by the Holy Spirit,* whom he has given us.

216. I can come to believe in Jesus only by the work of the Holy Spirit in me.

217. What more, then, has God done in his great love for me?

1017) Joel 2:28. And *afterward,* I will *pour out my Spirit* on all people.

1018) John 16:7,13. Unless I go away, the Counselor will not come to you; but if I go, *I will send him to you.* When he, the Spirit of truth, comes, he will guide you into all truth.

1019) Acts 2:1-13. (Jesus sent the Holy Spirit on the day of Pentecost.)

217. God in his love promised and sent the Holy Spirit.

THE THIRD ARTICLE

(Sanctification)

I believe in the Holy Spirit; the holy Christian church, the communion of saints; the forgiveness of sins; the resurrection of the body; and the life everlasting. Amen.

What does this mean?

I believe that I cannot by my own thinking or choosing believe in Jesus Christ, my Lord, or come to him.

But the Holy Spirit has called me by the gospel, enlightened me with his gifts, sanctified and kept me in the true faith. In the same way he calls, gathers, enlightens, and sanctifies the whole Christian church on earth, and keeps it with Jesus Christ in the one true faith.

In this Christian church he daily and fully forgives all sins to me and all believers.

On the Last Day he will raise me and all the dead and give eternal life to me and all believers in Christ.

This is most certainly true.

The Holy Spirit Is God

218. Who is the Holy Spirit?

1020) Acts 2:1-21. (The Holy Spirit came with power on Pentecost in fulfillment of Joel's prophecy.)

1021) Matthew 28:19. Go and make disciples of all nations, baptizing them in the name of the *Father* and of the *Son* and of the *Holy Spirit.*

1022) 2 Corinthians 13:14. May the grace of the *Lord Jesus Christ,* and the love of *God,* and the fellowship of the *Holy Spirit* be with you all.

1023) Matthew 3:16,17. (The Trinity was present at Jesus' baptism.)

218. The Holy Spirit is one of the three persons of the triune God.

219. Why do I believe that the Holy Spirit is true God?

1024) Acts 5:3,4. Then Peter said, "Ananias, how is it that Satan has so filled your heart that you have lied to the Holy Spirit . . . ? You have not *lied to* men but to *God.*"

1025) 1 Corinthians 12:6,11. *The same God* works all of them in all men. All these are the work of one and *the same Spirit.*

1026) 1 Corinthians 3:16. Don't you know that you yourselves are *God's temple* and that *God's Spirit* lives in you?

1027) 2 Corinthians 3:17. Now *the Lord* is *the Spirit.*

1028) Matthew 12:28. If I drive out demons by the *Spirit of God,* then the kingdom of God has come upon you.

219a. I believe that the Holy Spirit is true God because the Bible calls him God. (divine names)

1029) Psalm 139:7,8. Where can I go *from your Spirit?* Where can I flee *from your presence?* If I go up to the heavens, *you are there;* if I make my bed in the depths, *you are there.*

1030) Hebrews 9:14. Christ . . . through the *eternal* Spirit offered himself unblemished to God.

1031) 1 Corinthians 2:10,11. The Spirit *searches all* things, even the deep things of God. . . . no one *knows the thoughts of God* except the Spirit of God.

1032) Psalm 51:11. Do not cast me from your presence or take your *Holy* Spirit from me.

HOLY SPIRIT

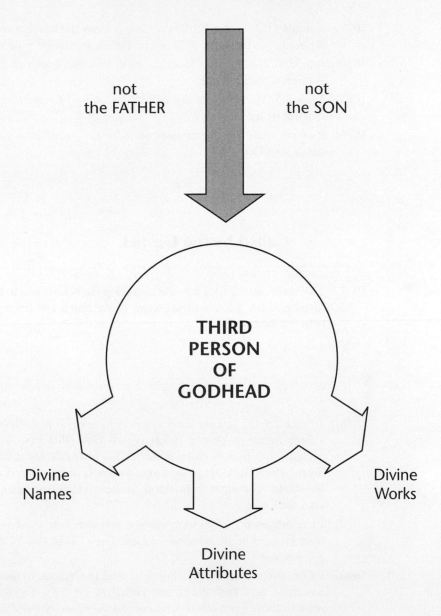

not
the FATHER

not
the SON

THIRD
PERSON
OF
GODHEAD

Divine
Names

Divine
Works

Divine
Attributes

219b. I believe that the Holy Spirit is true God because he has characteristics which only God has. (divine attributes)

> 1033) Genesis 1:1,2. In the beginning *God created* the heavens and the earth. . . . the *Spirit of God was hovering* over the waters.
>
> 1034) Job 33:4. The Spirit of God has *made me;* the breath of the Almighty gives me life.
>
> 1035) Titus 3:5. He saved us through *the washing of rebirth* and renewal by the Holy Spirit.
>
> 1036) Romans 8:27. The Spirit *intercedes for the saints* in accordance with God's will.

219c. I believe that the Holy Spirit is true God because he does things which only God can do. (divine works)

Called by the Gospel

220. What is the work of the Holy Spirit called?

> 1037) 2 Thessalonians 2:13. From the beginning God chose you to be saved through the *sanctifying work of the Spirit* and through belief in the truth.

220. The work of the Holy Spirit is called sanctification.

221. Why do I say that the Holy Spirit sanctifies me when he brings me to faith in Jesus?

> 1038) 1 Peter 2:9,11. You are a *chosen people,* a royal priesthood, a *holy* nation, a people *belonging to God,* that you may declare the praises of him who *called you out of darkness* into his wonderful light. . . . I urge you, as *aliens and strangers in the world,* to abstain from sinful desires, which war against your soul.
>
> 1039) 1 Corinthians 6:11. You were *washed,* you were *sanctified,* you were *justified* in the name of the Lord Jesus Christ and *by the Spirit of our God.*
>
> 1040) 1 Corinthians 1:2. To the church of God in Corinth, to those *sanctified in Christ Jesus* and *called to be holy,* together with all those everywhere *who call on the name of our Lord Jesus Christ.*

1041) 1 Thessalonians 5:23. May God himself, the God of peace, *sanctify you through and through*. May your whole spirit, soul and body *be kept blameless* at the coming of our Lord Jesus Christ.

221. I say that the Holy Spirit sanctifies me when he brings me to faith in Jesus because he calls me out of the unbelieving world to be holy. (sanctified in the wider meaning of this word)

222. By what means did the Holy Spirit call me to faith in Christ?

1042) John 17:17. *Sanctify* them *by the truth; your word* is truth.

1043) 2 Thessalonians 2:13,14. From the beginning God chose you to be saved through the sanctifying work of the Spirit and through belief in the truth. *He called you* to this *through our gospel,* that you might share in the glory of our Lord Jesus Christ.

1044) Acts 2:38-47. (Believers were added to the church through the Word, which the apostles taught.)

1045) Acts 8:35-39. (The Ethiopian eunuch heard the gospel and was baptized.)

1046) Acts 10:44-48. (The Holy Spirit came to all those in Cornelius' house who heard the Word, and they were baptized.)

1047) Romans 10:17. Faith comes *from hearing the message,* and the message is heard *through the word of Christ.*

1048) 2 Timothy 3:15. From infancy you have known the *holy Scriptures,* which are *able to make you wise for salvation through faith* in Christ Jesus.

1049) Acts 2:38. Peter replied, "Repent and *be baptized,* every one of you, in the name of Jesus Christ for the *forgiveness of your sins.* And you will receive the *gift of the Holy Spirit.*"

1050) Matthew 26:26-28. (Jesus gives us his body and blood in the Lord's Supper to assure us of our forgiveness.)

222. The Holy Spirit called me to faith in Christ by the gospel in Word and sacraments. (means of grace)

223. How does the Bible picture the miracle the Holy Spirit works in me when he calls me to faith by the gospel?

SANCTIFICATION

by the

HOLY SPIRIT

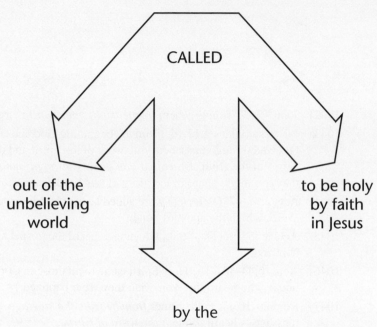

CALLED

out of the
unbelieving
world

to be holy
by faith
in Jesus

by the

GOSPEL

in the
WORD

in the
SACRAMENTS

the
MEANS OF
GRACE

1051) 1 Peter 2:25. You were like sheep *going astray,* but now you have *returned* to the Shepherd and Overseer of your souls.

1052) Acts 11:21. The Lord's hand was with them, and a great number of people *believed and turned* to the Lord.

1053) Acts 3:19. Repent . . . and *turn to God,* so that your sins may be wiped out.

1054) Psalm 51:13. I will teach transgressors your ways, and sinners will *turn back to you.*

1055) Acts 15:3. They told how the Gentiles had been *converted.*

223a. The Bible pictures the miracle of faith that the Holy Spirit works in me as turning me from unbelief to faith in God. (conversion)

1056) John 3:3,6. Jesus declared, "I tell you the truth, no one can see the kingdom of God unless he is *born again.* Flesh gives birth to flesh, but the *Spirit gives birth* to spirit.

1057) Titus 3:5. He saved us through the washing of *rebirth* and renewal by the Holy Spirit.

1058) 1 Peter 1:23. You have been *born again,* not of perishable seed, but of imperishable, through the living and enduring word of God.

223b. The Bible pictures the miracle of faith that the Holy Spirit works in me as giving me a second birth. (regeneration, rebirth)

1059) Ephesians 2:4,5. God, who is rich in mercy, *made us alive* with Christ even *when we were dead* in transgressions.

1060) Colossians 2:13. When you were *dead in your sins* and in the uncircumcision of your sinful nature, God *made you alive* with Christ.

223c. The Bible pictures the miracle of faith that the Holy Spirit works in me as raising me from death to life. (quickening)

Enlightened with His Gifts

224. What do the words "enlightened me with his gifts" explain about the work of the Holy Spirit?

187

1061) John 8:12. [Jesus] said, "I am the light of the world. Whoever follows me will *never walk in darkness,* but will *have the light of life.*"

1062) Acts 26:17,18. I am sending you to them to *open their eyes* and *turn them from darkness to light,* and from the power of Satan to God, *so that* they may receive forgiveness of sins and a place among those who are sanctified by faith in me.

1063) 2 Corinthians 4:4,6. The god of this age has *blinded the minds* of unbelievers, so that they *cannot see the light of the gospel* of the glory of Christ. . . . God . . . *made his light shine in our hearts* to give us *the light of the knowledge of the glory of God* in the face of Christ.

1064) Luke 10:23. Blessed are the *eyes that see* what you see.

224. These words explain that the Holy Spirit brought me out of the darkness of unbelief into the light of faith, so that I now see all the gifts God gives me in Christ.

225. **What are some of God's gifts that the Holy Spirit enlightened me to see by faith?**

1065) Ephesians 1:7. In him we have redemption through his blood, the *forgiveness* of sins, in accordance with the riches of God's grace.

1066) Romans 15:13. May the God of hope fill you with all *joy* and *peace* as you trust in him, so that you may overflow with *hope* by the power of the Holy Spirit.

1067) Romans 5:1. Since we have been justified through faith, we have *peace with God* through our Lord Jesus Christ.

1068) Isaiah 32:17. The fruit of righteousness will be *peace;* the effect of righteousness will be *quietness and confidence forever.*

1069) Psalm 71:5. For you have been *my hope,* O Sovereign LORD, *my confidence* since my youth.

1070) Romans 8:24,25. Hope that is seen is no hope at all. Who hopes for what he already has? But if we *hope for what we do not yet have,* we wait for it patiently.

1071) Titus 2:13. We wait for the *blessed hope*—the glorious appearing of our great God and Savior, Jesus Christ.

1072) Isaiah 61:10. I delight greatly in the LORD; my soul *rejoices* in my God. For he has clothed me with garments of salvation and arrayed me in a robe of righteousness.

ENLIGHTENED
by the
HOLY SPIRIT

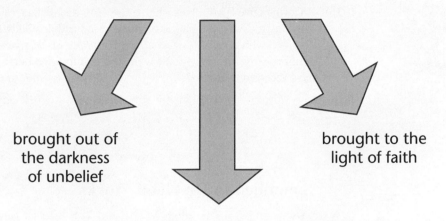

brought out of
the darkness
of unbelief

brought to the
light of faith

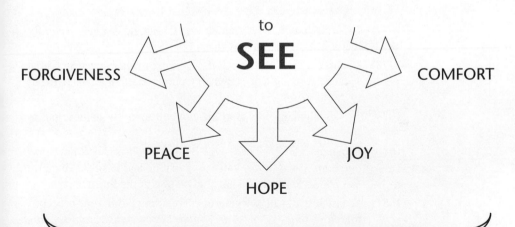

to
SEE

FORGIVENESS

COMFORT

PEACE

JOY

HOPE

**God's gifts
to me
IN CHRIST**

1073) Luke 2:10. The angel said to them, "Do not be afraid. I bring you good news of *great joy* that will be for all the people."

1074) Romans 5:2,3. We rejoice in the hope of the glory of God. Not only so, but we also *rejoice in our sufferings.*

1075) Psalm 119:50. My *comfort* in my suffering is this: Your promise preserves my life.

1076) 2 Corinthians 1:3,4. Praise be to the God and Father of our Lord Jesus Christ, the Father of compassion and the God of all comfort, who *comforts us in all our troubles,* so that we can comfort those in any trouble with the comfort we ourselves have received from God.

225. The Holy Spirit enlightened me to see by faith such wonderful gifts of God as forgiveness, peace, hope, joy, and comfort.

Sanctified to Do Good Works

226. What change does the Holy Spirit work in me when he sanctifies me by the gospel?

1077) 2 Corinthians 5:17. If anyone is in Christ, he is *a new creation;* the old has gone, the new has come!

1078) Ephesians 2:10. We are *God's workmanship,* created in Christ Jesus *to do good works,* which God prepared in advance for us to do.

1079) 1 Thessalonians 4:7. God did *not* call us *to be impure,* but *to live a holy life.*

1080) Galatians 5:24,25. Those who belong to Christ Jesus have *crucified the sinful nature* with its passions and desires. Since we *live by the Spirit,* let us keep in step with the Spirit.

1081) Psalm 119:104,112. I gain understanding from your precepts; therefore *I hate every wrong path.* My *heart is set on keeping* your decrees to the very end.

1082) Titus 2:14. [Jesus] gave himself for us to redeem us from all wickedness and to purify for himself a people that are his very own, *eager to do what is good.*

1083) Psalm 40:8. *I desire to do your will,* O my God.

226. When the Holy Spirit sanctifies me by the gospel, he leads me to hate sin and to be eager to live a holy life

SANCTIFICATION

by the

HOLY SPIRIT

leads me

to be eager

to do

GOOD WORKS

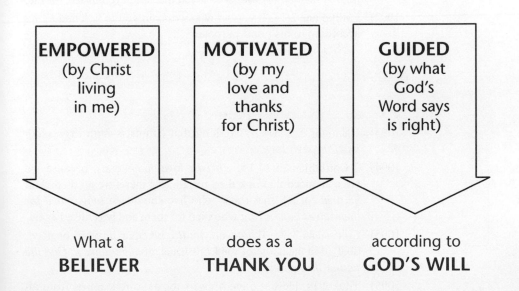

EMPOWERED	MOTIVATED	GUIDED
(by Christ living in me)	(by my love and thanks for Christ)	(by what God's Word says is right)

What a
BELIEVER

does as a
THANK YOU

according to
GOD'S WILL

filled with good works. (sanctified in the narrow meaning of this word)

227. Why am I able to do good works?

1084) Psalm 51:10. Create in me a *pure heart,* O God, and renew a steadfast spirit within me.

1085) Romans 8:5-10. (It is only when the Holy Spirit puts a new mind in me by faith in Jesus that I seek to do God's will.)

1086) Psalm 119:32. I run in the path of your commands, for you have *set my heart free.*

1087) Hebrews 11:6. *Without faith* it is *impossible* to please God.

1088) 2 Corinthians 5:17. If anyone is *in Christ,* he is *a new creation;* the old has gone, the new has come!

1089) Ephesians 2:10. We are God's workmanship, *created in Christ Jesus* to do good works.

1090) John 15:5. I am the vine; you are the branches. If a man *remains in me and I in him,* he will bear much fruit; apart from me you can do nothing.

1091) Galatians 2:20. I have been crucified with Christ and I no longer live, but *Christ lives in me.* The life I live in the body, I live *by faith in the Son of God,* who loved me and gave himself for me.

1092) Philippians 2:13. It is *God* who *works* in you *to will* and *to act* according to his good purpose.

227. I am able to do good works because the Holy Spirit gives me a pure heart in which Christ lives by faith.

228. Why do I gladly do good works?

1093) Galatians 5:6. The only thing that counts is faith *expressing itself through love.*

1094) 2 Corinthians 5:14,15. *Christ's love compels us,* because we are convinced that one died for all, and therefore all died. And he died for all, that those who live should *no longer live for themselves but for him* who died for them and was raised again.

1095) Colossians 3:17. *Whatever you do,* whether in word or deed, do it all in the name of the Lord Jesus, *giving thanks to God the Father through him.*

1096) Titus 2:14. [Jesus] gave himself for us to redeem us from all wickedness and to purify for himself a people that are his very own, *eager to do what is good.*

228. I gladly do good works to express my love and thanks to God for all his goodness to me. (Good works are the fruit of faith.)

229. What is my guideline in doing good works?

1097) Psalm 119:105. *Your word* is a lamp to my feet and a light for my path.

1098) Psalm 119:9. How can a young man keep his way pure? By *living according to your word*.

1099) Luke 11:28. Blessed . . . are those who hear the word of God and *obey it*.

1100) Romans 12:2. Do not conform any longer to the pattern of this world, but be transformed by the renewing of your mind. Then you will be able to *test and approve what God's will is*—his good, pleasing and perfect will.

229. My guideline in doing good works is God's will as it is written in his Word.

230. What, then, is a good work?

1101) Galatians 2:20. The life I live in the body, I live *by faith* in the Son of God.

1102) Psalm 119:105. *Your word* is a lamp to my feet.

1103) Colossians 3:17. Do it all in the name of the Lord Jesus, *giving thanks* to God the Father through him.

1104) Mark 12:41-44. (Jesus praised the poor widow's offering as an act of faith and love.)

1105) Mark 14:3-9. (Jesus praised Mary's anointing of him as a beautiful thing she did in love for her Savior.)

1106) Luke 19:1-10. (When Zacchaeus became a believer, he showed his love and thanks to Jesus by what he did.)

1107) Genesis 4:3-5; Hebrews 11:4. (Although Cain and Abel both offered a sacrifice, only Abel's was acceptable to God.)

230. A good work is whatever a believer does according to God's Word out of love and thanks for all of God's goodness.

231. Why does God consider such works done by a believer as good?

1108) Isaiah 64:6. All of us have become like *one who is unclean,* and all our righteous acts are *like filthy rags.*

1109) Romans 9:16. It does not . . . depend on *man's desire or effort,* but on *God's mercy.*

1110) Psalm 147:11. *The LORD delights* in those who fear him, who put their hope in his unfailing love.

1111) Colossians 3:17. Whatever you do, whether in word or deed, *do it all in the name of the Lord Jesus,* giving thanks to God the Father *through him.*

231. God considers such works as good only because in his mercy he delights in everything a believer does out of love for Jesus.

232. How many good works does God want me to do?

1112) Matthew 18:21,22. Then Peter came to Jesus and asked, "Lord, *how many times* shall I forgive my brother when he sins against me? *Up to* seven times?" Jesus answered, "I tell you, not seven times, but seventy-seven times."

1113) 2 Corinthians 9:8. God is able to make all grace abound to you, so that *in all things at all times,* having all that you need, you will *abound in every good work.*

1114) Titus 3:8. I want you to stress these things, so that those who have trusted in God may *be careful to devote themselves* to doing what is good.

1115) Galatians 6:10. Therefore, *as we have opportunity,* let us do good to all people, especially to those who belong to the family of believers.

232. God does not want me to keep a count of my good works but rather to make use of every opportunity I have to do them.

Kept in True Faith

233. What enemies try to weaken my faith and keep me from doing good works?

1116) 2 Corinthians 11:3. I am afraid that just as Eve was deceived *by the serpent's cunning,* your minds may somehow be *led astray* from your sincere and pure devotion to Christ.

THE
HOLY SPIRIT

HELPS ME
AGAINST
THE

ENEMIES OF
FAITH
AND
GOOD WORKS

DEVIL   SINFUL WORLD   SINFUL NATURE

by

strengthening
my faith

renewing my zeal
to do good works

1117) Ephesians 6:11,12. Put on the full armor of God so that you can take your stand against *the devil's schemes.* For our *struggle* is not against flesh and blood, but against the rulers, against the authorities, against the powers of this dark world and *against the spiritual forces of evil* in the heavenly realms.

1118) 1 John 2:15. *Do not love the world* or anything in the world. If anyone loves the world, the love of the Father is not in him.

1119) Galatians 5:17. The *sinful nature* desires what is *contrary to the Spirit,* and the Spirit what is contrary to the sinful nature. They are in conflict with each other, so that *you do not do what you want.*

1120) Romans 7:18-23. (I often fall into sin because my old Adam constantly opposes my new man.)

233. The devil, the world, and my own sinful nature try to weaken my faith and keep me from doing good works.

234. What, therefore, does the Holy Spirit do besides bringing me to faith?

1121) Isaiah 41:10. Do not fear, for I am with you; do not be dismayed, for I am your God. *I will strengthen you and help you; I will uphold you* with my righteous right hand.

1122) Ephesians 3:16. I pray that out of his glorious riches he may *strengthen you* with power through his Spirit in your inner being.

1123) 1 Peter 1:5. [You] through faith are *shielded* by God's power *until the coming of the salvation* that is ready to be revealed in the last time.

1124) 1 Peter 5:10. The God of all grace, who called you to his eternal glory in Christ, after you have suffered a little while, will himself *restore you* and *make you strong, firm and steadfast.*

1125) Psalm 51:10-12. Create in me a pure heart, O God, and *renew a steadfast spirit* within me. *Do not* cast me from your presence or *take your Holy Spirit from me.* Restore to me the joy of your salvation and *grant me a willing spirit,* to sustain me.

234. The Holy Spirit also strengthens my faith and renews my love to do God's will until I enter heaven.

The Holy Christian Church, the Communion of Saints

235. What is the holy Christian church?

1126) Acts 2:47. The Lord *added to their number* daily those who were being saved.

1127) Acts 5:14. More and more men and women *believed in the Lord* and were added to their number.

1128) Ephesians 5:23. Christ is the head of the *church,* his body, *of which he is the Savior.*

1129) 1 Corinthians 1:2. To the church of God in Corinth, to those sanctified in Christ Jesus and called to be holy, *together with all those everywhere* who call on the name of our Lord Jesus Christ.

235. The holy Christian church is all those everywhere who believe in Jesus as the Savior.

NOTE: The Bible also gives other names to all who believe in Jesus, such as the city of God (Psalm 46:4), the people of God (1 Peter 2:9,10), the temple of God (1 Corinthians 3:16,17), Mount Zion (Psalm 48:2), the bride of Christ (Revelation 21:2), and the body of Christ (Ephesians 1:22,23). The terms "the kingdom of God" and "the Lord's vineyard" are also applied to the holy Christian church.

236. Why are all believers everywhere called the *holy* Christian church and the communion of *saints*?

1130) Romans 1:7. To all in Rome who are loved by God and *called to be saints.*

1131) 1 Corinthians 1:2. To the church of God in Corinth, to those *sanctified in Christ Jesus* and *called to be holy,* together with all those everywhere who call on the name of our Lord Jesus Christ.

1132) Ephesians 5:25-27. *Christ* loved the church and *gave himself up* for her *to make her holy,* cleansing her by the washing with water through the word, and to present her to himself as a radiant church, *without stain or wrinkle or any other blemish,* but holy and blameless.

1133) Revelation 1:5,6. To him who loves us and has *freed us from our sins by his blood,* and has *made us to be a kingdom and priests* to serve his God and Father—to him be glory and power for ever and ever!

197

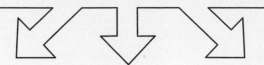

ALL BELIEVERS

"holy"
or
"saints"
(sins
washed
away by
Jesus)

"Christian"
(trust
only in
Christ)

"communion"
(united
by faith
in Christ
into one
body)

invisible

THE HOLY CHRISTIAN CHURCH

or

THE COMMUNION OF SAINTS

236. All believers everywhere are called *holy* and *saints* because by faith in Jesus their sins are all washed away.

237. Why are all believers everywhere called the holy *Christian* church?

1134) Ephesians 2:19,20. You are no longer foreigners and aliens, but fellow citizens with God's people and members of God's household, built on the foundation of the apostles and prophets, with *Christ Jesus* himself as the *chief cornerstone.*

1135) Acts 11:26. The disciples were called *Christians* first at Antioch.

1136) 1 Corinthians 3:11. *No one* can lay *any foundation other* than the one already laid, which is Jesus Christ.

1137) 1 Timothy 1:1. Paul, an apostle of Christ Jesus by the command of God our Savior and of *Christ Jesus our hope.*

237. All believers everywhere are called *Christian* because their entire hope is founded on Christ.

238. Why is the holy Christian church called a *communion* of saints?

1138) John 10:16. I have other sheep that are not of this sheep pen. I must bring them also. They too will *listen to my voice,* and there shall be *one flock* and *one shepherd.*

1139) 1 Corinthians 12:13. We were all baptized *by one Spirit into one body.*

1140) Romans 12:5. In Christ we who are many form one body, and *each member belongs to all the others.*

1141) Ephesians 5:23. *Christ is the head* of the church, his body.

1142) Ephesians 4:3-6. Make every effort to keep *the unity of the Spirit* through the bond of peace. There is *one body and one Spirit*—just as you were called to one hope when you were called—*one Lord, one faith,* one baptism; one God and Father of all, who is over all and through all and in all.

238. The holy Christian church is called a *communion* because by faith in Christ the Holy Spirit gathers all believers into one spiritual body.

239. Why is God the only one who knows the members of the holy Christian church?

1143) 1 Kings 19:9-18. (Elijah thought he was the only believer left, but God said there were 7,000.)

1144) Luke 17:20,21. The kingdom of God does *not come with your careful observation,* nor will people say, "Here it is," or "There it is," because the kingdom of God is *within you.*

1145) 1 Samuel 16:7. Man looks at the outward appearance, but the LORD *looks at the heart.*

1146) 2 Timothy 2:19. The Lord knows those who are his.

239. **God alone knows the members of the holy Christian church because he alone knows who has faith in his heart. (the invisible church)**

240. **By what means does the Holy Spirit call, gather, enlighten, and sanctify the whole Christian church on earth and keep it with Jesus Christ in the one true faith?**

1147) Acts 2:38-47. (Believers were added to the church through the Word, which the apostles taught.)

1148) Ephesians 5:25,26. Christ loved the church and gave himself up for her to make her holy, cleansing her by the *washing with water through the word.*

1149) John 10:16. I have other sheep that are not of this sheep pen. I must *bring them* also. They too will *listen to my voice,* and there shall be one flock and one shepherd.

240. **The Holy Spirit calls, gathers, enlightens, sanctifies, and keeps the holy Christian church by the gospel in Word and sacraments (see Question 222).**

241. **Where, then, is the holy Christian church only to be found?**

1150) Matthew 28:19,20. Go and make disciples of *all nations, baptizing* them in the name of the Father and of the Son and of the Holy Spirit, *and teaching* them to obey everything I have commanded you.

1151) Isaiah 55:10,11. As the rain and the snow come down from heaven, and do not return to it without watering the earth and making it bud and flourish, so that it yields seed for the sower and bread for the eater, so is *my word* that goes out from my mouth: It will *not return to me empty,* but will *accomplish what I desire* and achieve the purpose for which I sent it.

1152) Matthew 18:20. Where two or three *come together in my name,* there am I with them.

241. The holy Christian church is found only where the gospel is preached and the sacraments are used.

Visible Christian Churches

242. Why do we call a group of people who come together to hear the gospel a church?

1153) Acts 13:1; 14:23; 15:41; 16:5. (The congregations in various cities were called churches.)

1154) Isaiah 55:11. [My word] will *not return to me empty,* but will accomplish what I desire and achieve the purpose for which I sent it.

1155) Revelation 3:4. Yet you have *a few people* in Sardis who have not soiled their clothes. They will *walk with me,* dressed in white, for they are worthy.

242. We call a group of people who come together to hear the gospel a church because we know the Holy Spirit will use the gospel to bring people in that group to faith. (a visible church, a congregation, a church body)

243. What does God want us to do with every visible church that teaches his Word?

1156) 1 John 4:1. Dear friends, do not believe every spirit, but *test* the spirits to see *whether they are from God,* because many false prophets have gone out into the world.

1157) 1 Thessalonians 5:21,22. *Test everything.* Hold on to the good. Avoid every kind of evil.

243. God wants us to test every visible church very carefully.

244. What does God want us to examine when we test a visible church?

1158) Matthew 28:19,20. Go and make disciples of all nations, . . . teaching them *to obey everything I have commanded you.*

1159) John 8:31. To the Jews who had believed him, Jesus said, "If you *hold to my teaching,* you are *really* my disciples."

1160) Revelation 3:8-10. (Jesus praised the church in Philadelphia because it kept God's Word.)

1161) Revelation 2:13-16. (Jesus faulted the church at Pergamum because it allowed false doctrine to be taught in addition to God's Word.)

1162) 2 Timothy 4:3,4. The time will come when men will *not put up with sound doctrine.* Instead, to suit their own desires, they will gather around them a great number of teachers to say what their itching ears want to hear. They will *turn their ears away from the truth* and turn aside to myths.

1163) Hebrews 13:9. Do not be carried away by *all kinds of strange teachings.*

1164) 2 John 9. Anyone who *runs ahead and does not continue in the teaching of Christ* does not have God; whoever *continues in the teaching* has both the Father and the Son.

1165) Revelation 22:18,19. (Nothing is to be added to or subtracted from God's Word.)

244. When we test a visible church, God wants us to examine whether it holds to his pure Word or whether it allows anything false to be mixed together with his Word. (true and false visible churches)

The Need for Confessions

Since we cannot know whether the people in a church have faith in their hearts or not (see Question 239), our testing of a church will have to be made on the basis of what a church confesses (Romans 10:10; Matthew 12:37).

Most churches have a written statement of what they believe and teach. These statements are called confessions. But since churches don't always practice what they preach or confess, we will also have to test a church's practice as well as its confessional statement.

Sometimes people will say that they don't agree with the errors in the confession or practice of the church to which they belong. But if they continue to attend and support a false church, then they are holding to the confession of that church (2 John 10,11).

Our Lutheran church has a number of confessions. They are the following:

1. The Small Catechism (written by Luther in 1529)
2. The Large Catechism (written by Luther in 1529)
3. The Augsburg Confession (written by Melanchthon in 1530)
4. The Apology (written by Melanchthon in 1530)
5. The Smalcald Articles (written by Luther in 1537)
6. The Formula of Concord (written by a committee of Lutherans in 1577)

These were all written at the time of the Reformation and were published together in the *Book of Concord* in 1580.

Since some new errors have troubled the Lutheran church in the 1900s, our Wisconsin Synod has published a confessional tract called *This We Believe.* This tract confesses what is truth and what is error according to God's Word in regard to these new matters that are troubling the church today.

A true Lutheran church will always want to confess the whole truth of God's Word and reject everything that is false (see Question 12).

245. What does God want us to do when we find people who hold to his pure Word?

1166) John 8:31. To the Jews who had believed him, Jesus said, "If you *hold to my teaching,* you are really my disciples."

1167) John 17:20,21. I pray also for those who will believe in me through their message, that *all of them may be one.*

1168) Acts 2:41-47. (The believers formed a congregation under the leadership of the apostles.)

1169) Acts 11:22,29. (The churches in Antioch and Jerusalem helped one another.)

1170) Acts 15. (The churches acted together in obedience to God's Word when there was a question about doctrine.)

1171) 1 John 1:3. We proclaim to you what we have seen and heard, so that you also may have *fellowship with us.*

245. God wants us to join in fellowship with all those who hold to his pure Word.

246. How do we join in fellowship with those who hold to God's pure Word?

1172) Colossians 3:16. Let the word of Christ dwell in you richly *as you teach and admonish one another* with all wisdom, *and as you sing* psalms, hymns and spiritual songs with gratitude in your hearts to God.

1173) Hebrews 10:24,25. Let us consider how we may *spur one another on toward love and good deeds.* Let us *not give up meeting together,* as some are in the habit of doing, but let us *encourage one another*—and *all the more* as you see the Day approaching.

1174) Romans 1:11,12. I long to see you so that . . . you and I may be *mutually encouraged by each other's faith.*

1175) Galatians 6:2. *Carry each other's burdens,* and in this way you will fulfill the law of Christ.

1176) 1 Thessalonians 5:11. Therefore *encourage one another* and *build each other up,* just as in fact you are doing.

1177) Ephesians 4:11-16. (As members of one body we grow stronger together by our fellowship in Christ.)

246a. We join in fellowship by worshiping and studying God's Word regularly together. (church fellowship)

1178) Acts 1:14. They all *joined* together constantly *in prayer.*

1179) Acts 2:42. *They devoted themselves* to the apostles' teaching and to the fellowship, to the breaking of bread and *to prayer.*

1180) 1 Timothy 2:1-4,8. (Paul instructs Christians to join with one another in prayers of all kinds.)

1181) James 5:16. Therefore confess your sins to each other and *pray for each other* so that you may be healed.

246b. We join in fellowship by praying with each other and for each other. (prayer fellowship)

1182) Psalm 78:4-7. We will *tell the next generation* the praiseworthy deeds of the LORD, his power, and the wonders he has done. He decreed statutes for Jacob and established the law in Israel, which he commanded our forefathers to *teach their children, so the next generation would know* them, even the children yet to be born, and *they in turn would tell their children.* Then they would put their trust in God and would not forget his deeds but would keep his commands.

1183) Joel 1:3. Tell it *to your children,* and let your children tell it *to their children,* and their children *to the next generation.*

1184) John 21:15. Feed my lambs.

1185) Mark 10:14,15. Let the little children come to me, and do not hinder them, for the kingdom of God belongs to such as these. I tell you the truth, anyone who will not *receive the kingdom of God like a little child* will never enter it.

1186) 2 Timothy 3:15. *From infancy* you have known the holy Scriptures, which are able to make you wise for salvation through faith in Christ Jesus.

1187) Proverbs 22:6. *Train a child* in the way he should go, and when he is old he will not turn from it.

246c. We join in fellowship by working together to help parents teach God's Word to their children. (Christian education)

1188) Matthew 28:19. Go and make disciples of *all nations.*

1189) Mark 16:15. Go into *all the world* and preach the good news to all creation.

1190) Acts 8:4. Those who had been scattered *preached* the word *wherever they went.*

1191) Acts 6:1-7. (Men were chosen to help the apostles so that the apostles could devote themselves full time to the ministry of the Word.)

1192) Philippians 4:14-16. (The Philippians sent money so that Paul could spend all his time in preaching God's Word.)

1193) 3 John 5-8. (John commended Gaius for helping those missionaries who worked among the pagans and so had little or no income.)

246d. We join in fellowship by working together to help spread the gospel to all people. (mission work)

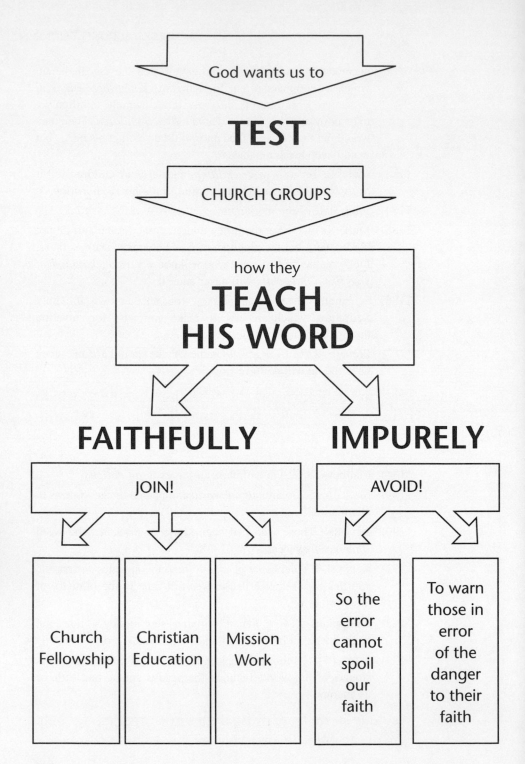

God wants us to

TEST

CHURCH GROUPS

how they

TEACH HIS WORD

FAITHFULLY

IMPURELY

JOIN!

AVOID!

Church Fellowship

Christian Education

Mission Work

So the error cannot spoil our faith

To warn those in error of the danger to their faith

247. **What does God want us to do if people who are not members of our church ask us about our faith?**

1194) 1 Peter 3:15. *Always be prepared to give an answer to everyone* who asks you to give the reason for the hope that you have. But do this with gentleness and respect.

1195) 2 Timothy 2:14. *Warn them* before God *against quarreling* about words; it is of no value, and only *ruins those who listen.*

1196) Matthew 7:6. Do not give dogs what is sacred; *do not throw your pearls to pigs.* If you do, they may trample them under their feet, and then *turn and tear you* to pieces.

1197) 1 John 1:3. We proclaim to you what we have seen and heard, *so that* you also may *have fellowship with us.* And our fellowship is with the Father and with his Son, Jesus Christ.

247. God wants us to be ready to share our faith with everyone who asks us about it.

248. **What does God tell us if we find people who persist in mixing something false with God's Word?**

1198) Romans 16:17. *Watch out* for those who cause divisions and put obstacles in your way that are contrary to the teaching you have learned. *Keep away from them.*

1199) 2 Corinthians 6:14,17; 7:1. *Do not be yoked together* with unbelievers. . . . "come out from them and *be separate,*" says the Lord. . . . let us *purify ourselves from everything* that contaminates body and spirit, perfecting holiness out of reverence for God.

1200) Titus 3:10. Warn a divisive person once, and then warn him a second time. After that, *have nothing to do with him.*

1201) 2 John 10,11. If *anyone* comes to you and does not bring this teaching, *do not take him into your house or welcome him.* Anyone who welcomes him shares in his wicked work.

248. God forbids us to join in fellowship with anyone who persists in mixing anything false with God's Word.

249. **Why does God want us to separate ourselves from anyone who persists in mixing anything false with God's Word?**

1202) 1 John 1:5,6. *God is light;* in him there is *no darkness* at all. If we claim to have *fellowship with him* yet walk in the darkness, we lie and do not live by the truth.

1203) 2 Corinthians 13:8. We *cannot do anything against* the truth, but *only for* the truth.

1204) Psalm 119:30,31,103-105. I have *chosen the way of truth.* . . . I hold fast to your statutes, O LORD. . . . *How sweet* are your words to my taste, sweeter than honey to my mouth! *I gain understanding* from your precepts; therefore *I hate every wrong path.* Your word is a lamp to my feet and a light for my path.

249a. God wants us to separate ourselves because we are his children who love the truth and hate anything false. (separation out of love for the truth of God's Word)

1205) Matthew 7:15. Watch out for false prophets. They *come* to you in *sheep's clothing,* but inwardly they are *ferocious wolves.*

1206) 2 John 11. Anyone who welcomes him *shares in his wicked work.*

1207) 2 Corinthians 7:1. Let us purify ourselves from everything that *contaminates body and spirit.*

1208) 2 Timothy 2:17. Their teaching will *spread like gangrene.*

1209) Galatians 5:9. A little yeast *works through* the whole batch of dough.

1210) 2 Corinthians 11:3. I am afraid that just as Eve was deceived by the serpent's cunning, *your minds may somehow be led astray* from your sincere and pure devotion to Christ.

249b. God wants us to separate ourselves because that which is false will spread to us and weaken or destroy our faith. (separation out of love for our own souls)

1211) Revelation 22:18,19. (Adding or subtracting anything in regard to God's Word endangers one's salvation.)

1212) 2 Timothy 2:16-18. Avoid godless chatter, because those who indulge in it will *become more and more ungodly.* Their teaching will *spread like gangrene.* Among them are Hymenaeus and Philetus, who have wandered away from the truth. They say that the resurrection has already taken place, and they *destroy the faith of some.*

1213) Titus 1:11. They must be silenced, because they are *ruining whole households* by teaching things they ought not to teach.

1214) 2 Peter 2:1. False teachers . . . will secretly introduce *destructive* heresies.

1215) Titus 3:10. *Warn* a divisive person once, and then *warn* him a second time. After that, have nothing to do with him.

1216) Titus 1:13,14. Rebuke them sharply, *so that they will be sound in the faith* and will *pay no attention* to Jewish myths or to the commands of those who reject the truth.

1217) James 5:19,20. If one of you should wander from the truth and someone should *bring him back*, remember this: Whoever *turns a sinner from the error of his way* will *save him from death* and cover over a multitude of sins.

249c. God wants us to separate ourselves from those who mix something false with God's Word to warn them about the great danger to their souls. (separation out of love for their souls)

250. Why is it possible that people in a false visible church can be saved if God's Word is used there?

1218) 1 Kings 19:14-18. (When false teachers led most of Israel astray and Elijah thought he was the only believer left, God said he still had kept 7,000 faithful.)

1219) Isaiah 55:11. [My word] will *not return to me empty*, but will *accomplish* what I desire and *achieve* the purpose for which I sent it.

250. This is possible because even in a false visible church the Holy Spirit can use God's Word to work faith.

The Forgiveness of Sins

251. How does God forgive sins?

1220) Romans 4:6-8. David . . . speaks of the blessedness of the man to whom *God credits righteousness* apart from works: "Blessed are they whose transgressions are forgiven, whose sins are *covered*. Blessed is the man *whose sin the Lord will never count against him*."

1221) 2 Corinthians 5:19. God was reconciling the world to himself in Christ, *not counting men's sins against them*.

1222) Psalm 51:9. *Hide your face from* my sins and *blot out* all my iniquity.

1223) Psalm 85:2,3. You forgave the iniquity of your people and *covered* all their sins. You *set aside all your wrath* and *turned from your fierce anger.*

1224) Jeremiah 31:34. I will forgive their wickedness and will *remember their sins no more.*

1225) 1 John 1:9. He . . . will forgive us our sins and *purify us from all unrighteousness.*

1226) Romans 8:33. *Who will bring any charge against* those whom God has chosen? It is *God* who *justifies.*

251. God forgives sins like a judge in a courtroom who tells a criminal that there is no longer any charge against him and so declares him innocent or not guilty. (declare righteous, justify)

252. On what basis did God declare guilty sinners to be righteous?

1227) Isaiah 53:5,6. *He was pierced* for our transgressions, *he was crushed* for our iniquities; *the punishment* that brought us peace *was upon him,* and *by his wounds* we are healed. We all, like sheep, have gone astray, each of us has turned to his own way; and the *LORD has laid on him* the iniquity of us all.

1228) 2 Corinthians 5:19,21. God was reconciling the world to himself *in Christ,* not counting men's sins against them. . . . *God made him* who had no sin *to be sin for us,* so that *in him* we might become the righteousness of God.

1229) Romans 3:23-26. (So that God could be a good judge and still declare sinners righteous, he had Christ pay the debt which sinners owed for all their sins.)

252. God declared guilty sinners to be righteous because Jesus served as their substitute and paid for their sins in full.

253. How many people did God declare righteous?

1230) 1 Timothy 2:3,4. God our Savior . . . wants *all men* to be saved and to come to a knowledge of the truth.

1231) Mark 16:15. Go into all the world and preach the good news to all *creation.*

1232) John 3:17. God did not send his Son into the world to condemn the world, but to *save the world* through him.

1233) Romans 5:18. Just as the result of one trespass was condemnation for all men, so also the result of one act of righteousness was *justification* that brings life *for all men.*

1234) 2 Corinthians 5:19. God was reconciling *the world* to himself in Christ, not counting men's sins against them.

1235) 1 John 2:2. He is the atoning sacrifice for our sins, and not only for ours but also for the *sins of the whole world.*

1236) John 1:29. Look, the Lamb of God, who takes away *the sin of the world!*

253. God declared all people righteous. (objective justification)

254. How do many people reject this perfect righteousness that Jesus obtained for them?

1237) Luke 14:16-24. (Many rejected the invitation to the banquet.)

1238) Romans 10:3. Since they did not know the righteousness that comes from God and *sought to establish their own,* they did not submit to God's righteousness.

1239) Romans 4:6. God credits righteousness *apart from works.*

1240) Galatians 5:4. You who are trying to be justified by law have been *alienated from Christ;* you have *fallen away from grace.*

1241) Romans 11:6. If *by grace,* then it is *no longer by works;* if it were, grace would no longer be grace.

1242) Titus 3:5. He saved us, not because of righteous things we had done, but because of *his mercy.*

254. Many people reject this perfect righteousness by trying to earn righteousness before God by their own works. (self-righteousness, work-righteousness)

255. Why is it important, then, that the Holy Spirit work faith in me?

1243) Philippians 3:7-11. (Paul considered all his own works rubbish and trusted only in what Christ did for him.)

1244) Ephesians 2:8,9. It is *by grace* you have been saved, through faith—and this *not from yourselves,* it is the *gift of God—not by works,* so that *no one can boast.*

FORGIVENESS OF SINS

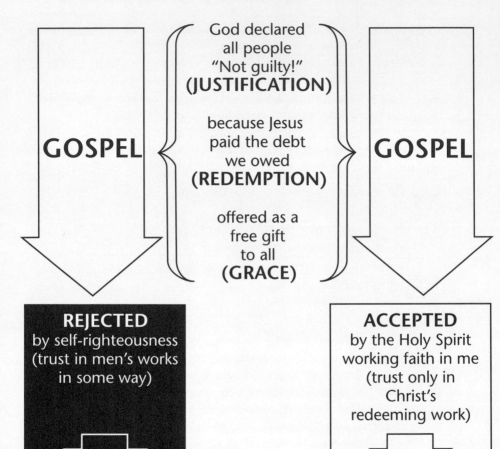

GOSPEL

God declared
all people
"Not guilty!"
(JUSTIFICATION)

because Jesus
paid the debt
we owed
(REDEMPTION)

offered as a
free gift
to all
(GRACE)

GOSPEL

REJECTED
by self-righteousness
(trust in men's works
in some way)

ACCEPTED
by the Holy Spirit
working faith in me
(trust only in
Christ's
redeeming work)

**Forgiveness
and
Salvation
are
lost!**

**Daily Forgiveness
and
Eternal Life
are
certain!**

1245) Galatians 3:26,27. You are all sons of God *through faith* in Christ Jesus, for all of you who were baptized into Christ have *clothed yourselves with Christ.*

1246) Romans 3:22,28. This righteousness from God comes *through faith* in Jesus Christ *to all who believe.* . . . . a man is justified by faith *apart from observing the law.*

1247) Romans 4:5. To the man who *does not work but trusts God* who justifies the wicked, his *faith is credited as righteousness.*

1248) Romans 1:17. In the gospel a righteousness from God is revealed, a righteousness that is *by faith from first to last,* just as it is written: "The righteous will live by faith."

255. It is important that the Holy Spirit work faith in me so that I do not trust in my own works but only in the righteousness God gives me by grace in Christ. (subjective justification)

256. Why can I as a believer be certain of God's forgiveness?

1249) Romans 4:16. The promise comes by faith, so that it may be *by grace* and may be *guaranteed* to all Abraham's offspring.

1250) Philippians 3:8,9. I consider them [all things] rubbish, that I may gain Christ and be found in him, *not* having *a righteousness of my own* that comes from the law, *but* that which is through faith in Christ—*the righteousness that comes from God* and is by faith.

1251) Galatians 2:16. We, too, have put our faith in Christ Jesus that we may be *justified by faith in Christ* and *not by observing the law,* because by observing the law no one will be justified.

1252) Ephesians 3:12. *In him* and *through faith in him* we may approach God with *freedom and confidence.*

256. I can be certain of God's forgiveness because it does not depend on anything I do but completely on what Christ has done for me.

257. Why is this certainty a great blessing to me?

1253) Romans 7:14-25. (We sin daily because of our old Adam—"sinful nature.")

1254) Psalm 32:1-5. (The forgiveness of sins removes the torment we go through because of our guilt.)

1255) Matthew 11:28,29. Come to me, all you who are weary and burdened, and *I will give you rest.* Take my yoke upon you and learn from me, for I am gentle and humble in heart, and you will find *rest for your souls.*

1256) Lamentations 3:22,23. Because of the LORD's great love we are not consumed, for *his compassions* never fail. They are *new every morning;* great is your faithfulness.

257a. This certainty is a great blessing to me because I need the assurance of God's forgiveness every day.

1257) Romans 5:20,21. Where sin increased, *grace increased all the more,* so that, just as sin reigned in death, so also grace might reign through righteousness to *bring eternal life* through Jesus Christ our Lord.

1258) Titus 3:7. [He saved us] so that, having been *justified by his grace,* we might become *heirs* having the hope *of eternal life.*

1259) Ephesians 1:13,14. Having believed, you were marked in him with a seal, the promised Holy Spirit, who is *a deposit guaranteeing our inheritance.*

257b. This certainty is a great blessing to me because I have the assurance that I am an heir of eternal life.

The Resurrection to Eternal Life

258. What happens when a person dies?

1260) Ecclesiastes 12:7. The *dust returns to the ground* it came from, and the *spirit returns to God* who gave it.

1261) Job 19:26; John 11:39. (The body decays.)

1262) Luke 16:22,23. The time came when the beggar died and the angels carried him to Abraham's side. The rich man also *died* and was buried. *In hell,* where he was in torment, he looked up and saw Abraham far away, with Lazarus by his side.

1263) Luke 23:43. I tell you the truth, *today* you will be *with me in paradise.*

1264) Luke 23:46. (Jesus commended his spirit to God.)

1265) 2 Corinthians 5:8. We are confident . . . and would prefer to be *away from the body* and *at home with the Lord.*

1266) Philippians 1:23,24. I am torn between *the two:* I desire to depart and *be with Christ,* which is better by far; but it is more necessary for you that I *remain in the body.*

258. When a person dies, his body decays, but his soul is either in hell or with God in heaven.

259. What will happen in the resurrection on the Last Day?

1267) John 5:28,29. A time is coming when *all who are in their graves* will hear his voice and *come out*—those who have done good will rise to live, and those who have done evil will rise to be condemned.

1268) Daniel 12:2. *Multitudes who sleep* in the dust of the earth *will awake: some* to everlasting life, *others* to shame and everlasting contempt.

1269) Acts 24:15. There will be *a resurrection of both* the righteous and the wicked.

1270) Job 19:25-27. I know that my Redeemer lives, and that *in the end* he will stand upon the earth. And after my skin has been destroyed, yet *in my flesh* I will see God; I *myself* will see him with my own eyes—*I, and not another.* How my heart yearns within me!

1271) John 6:40. My Father's will is that everyone who looks to the Son and believes in him shall have eternal life, and I will raise him up *at the last day.*

1272) Revelation 20:13. The sea gave up the dead that were in it.

1273) 1 Corinthians 6:14. By *his power* God raised the Lord from the dead, and he will raise us also.

259. On the Last Day God will use his power to raise the bodies of all people from the dead.

260. What will happen to the unbelievers who rejected God's gracious forgiveness?

1274) Mark 16:16. Whoever does not believe will be *condemned.*

1275) Matthew 25:41,46. Then he will say to those on his left, "*Depart from me,* you who are cursed, into the eternal fire prepared for the devil and his angels." . . . Then they will go away to *eternal punishment.*

1276) Revelation 20:15. If anyone's name was not found written in the book of life, he was *thrown into the lake of fire.*

1277) Luke 16:23,24. *In hell,* where he was *in torment,* he looked up and saw Abraham far away, with Lazarus by his side. So he called to him, "Father Abraham, have pity on me and send Lazarus to dip the tip of his finger in water and cool my tongue, because I am *in agony in this fire.*"

1278) Matthew 22:10-13. (In the parable of the wedding banquet, Jesus teaches that those who reject God's grace will be cast out into darkness where there is weeping and gnashing of teeth.)

1279) Isaiah 66:24. Their worm will not die, nor will their fire be quenched, and they will be *loathsome* to all mankind.

260. The unbelievers will be separated from God to suffer eternal torment in the fires of hell.

261. What will happen to the believers in whom the Holy Spirit worked faith in Christ?

1280) Matthew 25:34,46. Then the King will say to those on his right, "*Come,* you who are blessed by my Father; *take your inheritance,* the kingdom prepared for you since the creation of the world." Then . . . the righteous [will go away] to *eternal life.*

1281) 1 Thessalonians 4:17. So we will be *with the Lord forever.*

1282) Psalm 23:6. I will dwell *in the house of the LORD* forever.

261. The believers will be taken by Christ to be with him forever in heaven.

262. What will my life be like when I am with God in heaven?

1283) Revelation 7:15-17. (Those with God in heaven are free from every trouble and sorrow of life here on earth.)

1284) Revelation 21:3,4. Now the dwelling of God is with men, and he will live with them. . . . He will *wipe every tear* from their eyes. There will be *no more death or mourning or crying or pain,* for the old order of things has passed away.

1285) Hebrews 4:9,10. There remains . . . *a Sabbath-rest* for the people of God; for anyone who enters God's rest also *rests from his own work,* just as God did from his.

217

262a. When I am with God in heaven, I will have rest from all the labors, troubles, and sorrows of my life on earth.

> 1286) Revelation 14:13. *Blessed* are the dead who die in the Lord *from now on.*
>
> 1287) Revelation 19:9. Blessed are those who are invited to the *wedding supper* of the Lamb!
>
> 1288) Psalm 16:11. You will *fill me with joy* in your presence, with *eternal pleasures* at your right hand.
>
> 1289) Colossians 3:4. When Christ, who is your life, appears, then you also will appear with him *in glory.*

262b. When I am with God in heaven, I will live in glory and have joy and pleasures forever.

263. How will Christ change my body so that I can live with him in heaven?

> 1290) 2 Corinthians 5:1,2. Now we know that if the earthly tent we live in is destroyed, we have *a building from God,* an eternal house in heaven, not built by human hands. Meanwhile we groan, longing to be *clothed with our heavenly dwelling.*
>
> 1291) Philippians 3:21. [Christ] will transform our lowly bodies so that they will be *like his glorious body.*
>
> 1292) 1 Corinthians 15:52,53. The trumpet will sound, the dead will be raised imperishable, and *we will be changed.* For the perishable must clothe itself with the *imperishable,* and the mortal with *immortality.*
>
> 1293) 1 Corinthians 15:42-44. So it will be with the resurrection of the dead. The body that is sown is perishable, it is raised *imperishable;* it is sown in dishonor, it is raised *in glory;* it is sown in weakness, it is raised *in power;* it is sown a natural body, it is raised a *spiritual body.*

263. Christ will change my body so that it is a glorious body like his, which is able to live forever in heaven with him.

264. How do I look forward to the Last Day because the Holy Spirit brought me to faith?

1294) 2 Thessalonians 2:13. From the beginning God chose you to be *saved* through the sanctifying *work of the Spirit* and through belief in the truth.

1295) Luke 21:28. When these things begin to take place, *stand up and lift up your heads,* because your redemption is drawing near.

1296) Philippians 3:20. Our citizenship is in heaven. And we *eagerly await* a Savior from there, the Lord Jesus Christ.

1297) 2 Timothy 4:8. Now there is in store for me the crown of righteousness, which the Lord, the righteous Judge, will award to me on that day—and not only to me, but also *to all who have longed for his appearing.*

1298) Revelation 22:20. He who testifies to these things says, "Yes, I am coming soon." Amen. *Come, Lord Jesus.*

264. Because the Holy Spirit brought me to faith, I look forward to the Last Day with longing and eager anticipation.

THE MEANS OF GRACE: THE GOSPEL IN WORD AND SACRAMENTS

In the Bible, the expression "grace of God" usually means "God's undeserved love, which provides free forgiveness of sins, life, and salvation for all people." In the study of the three articles, we learned that it is only through Christ that God in his grace forgives all sins and thus also gives life and salvation. Now we want to ask, "By what means do we learn to know the grace of God?" It is by the study of God's Word. So we say that the *means* by which God makes known and gives his *grace* to us is his Word.

But earlier we learned that God's Word is made up of two basic teachings or doctrines, the law and the gospel. Of these two doctrines it is the gospel that tells us about God's grace. So to be more exact we say that the *means* by which God offers and gives his *grace* to us is the gospel in his Word.

We might use a water pipe as an illustration of the means of grace. The water pipe is the means by which the water from a water tower or well is brought to the faucet in our sinks. In a similar way the gospel in God's Word is the means by which God's grace (forgiveness of sins and eternal life) is offered and given to us.

In the Third Article we learned how the gospel in God's Word serves as a means of grace. Now we are going to begin the study of two sacred acts in which the gospel is also used as a means of grace. They are called the Sacrament of Holy Baptism and the Sacrament of Holy Communion.

When we use the term "sacrament," we mean a sacred act that has three basic characteristics:

1. A sacrament is *a sacred act that Christ established* or instituted for Christians to do.

2. A sacrament is a sacred act in which *Christ tells us to use earthly elements* (water, bread, and wine) *together with God's Word.*

3. A sacrament is a sacred act in which *Christ offers, gives, and seals to us the forgiveness of sins* and thus also life and salvation.

In our study of the sacraments that follows, each of these three characteristics will be stressed. But note especially the third characteristic, which reminds us that the gospel used in the sacraments is the means by which God offers and gives us his grace.

In summary, then, if we ask, "What do we mean by the means of grace?" the answer is this: The means of grace is that means by which God offers and gives us the forgiveness of sins, life, and salvation. And if we ask, "What is that means of grace?" the answer is this: The means of grace is the gospel in Word and sacraments.

Holy Baptism

THE INSTITUTION OF BAPTISM

First: *What is Baptism?*

Baptism is not just plain water, but it is water used by God's command and connected with God's Word.

What is that word of God?

Christ our Lord says in the last chapter of Matthew, "Go and make disciples of all nations, baptizing them in the name of the Father and of the Son and of the Holy Spirit."

265. How was the Sacrament of Holy Baptism instituted?

1299) Matthew 28:18,19. *Jesus* came to them and *said,* "All authority in heaven and on earth has been given to me. Therefore go and make disciples of *all nations, baptizing them* in *the name of the Father and of the Son and of the Holy Spirit.*"

265. The Sacrament of Holy Baptism was instituted by Jesus' command to baptize all nations in the name of the triune God.

266. What does the Greek word "baptize" mean?

1300) Mark 1:8. I baptize you *with water.*

1301) Mark 7:3,4. The Pharisees and all the Jews do not eat unless they give their hands a ceremonial washing [Greek: washing], holding to the tradition of the elders. When they come from the marketplace they do not eat unless they *wash* [Greek: baptize]. And they observe many other traditions, such as the *washing* [Greek: baptizing] of cups, pitchers and kettles [footnote: and dining couches].

266. The Greek word "baptize" means to use water in various ways: immerse, wash, pour, or sprinkle.

267. Why is the Sacrament of Holy Baptism not just the use of plain water?

1302) Matthew 28:19. *[Jesus said],* "Go and make disciples of all nations, baptizing them."

267a. The Sacrament of Baptism is not just the use of plain water since it is water used by God's command.

1303) Matthew 28:19. Baptizing them *in the name of the Father and of the Son and of the Holy Spirit.*

1304) Ephesians 5:25,26. Christ loved the church and gave himself up for her to make her holy, cleansing her by the *washing with water through the word.*

267b. The Sacrament of Baptism is not just the use of plain water since it is water connected with God's Word.

268. What does it mean to baptize "in the name of" the triune God?

1305) Numbers 6:27. So they will *put my name on* the Israelites, and I will *bless them.*

1306) Galatians 3:27. All of you who were *baptized into Christ* have clothed yourselves with Christ.

1307) 1 Corinthians 12:13. We were all *baptized* by one Spirit *into one body.*

1308) Ephesians 2:19. You are no longer foreigners and aliens, but *fellow citizens with God's people* and *members of God's household.*

268. To baptize "in the name of" the triune God means that God makes us members of his blessed family.

269. What does Jesus' command to baptize "all nations" mean?

1309) Acts 2:38,39. Repent and be baptized, every one of you. . . . The promise is *for you and your children.*

1310) Acts 8:26-40. (The Ethiopian requested Baptism for himself.)

1311) Acts 16:29-34. (The jailer requested Baptism for himself and his whole family.)

269. Jesus' command to baptize "all nations" means we are to baptize all who request baptism for themselves or for their children.

270. What does the Bible teach us to do before we baptize adults?

1312) Acts 8:26-40. (The Ethiopian was instructed about Jesus and then baptized.)

1313) Acts 16:29-34. (The jailer of Philippi was instructed about Jesus and then baptized.)

270. The Bible teaches us to instruct adults about Jesus before we baptize them.

271. Why do we baptize little children?

1314) Matthew 28:19. Go and make disciples of *all nations, baptizing them* in the name of the Father and of the Son and of the Holy Spirit.

1315) Acts 2:39. The promise is for you and *your children.*

271a. We baptize little children because they are included in Christ's words "all nations."

1316) Psalm 51:5. Surely I was *sinful at birth,* sinful from the time my mother conceived me.

1317) John 3:5,6. No one can enter the kingdom of God *unless* he is *born of water and the Spirit. Flesh gives birth to flesh,* but the Spirit gives birth to spirit.

271b. We baptize little children because they are sinful by nature and must be born again in order to be saved.

1318) Matthew 18:6. If anyone causes one of these *little ones* who *believe in me* to sin, it would be better for him to have a large millstone hung around his neck and to be drowned in the depths of the sea.

1319) Luke 18:15-17. People were . . . bringing *babies* to Jesus to have him touch them. When the disciples saw this, they rebuked them. But Jesus called the children to him and said, "Let the little children come to me, and do not hinder them, for *the kingdom of God belongs to such as these.* I tell you the

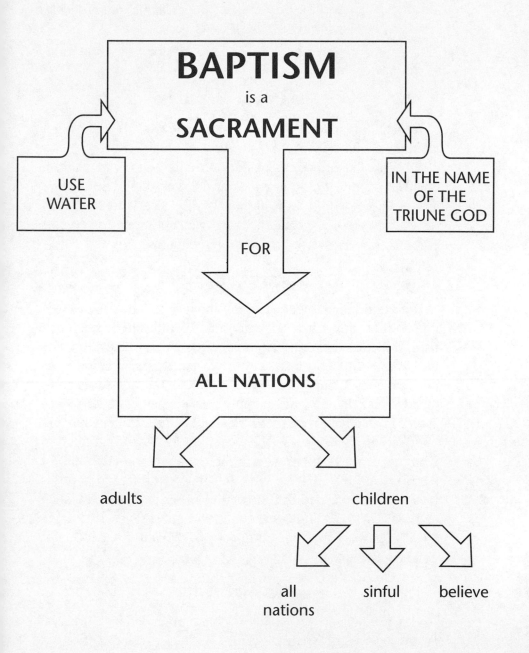

BAPTISM
is a
SACRAMENT

USE
WATER

IN THE NAME
OF THE
TRIUNE GOD

FOR

ALL NATIONS

adults

children

all
nations

sinful

believe

truth, anyone who will not *receive the kingdom of God like a little child* will never enter it."

271c. We baptize little children because they too can believe.

The Pastor Baptizes

Jesus commanded his disciples to baptize. This means that all believers have the right from Jesus to baptize (see Question 305). Why, then, does our pastor normally do the baptizing in our congregation? God urges us to do everything "in a fitting and orderly way" (1 Corinthians 14:40). Therefore, to avoid disorder in our congregation, when we call a man to serve as our pastor, we also ask him to do the baptizing.

Emergency Baptism

If a child is in danger of dying, however, and our pastor is not present, any Christian may and should administer Baptism. If the child lives, it is not necessary later to have the pastor baptize the child also. The important thing in Baptism is not who does it, but rather that it is done in the way Jesus commanded us, namely, by using water connected with God's Word. In an emergency, then, we should simply take water and pour or sprinkle or wash the water on the head of the child while we say, "I baptize you in the name of the Father and of the Son and of the Holy Spirit." If there is time, the baptism may also be preceded or followed by a Scripture reading such as Luke 18:15-17, a prayer, and the Lord's Prayer. (See page 14 of *Christian Worship: A Lutheran Hymnal* for a form for emergency baptism.)

Sponsors and Witnesses

Having sponsors for a baby is not commanded by God, so it is not a necessary part of Baptism. It is a custom that our church uses because of the special things a sponsor can do for a child.

The sponsor does not believe for the child, but the parents ask the sponsor to be concerned about the spiritual welfare of the child in various ways. The sponsor can remind the child of his or her baptism and the meaning of Baptism. The sponsor can assure the child it was baptized if this is ever in doubt. The sponsor can pray for the godchild and encourage the godchild to study God's Word faithfully. Thus the sponsor also assures the parents that if they should die, there would be someone to look after the spiritual needs of the child and bring the child up in the true faith.

The responsibility of a witness is different from that of a sponsor. If we ask someone to serve as a witness to a child's baptism, we are asking that person *only* to be a witness to the fact that the child was baptized. If a person is of another faith, we ask him to serve as a witness rather than a sponsor. We do this because we want to uphold the confession that God tells us to make to all with whom we are not in fellowship (see Questions 246 and 247).

THE BLESSINGS OF BAPTISM

Second: *What does Baptism do for us?*

Baptism works forgiveness of sin, delivers from death and the devil, and gives eternal salvation to all who believe this, as the words and promises of God declare.

What are these words and promises of God?

Christ our Lord says in the last chapter of Mark, "Whoever believes and is baptized will be saved, but whoever does not believe will be condemned."

272. **What blessings does God offer and give us in Baptism?**

> 1320) Acts 2:38. Repent and be baptized, every one of you, in the name of Jesus Christ *for the forgiveness of your sins.*
>
> 1321) Acts 22:16. Be baptized and *wash your sins away.*

272a. In Baptism God offers and gives us forgiveness of sins.

> 1322) Romans 6:3. Don't you know that all of us who were baptized into Christ Jesus were *baptized into his death?*
>
> 1323) Hebrews 2:14,15. He too shared in their humanity so that *by his death* he might *destroy* him who holds the power of death—that is, *the devil—and free those* who all their lives were *held in slavery by their fear of death.*

272b. In Baptism God offers and gives us deliverance from the power of death and the devil.

> 1324) Mark 16:16. Whoever believes and is *baptized will be saved.*
>
> 1325) 1 Peter 3:20,21. In it [Noah's ark] only a few people, eight in all, were saved through water, and this water symbolizes *baptism* that now *saves you* also.

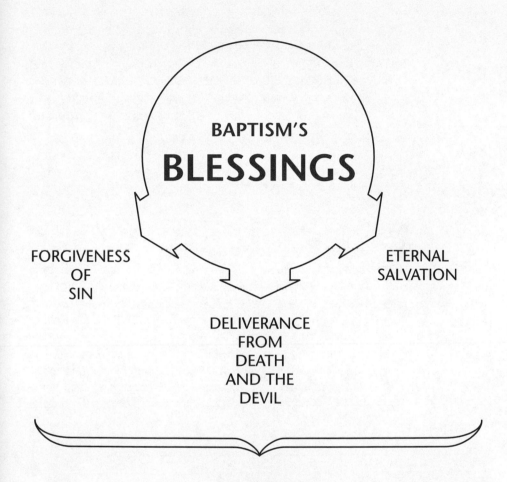

BAPTISM'S
BLESSINGS

FORGIVENESS
OF
SIN

ETERNAL
SALVATION

DELIVERANCE
FROM
DEATH
AND THE
DEVIL

GOD'S CHILD
and an
HEIR OF LIFE

272c. In Baptism God offers and gives us eternal salvation.

273. Why is Baptism, then, a means of grace?

1326) Romans 6:3. Don't you know that all of us who were baptized into Christ Jesus were *baptized into his death?*

1327) 1 Peter 3:21. *Baptism* . . . now saves you also—not the removal of dirt from the body but the *pledge of a good conscience toward God.* It saves you *by the resurrection of Jesus Christ.*

1328) Galatians 3:27. All of you who were *baptized into Christ* have *clothed yourselves with Christ.*

273. Baptism is a means of grace because in Baptism God offers and gives us all the blessings that Christ won for us.

274. Why, then, is my baptism such a great comfort to me?

1329) John 3:3,5. *Unless he is born again* . . . no one can enter the kingdom of God unless he is born of water and the Spirit.

1330) Galatians 3:26,27. You are all *sons of God* through faith in Christ Jesus, for all of you who were *baptized into Christ* have clothed yourselves with Christ.

1331) Titus 3:5-7. He *saved us* through the *washing of rebirth* and renewal by the Holy Spirit, whom he poured out on us generously through Jesus Christ our Savior, so that, having been *justified by his grace,* we might become *heirs* having the hope *of eternal life.*

274. My baptism is such a great comfort to me because it assures me that I am born again as a justified child of God and an heir of everlasting life.

THE POWER OF BAPTISM

Third: *How can water do such great things?*

It is certainly not the water that does such things, but God's Word which is in and with the water and faith which trusts this Word used with the water.

For without God's Word the water is just plain water and not Baptism. But with this Word it is Baptism, that is, a gracious water of life and a washing of rebirth by the Holy Spirit.

Where is this written?

St. Paul says in Titus, chapter 3, "[God] saved us through the washing of rebirth and renewal by the Holy Spirit, whom he poured out on us generously through Jesus Christ our Savior, so that, having been justified by his grace, we might become heirs having the hope of eternal life. This is a trustworthy saying."

275. **Why is Baptism able to offer and give such great blessings?**

    1332) John 3:5. No one can enter the kingdom of God unless he is born of water *and the Spirit.*

    1333) Acts 2:38. Repent and be *baptized,* every one of you, in the name of Jesus Christ for the forgiveness of your sins. And *you will receive the gift of the Holy Spirit.*

    1334) Titus 3:5. He saved us through the washing of rebirth and renewal *by the Holy Spirit.*

275. Baptism is able to offer and give such great blessings because the Holy Spirit is at work in Baptism.

BAPTISM'S
POWER

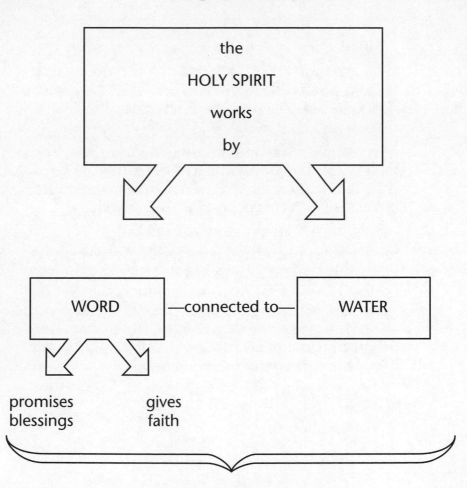

the

HOLY SPIRIT

works

by

WORD —connected to— WATER

promises   gives
blessings   faith

"WASHING OF REBIRTH"
(Means of Grace)

276. Through what does the Holy Spirit do his work in Baptism?

1335) Ephesians 5:25,26. Christ loved the church and gave himself up for her to make her holy, cleansing her by the washing with water *through the word.*

1336) 1 Peter 1:23. You have been *born again,* not of perishable seed, but of imperishable, *through the living* and enduring *word of God.*

276. The Holy Spirit does his work in Baptism through the Word of God connected with the water.

277. What does the Holy Spirit do through the Word of God in Baptism?

1337) Acts 2:38,39. Repent and *be baptized,* every one of you, in the name of Jesus Christ for the forgiveness of your sins. *And you will receive* the gift of the Holy Spirit. *The promise* is for you and your children.

277a. Through the Word of God in Baptism the Holy Spirit promises us blessings.

1338) Mark 16:16. *Whoever believes* and is baptized will be saved.

1339) Colossians 2:12. [You have] been buried with him in baptism and raised with him *through your faith.*

1340) Titus 3:5,7. He saved us through the washing of *rebirth* and renewal by the Holy Spirit . . . *so that,* having been justified by his grace, we might become heirs having the hope of eternal life.

1341) Acts 8:26-39. (By Baptism the Ethiopian was strengthened in faith, so that he went away rejoicing.)

277b. Through the Word of God in Baptism the Holy Spirit creates or strengthens faith in us, so that we trust God's promise and make the blessings of Baptism our own.

278. What, then, does the Word of God make Baptism?

1342) 1 Peter 3:21. Baptism . . . now saves you also—*not the removal of dirt* from the body *but the pledge of a good conscience* toward God.

1343) Titus 3:5-7. He saved us through the *washing of rebirth and renewal by the Holy Spirit,* whom he poured out on us *generously through Jesus Christ our Savior,* so that, having been *justified by his grace,* we might become heirs having *the hope of eternal life.*

278. The Word of God makes Baptism a gracious water of life and a washing of rebirth by the Holy Spirit.

THE MEANING OF BAPTISM
FOR OUR DAILY LIFE

Fourth: *What does baptizing with water mean?*

Baptism means that the old Adam in us should be drowned by daily contrition and repentance, and that all its evil deeds and desires be put to death. It also means that a new person should daily arise to live before God in righteousness and purity forever.

Where is this written?

Saint Paul says in Romans, chapter 6, "We were . . . buried with [Christ] through baptism into death in order that, just as Christ was raised from the dead through the glory of the Father, we too may live a new life."

279. **What new desire does the Holy Spirit work in me by Baptism?**

    1344) Romans 6:3,6. Don't you know that all of us who were baptized into Christ Jesus were *baptized into his death?* For we know that our old self was crucified with him *so that* the body of sin might be done away with, that *we should no longer be slaves to sin.*

    1345) Romans 6:4,5. We were therefore buried with him through baptism into death *in order that,* just as Christ was raised from the dead through the glory of the Father, *we too may live a new life.* If we have been united with him in his death, we will *certainly also* be *united* with him *in his resurrection.*

279. By Baptism the Holy Spirit works in me the desire to throw off the slavery of sin and live a new life.

280. How does the old Adam oppose this new desire in me? (See Questions 126 and 127 for an explanation of old Adam.)

1346) Galatians 5:17. The *sinful nature desires what is contrary to the Spirit,* and the Spirit what is contrary to the sinful nature. They are in *conflict with each other,* so that you *do not do what you want.*

1347) Galatians 5:19-21. *The acts of the sinful nature* are obvious: sexual immorality, impurity and debauchery; idolatry and witchcraft; hatred, discord, jealousy, fits of rage, selfish ambition, dissensions, factions and envy; drunkenness, orgies, and the like.

280. The old Adam opposes this new desire in me by trying to lead me into many kinds of evil deeds and desires.

281. What does my baptism remind me to do with the old Adam every day?

1348) Colossians 2:11,12. In him you were also circumcised, in the *putting off of the sinful nature,* not with a circumcision done by the hands of men but with the circumcision done by Christ, *having been buried with him in baptism* and raised with him through your faith.

1349) Romans 6:2,3,6,12,13. We *died to sin;* how can we live in it any longer? Or don't you know that all of us who were baptized into Christ Jesus were *baptized into his death?* For we know that *our old self was crucified with him* so that the body of sin might be done away with, that we should no longer be slaves to sin. Therefore *do not let sin reign* in your mortal body so that you obey its evil desires. *Do not offer the parts of your body to sin,* as instruments of wickedness.

281. My baptism reminds me to put off the old Adam every day.

282. How do I put off the old Adam every day?

1350) Psalm 38:18. I *confess* my iniquity; I am *troubled* by my sin.

1351) Luke 15:21. The son said to him, "Father, *I have sinned against heaven* and against you. I am *no longer worthy* to be called your son."

BAPTISM'S
MEANING

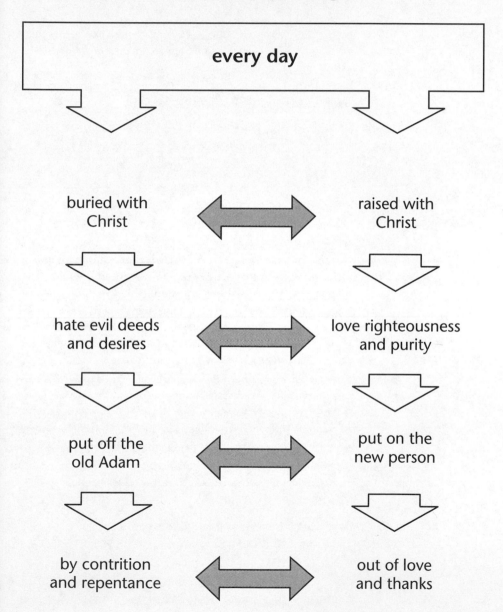

every day

buried with Christ ⟷ raised with Christ

hate evil deeds and desires ⟷ love righteousness and purity

put off the old Adam ⟷ put on the new person

by contrition and repentance ⟷ out of love and thanks

1352) Psalm 51:4,17. *Against you, you only,* have I sinned and done what is evil *in your sight.* . . . a *broken and contrite heart,* O God, you will not despise.

1353) 2 Corinthians 7:10. *Godly sorrow brings repentance* that leads to salvation.

1354) Acts 20:21. I have declared to both Jews and Greeks that they must turn to God in repentance and *have faith in our Lord Jesus.*

1355) Matthew 26:75; John 21:15-17. (Peter wept over his sin and confessed his love of Jesus his Savior.)

282. I put off the old Adam every day by being sorry for my sins and by believing that God forgives my sins for Jesus' sake. (contrition and repentance)

283. Of what does my baptism remind me every day concerning my new person? (See Question 130 for an explanation of new man or new person.)

1356) Romans 6:4. We were . . . buried with him through baptism into death in order that, *just as Christ was raised* from the dead through the glory of the Father, *we too may live a new life.*

1357) Ephesians 4:22-24. You were taught, with regard to your former way of life, to put off your old self . . . ; *to be made new* in the attitude of your minds; and to *put on the new self,* created to be *like God in true righteousness and holiness.*

1358) Romans 6:13. Do not offer the parts of your body to sin, as instruments of wickedness, but rather *offer yourselves to God,* as those who have *been brought from death to life;* and *offer the parts of your body to him* as instruments of righteousness.

1359) Luke 19:1-10. (Zacchaeus' repentance led to a new life.)

1360) Galatians 5:22,23. *The fruit of the Spirit* is love, joy, peace, patience, kindness, goodness, faithfulness, gentleness and self-control.

283. My baptism reminds me that a new person should daily arise to live before god in righteousness and purity forever.

284. Why does my baptism renew in me day by day the desire to live a new and holy life?

1361) Galatians 3:27. All of you who were *baptized into Christ* have *clothed yourselves with Christ.*

1362) 2 Corinthians 5:14,15. *Christ's love compels us.* . . . He died for all, that those who live should no longer *live for* themselves but for *him who died for them and was raised again.*

1363) Colossians 2:6,7. So then, just as you received Christ Jesus as Lord, *continue to live in him,* rooted and built up in him, strengthened in the faith as you were taught, and *overflowing with thankfulness.*

284. My baptism renews this desire in me day by day because the blessings Christ gives me in Baptism lead me to want to thank him with my whole life.

Holy
Communion

THE INSTITUTION OF HOLY COMMUNION

First: *What is the Sacrament of Holy Communion?*

It is the true body and blood of our Lord Jesus Christ under the bread and wine, instituted by Christ for us Christians to eat and to drink.

Where is this written?

The holy evangelists Matthew, Mark, Luke, and the apostle Paul tell us: Our Lord Jesus Christ, on the night he was betrayed, took bread; and when he had given thanks, he broke it and gave it to his disciples, saying, "Take and eat; this is my body, which is given for you. Do this in remembrance of me."

Then he took the cup, gave thanks, and gave it to them, saying, "Drink from it, all of you; this is my blood of the new covenant, which is poured out for you for the forgiveness of sins. Do this, whenever you drink it, in remembrance of me."

285. How was the Sacrament of Holy Communion instituted?

1364) Matthew 26:26-29; Mark 14:22-25; Luke 22:14-20. (Christ instituted Holy Communion while eating the Passover meal with his disciples.)

1365) 1 Corinthians 11:23-25. *The Lord Jesus, on the night he was betrayed,* took bread, and when he had given thanks, he broke it and *said,* "This is my body, which is for you; *do this* in remembrance of me." In the same way, after supper he took the cup, saying, "This cup is the new covenant in my blood; *do this,* whenever you drink it, in remembrance of me."

244

285. The Sacrament of Holy Communion was instituted by the command of Jesus to do what he did on the night he was betrayed.

> NOTE: Holy Communion is also called the Lord's Supper (1 Corinthians 11:20), the Lord's Table (1 Corinthians 10:21), the Sacrament of the Altar, and the Eucharist (1 Corinthians 11:24).

286. What does Jesus tell us to do in the Sacrament of Holy Communion?

> 1366) Matthew 26:26-29. Jesus took *bread,* gave thanks and broke it, and gave it to his disciples, saying, "Take and *eat;* this is my body." Then he took *the cup,* gave thanks and offered it to them, saying, *"Drink from it,* all of you. This is my blood of the covenant, which is poured out for many for the forgiveness of sins. I tell you, I will not drink of *this fruit of the vine* from now on until that day when I drink it anew with you in my Father's kingdom."

286. Jesus tells us to eat bread and to drink wine.

287. What does Jesus tell us is present with the bread and the wine in Holy Communion?

> 1367) Mark 14:22-24. Jesus took bread, gave thanks and broke it, and gave it to his disciples, saying, "Take it; *this is my body."* Then he took the cup, gave thanks and offered it to them, and they all drank from it. *"This is my blood* of the covenant, which is poured out for many," he said.
>
> 1368) Luke 22:19,20. He took bread, gave thanks and broke it, and gave it to them, saying, "This is my body *given for you;* do this in remembrance of me." In the same way, after the supper he took the cup, saying, "This cup is the new covenant in my blood, *which is poured out for you."*

287. Jesus tells us that his real body is present with the bread and that his real blood is present with the wine. (real presence)

288. What do we receive, therefore, in, with, and under the bread and the wine in Holy Communion?

1369) 1 Corinthians 10:16. Is not the cup of thanksgiving for which we give thanks *a participation in* [Greek: a sharing in] the blood of Christ? And is not the bread that we break *a participation in* [Greek: a sharing in] the body of Christ?

1370) 1 Corinthians 11:27. Whoever eats the bread or drinks the cup of the Lord in an unworthy manner will be *guilty of sinning against the body and blood of the Lord.*

288. In Holy Communion we receive the true body of Christ in, with, and under the bread and the true blood of Christ together with the wine.

289. Why do we believe this teaching about the real presence of Jesus' true body and blood in Holy Communion even though we cannot explain it?

1371) Luke 1:34-37. (Faith does not understand God's miracles, but it knows that God is able to do everything he says.)

1372) Numbers 23:19. God is *not a man,* that he should *lie.*

1373) Psalm 33:4. The *word* of the LORD is *right and true;* he is *faithful in all he does.*

289. We believe this teaching of the real presence because God reveals it to us in his Word of Truth.

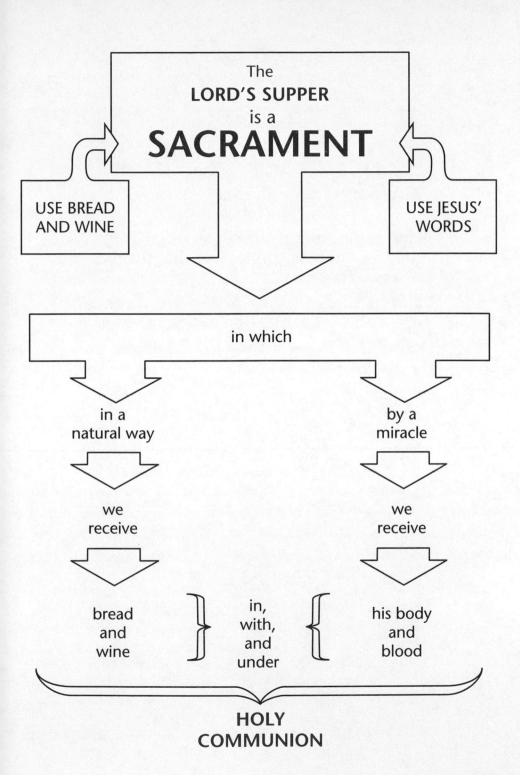

The
LORD'S SUPPER
is a
SACRAMENT

USE BREAD
AND WINE

USE JESUS'
WORDS

in which

in a
natural way

by a
miracle

we
receive

we
receive

bread
and
wine

in,
with,
and
under

his body
and
blood

**HOLY
COMMUNION**

THE BLESSINGS OF HOLY COMMUNION

Second: *What blessing do we receive through this eating and drinking?*

That is shown us by these words: "Given" and "poured out for you for the forgiveness of sins."

Through these words we receive forgiveness of sins, life, and salvation in this sacrament.

For where there is forgiveness of sins, there is also life and salvation.

290. Why did Jesus give his body into death and pour out his blood for us?

1374) 1 Peter 2:24. He himself *bore our sins in his body* on the tree . . . ; by his wounds you have been *healed.*

1375) Ephesians 1:7. In him we have redemption *through his blood, the forgiveness of sins.*

290. Jesus gave his body into death and poured out his blood for the forgiveness of our sins.

291. What blessings does Jesus offer and give us by giving us his body and blood in Holy Communion?

1376) Matthew 26:28. This is *my blood of the covenant,* which is *poured out* for many *for the forgiveness of sins.*

1377) Luke 22:19,20. This is my body *given for you.* . . . This cup is the new covenant in my blood, which is *poured out for you.*

1378) 1 Corinthians 11:24,25. This is my body, which is for you. . . . This cup is *the new covenant* in my blood.

1379) Romans 11:27. This is my *covenant* with them when I *take away their sins.*

248

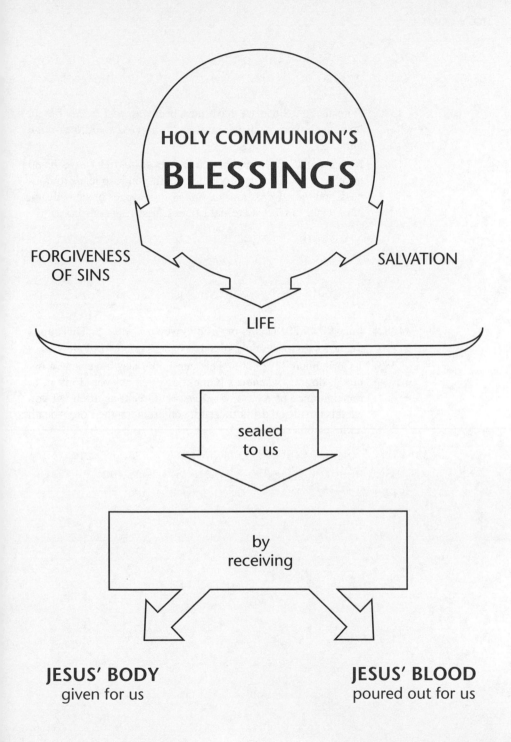

HOLY COMMUNION'S
BLESSINGS

FORGIVENESS
OF SINS

SALVATION

LIFE

sealed
to us

by
receiving

JESUS' BODY
given for us

JESUS' BLOOD
poured out for us

291a. By giving us his body and blood in Holy Communion, Jesus offers and gives us forgiveness of sins.

> 1380) Romans 5:9. Since we have now been *justified by his blood, how much more shall we be saved from God's wrath through him!*
>
> 1381) Romans 6:22,23. Now that you have been *set free from sin* and have become slaves to God, the benefit you reap leads to holiness, and *the result is eternal life.* For the wages of sin is death, but *the gift of God* is eternal life in Christ Jesus our Lord.

291b. In Holy Communion Jesus also offers and gives us life and salvation.

292. Why, then, is Holy Communion so comforting to me?

> 1382) Luke 22:19,20. This is my body given *for you.* . . . This cup is the new covenant in my blood, which is poured out *for you.*
>
> 1383) 1 Corinthians 11:25,26. "This cup is the new covenant in my blood; do this, *whenever* [Greek: as often as] you drink it, in remembrance of me." For *whenever* [Greek: as often as] you eat this bread and drink this cup, you proclaim the Lord's death until he comes.

292. Holy Communion is so comforting to me because in it Jesus again and again assures me personally of forgiveness, life, and salvation.

THE POWER OF HOLY COMMUNION

Third: *How can eating and drinking do such great things?*

It is certainly not the eating and drinking that does such things, but the words "Given" and "poured out for you for the forgiveness of sins."

These words are the main thing in this sacrament, along with the eating and drinking. And whoever believes these words has what they plainly say, the forgiveness of sins.

293. Why is Holy Communion able to offer and give such great blessings?

1384) 1 Corinthians 11:23-25. The *Lord* Jesus . . . took bread, and when he had given thanks, he broke it and *said,* "This is my body, which is for you; *do this* in remembrance of me." *In the same way,* after supper he took the cup, *saying,* "This cup is the new covenant in my blood; *do this,* whenever you drink it, in remembrance of me."

1385) John 6:63. *The words* I have spoken to you *are spirit* and they *are life.*

293. Holy Communion is able to offer and give such great blessings because of the words Jesus told us to use along with the eating and drinking.

294. What does Jesus do through his Word in Holy Communion?

1386) Matthew 26:26,28. Take and eat; *this is my body. This is my blood* of the covenant, which is poured out for many *for the forgiveness of sins.*

251

HOLY COMMUNION'S
POWER

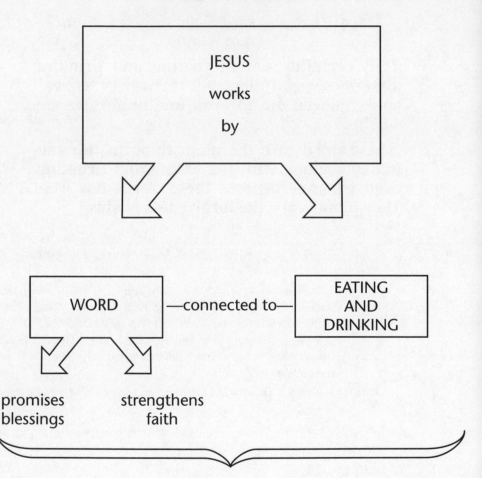

JESUS

works

by

WORD —connected to— EATING AND DRINKING

promises   strengthens
blessings   faith

Means of Grace

294a. Through his Word in Holy Communion, Jesus promises to give us his body and blood for the forgiveness of sins.

> 1387) Romans 10:17. *Faith* comes from hearing the message, and the message is heard *through the word of Christ.*
>
> 1388) Numbers 21:4-9. (Only those Israelites who looked to the bronze snake in faith were healed.)
>
> 1389) Hebrews 11:1. Faith is *being sure* of what we hope for and *certain of what we do not see.*

294b. Through his Word in Holy Communion, Jesus strengthens our faith so that we trust his promise and make the blessings of this sacrament our own.

295. What, therefore, does the Word of Christ make Holy Communion?

> 1390) 1 Corinthians 10:16. Is not the *cup* of thanksgiving for which we give thanks *a participation in the blood of Christ?* And is not the *bread* that we break *a participation in the body of Christ?*
>
> 1391) Romans 3:24,25. [All] are *justified freely by his grace through the redemption* that came *by Christ Jesus.* God presented him as a *sacrifice of atonement,* through faith in his blood.

295. The Word of Christ makes Holy Communion an eating and drinking through which God graciously gives us all the blessings that Christ won for us. (means of grace)

THE RECEPTION OF HOLY COMMUNION

Fourth: *Who, then, is properly prepared to receive this sacrament?*

Fasting and other outward preparations may serve a good purpose, but he is properly prepared who believes these words: "Given" and "poured out for you for the forgiveness of sins."

But whoever does not believe these words or doubts them is not prepared, because the words "for you" require nothing but hearts that believe.

296. Why do we prepare ourselves to receive Holy Communion?

    1392) 1 Corinthians 11:27,28. *Whoever eats* the bread *or drinks* the cup of the Lord *in an unworthy manner* will be *guilty of sinning* against the body and blood of the Lord. A man ought to *examine himself before* he eats of the bread and drinks of the cup.

296. We prepare ourselves so that we do not sin by receiving the body and blood of Christ in an unworthy manner.

297. What good purpose may fasting and other outward preparations serve in preparing to receive the Lord's Supper?

    1393) 1 Corinthians 11:20-22. (The Corinthians did not center their thoughts on the meaning of the Lord's Supper.)

    1394) Leviticus 23:26-32. (God wanted his people in the Old Testament to do no work and to deny themselves or fast in order to center all their thoughts on the meaning of the Day of Atonement.)

297a. Fasting and other outward preparations may help us center our thoughts on the meaning of the Lord's Supper.

> 1395) 1 Corinthians 10:21. *You* cannot *drink the cup of the Lord* and the cup of demons too; *you* cannot *have a part in* both *the Lord's table* and the table of demons.
>
> 1396) Exodus 19:10. (Moses was to have the people wash their clothes out of respect for the Lord, who was coming to them on Mt. Sinai.)

297b. Fasting and other outward preparations may be a way of showing respect for Jesus, who invites us to eat and drink at his table.

298. What, however, is the one and only thing that makes us properly prepared to receive the Lord's Supper?

> 1397) Luke 22:19,20. This is my body given *for you.* . . . This cup is the new covenant in my blood, which is poured out *for you.*
>
> 1398) 1 Corinthians 11:27-29. (God says that whoever eats the bread or drinks the cup of the Lord without recognizing the real presence of Christ's body and blood is sinning and so is unprepared to receive the Lord's Supper.)

298. The one and only thing which makes us properly prepared is faith, because Jesus' words "for you" require nothing but hearts that believe.

299. What are we confessing about our faith when we receive Holy Communion together with others?

> 1399) 1 Corinthians 11:24-26. "This is my body, which is for you; do this *in remembrance of me.*". . . "This cup is the new covenant in my blood; do this, whenever you drink it, *in remembrance of me.*" For whenever you eat this bread and drink this cup, you *proclaim the Lord's death* until he comes.
>
> 1400) 1 Corinthians 10:17. Because there is one loaf, *we, who are many,* are *one body,* for we all *partake of the one loaf.*

299. When we receive Holy Communion together with others, we are confessing our unity of faith in our Lord Jesus.

300. Why are we careful about whom we invite to receive Holy Communion?

1401) 1 Corinthians 11:27,29,30. Whoever eats the bread or drinks the cup of the Lord *in an unworthy manner* will be *guilty of sinning* against the body and blood of the Lord. . . . anyone who eats and drinks without recognizing the body of the Lord *eats and drinks judgment on himself.* That is why many among you are *weak and sick,* and a number of you have *fallen asleep.*

300. We are careful about whom we invite to receive Holy Communion because we do not want anyone to bring God's judgment on himself by receiving Holy Communion in an unworthy manner.

301. To whom does God want us to give Holy Communion?

1402) 1 John 1:8,9. If we claim to be without sin, we deceive ourselves and the truth is not in us. *If we confess our sins,* he . . . will forgive us our sins.

1403) Matthew 18:15-18. (God tells us to withhold forgiveness and fellowship from an unrepentant sinner.)

301a. God wants us to give Holy Communion only to repentant sinners.

1404) 1 Corinthians 11:24,26. "Do this *in remembrance of me."* . . . For whenever you eat this bread and drink this cup, *you proclaim the Lord's death* until he comes.

1405) Hebrews 5:13; 6:1. Anyone who *lives on milk,* being still an infant, is *not acquainted* with the teaching about righteousness. Therefore let us *leave the elementary teachings* about Christ and *go on to maturity.*

301b. God wants us to give Holy Communion only to those who are instructed so that they know the meaning of Christ's death. (confirmation instruction)

THE **RECEPTION**
of HOLY COMMUNION

1. HOW?

Prepared!
(faith)

Close
Communion

2. WHAT?

A confession!
(faith)

3. WHEN?

Often!

4. WHY?

Forgives sins!

Strengthens faith!

Encourages each other!

Gives strength for
Christian living!

1406) 1 Corinthians 11:28,29. A man ought to *examine himself* before he eats of the bread and drinks of the cup. For anyone who eats and drinks *without recognizing the body of the Lord* eats and drinks judgment on himself.

301c. God wants us to give Holy Communion only to those who are able to examine themselves. (See Christian Questions on page 318.)

1407) 1 Corinthians 10:17. Because there is one loaf, *we,* who are many, *are one body,* for we *all partake of the one loaf.*

1408) Romans 16:17. I urge you, brothers, to watch out for *those who cause divisions* and put obstacles in your way that are *contrary to the teaching you have learned. Keep away from them.*

1409) 2 John 10,11. If *anyone* comes to you and *does not bring this teaching,* do not take him into your house or welcome him. *Anyone who welcomes him shares in his wicked work.*

301d. God wants us to give Holy Communion only to those who are one with us in all we believe and teach.

302. Why does Jesus urge us to come to Holy Communion often?

1410) 1 Corinthians 11:25. This cup is the new covenant in my blood; do this, *whenever* [Greek: as *often* as] you drink it, in remembrance of me.

1411) Romans 4:7. *Blessed* are they whose transgressions are forgiven, whose *sins are covered.*

1412) Romans 7:19. What I do is not the good I want to do; no, the evil I do not want to do—this I *keep on doing.*

1413) Matthew 11:28. *Come to me,* all you who are weary and burdened, and *I will give you rest.*

302a. Jesus urges us to come often because by Holy Communion he wants to assure us that he forgives all our sins.

1414) Mark 9:24. I do believe; *help me* overcome my unbelief!

1415) Hebrews 4:15,16. We do not have a high priest who is unable *to sympathize with our weaknesses.* . . . Let us then approach the throne of grace with confidence, so that we may receive mercy and find grace to *help us in our time of need.*

302b. Jesus urges us to come often because by Holy Communion he wants to strengthen our weak faith.

1416) 1 Corinthians 11:26. *Whenever* you eat this bread and drink this cup, *you proclaim the Lord's death* until he comes.

1417) 1 Corinthians 10:17. *We,* who are many, *are one body,* for we all partake of the one loaf.

1418) Hebrews 10:23-25. Let us *hold* unswervingly *to the hope we profess.* . . . And let us consider how we may *spur one another on toward love and good deeds.* Let us *not give up meeting together,* as some are in the habit of doing, *but let us encourage one another*—and all the more as you see the Day approaching.

302c. Jesus urges us to come often because as we proclaim our unity of faith in our Lord's death, we also encourage each other in our Christian faith and lives.

303. Why will receiving the blessings of the Lord's Supper also strengthen us in Christian living?

1419) 1 Corinthians 10:21. *You cannot* drink the cup of the Lord and the cup of demons too; *you cannot have a part in both* the Lord's table and the table of demons.

1420) 2 Corinthians 5:14,15. *Christ's love compels us.* . . . He died for all, that those who live should no longer *live for* themselves but for *him who died for them and was raised again.*

1421) Colossians 2:6,7. So then, just as you received Christ Jesus as Lord, *continue to live in him,* rooted and built up in him, strengthened in the faith as you were taught, and *overflowing with thankfulness.*

303. Receiving the blessings of the Lord's Supper also strengthens us in Christian living because it renews our desire to thank Christ for all that he did in love for us.

The Use of the
Keys and Confession

THE KEYS

First: *What is the use of the keys?*

The use of the keys is that special power and right which Christ gave to his church on earth: to forgive the sins of penitent sinners but to refuse forgiveness to the impenitent as long as they do not repent.

Where is this written?

The holy evangelist John writes in chapter 20, "[Jesus] breathed on [his disciples] and said, 'Receive the Holy Spirit. If you forgive anyone his sins, they are forgiven; if you do not forgive them, they are not forgiven.'"

304. What does Christ mean when he speaks about the keys?

1422) Matthew 16:19. *I* will *give you the keys of the kingdom of heaven;* whatever *you bind* on earth will be bound in heaven, and whatever *you loose* on earth will be loosed in heaven.

1423) John 20:23. If *you forgive* anyone his sins, they are forgiven; if *you do not forgive* them, they are not forgiven.

304. By the keys Christ means the special power and right he gives us either to forgive sins (the loosing key) or to refuse to forgive sins (the binding key).

305. Why is the use of the keys called a "special power and right"?

1424) John 20:21-23. Jesus said, "Peace be with you! As the Father has sent me, *I am sending you.*" And with that he breathed on them and said, "Receive the Holy Spirit. If *you* forgive anyone his sins, they are forgiven; if *you* do not forgive them, they are not forgiven."

1425) 1 Peter 2:9. *You are a chosen people,* a *royal priesthood,* a *holy nation,* a *people belonging to God, that you may declare the praises* of him who called you out of darkness into his wonderful light.

1426) Matthew 18:18,20. Whatever *you* bind on earth will be bound in heaven, and whatever *you* loose on earth will be loosed in heaven. For where *two or three come together in my name,* there am I with them.

305. The use of the keys is called a "special power and right" because Christ gives the keys only to his holy people, namely, to all believers, or the church. (the priesthood of all believers)

306. How valid and certain is the use of the keys by believers?

1427) Matthew 18:18,20. *I tell you the truth,* whatever you bind on earth will be *bound in heaven,* and whatever you loose on earth will be *loosed in heaven.* For where two or three come *together in my name,* there am *I with them.*

306. The use of the keys by believers is as valid and certain in heaven also, as if Christ dealt with us himself.

307. How does God want us to use the binding key?

1428) 1 John 1:8,10. If we *claim to be without sin,* we deceive ourselves and the *truth is not in us.* If we claim we have not sinned, we make him out to be a liar and his *word has no place in our lives.*

1429) Luke 18:10-14. (The Pharisee was not justified before God because he was impenitent.)

1430) Matthew 18:15-18. (If a person refuses to listen when we tell him about a sin he is committing, he is to be told that he stands under God's judgment.)

1431) John 20:23. If *you do not forgive them,* they are *not forgiven.*

307. God wants us to use the binding key to refuse forgiveness to an impenitent person as long as he does not repent.

263

308. Why does God want us to use the binding key?

1432) Matthew 18:15,17. Go and *show him his fault.* . . . If he refuses to listen . . . *treat him* as you would *a pagan or a tax collector.*

1433) Matthew 18:15. *If he listens* to you, you have *won your brother over.*

1434) 1 Corinthians 5:5. *Hand* this man *over to Satan,* so that the *sinful nature may be destroyed* and his *spirit saved* on the day of the Lord.

1435) Matthew 18:18. Whatever *you bind* on earth will be *bound in heaven.*

308. God wants us to use the binding key to try to lead the impenitent sinner to repent by announcing God's terrible judgment on him.

309. How does God want us to use the loosing key?

1436) 1 John 1:9. *If we confess* our sins, he is faithful and just and will *forgive us* our sins and purify us from all unrighteousness.

1437) Luke 18:13,14. (The penitent tax collector went home justified before God.)

1438) Acts 3:19. *Repent* . . . and turn to God, so that your *sins* may be *wiped out.*

1439) John 20:23. If *you forgive* anyone his sins, they are *forgiven.*

309. God wants us to use the loosing key to forgive the sins of a penitent sinner.

310. Why does God want us to use the loosing key?

1440) Psalm 38:3-7,18,21,22. (David as a penitent sinner needed and desired the assurance of God's forgiveness for his sins.)

1441) Psalm 51:8,9. *Let me hear joy* and gladness; let the bones you have crushed rejoice. Hide your face from my sins and *blot out all my iniquity.*

1442) 2 Corinthians 2:7. You ought *to forgive and comfort him,* so that he will not be overwhelmed by excessive sorrow.

310. God wants us to use the loosing key to comfort the penitent sinner by announcing God's forgiveness to him.

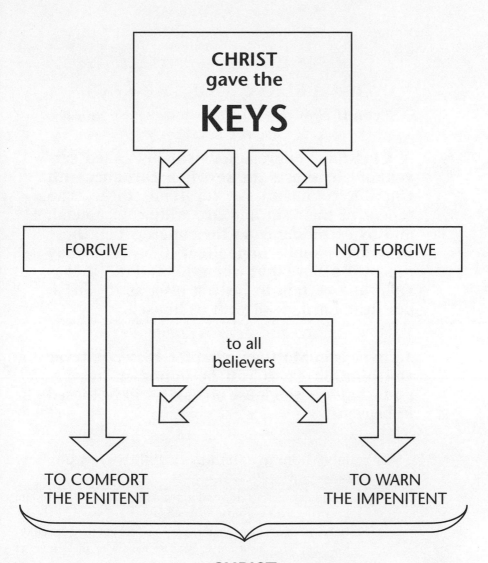

THE PUBLIC USE OF THE KEYS

Second: *How does a Christian congregation use the keys?*

A Christian congregation with its called servant of Christ uses the keys in accordance with Christ's command by forgiving those who repent of their sin and are willing to amend, and by excluding from the congregation those who are plainly impenitent that they may repent. I believe that when this is done, it is as valid and certain in heaven also, as if Christ, our dear Lord, dealt with us himself.

Where is this written?

Jesus says in Matthew, chapter 18, "Whatever you bind on earth will be bound in heaven, and whatever you loose on earth will be loosed in heaven."

311. **Through whom are the keys administered publicly in a congregation?**

   1443) 2 Corinthians 2:10. If you forgive anyone, *I also* forgive him . . . in the sight of Christ *for your sake.*

   1444) Hebrews 13:17. Obey your *leaders* and submit to their authority. They *keep watch over you* as men who must give an account.

311. The keys are administered publicly in a congregation through its pastor.

312. **Why do our congregations have pastors?**

   1445) Hebrews 13:17. Obey your *leaders* and submit to their *authority.*

266

1446) Ephesians 4:11. [Christ] gave some *to be . . . pastors and teachers.*

1447) Titus 1:5. The reason I left you in Crete was that you might straighten out what was left unfinished and appoint *elders in every town.*

1448) 1 Peter 5:2. Be *shepherds of God's flock* that is under your care, serving as *overseers.*

312. Our congregations have pastors because God ordained that there should be leaders in the church. (the office of the public ministry)

313. Who only may serve as pastors in our congregations?

1449) 1 Timothy 3:1-7; Titus 1:6-9. (God sets down specific qualifications that a pastor must have.)

1450) 1 Timothy 2:11-13. A woman should learn in quietness and full submission. I do *not* permit a woman to teach or *to have authority over a man;* she must be silent. *For Adam was formed first, then Eve.*

1451) 1 Corinthians 14:33,34,37. As in all the congregations of the saints, women should remain silent in the churches. They are not allowed to speak, but must *be in submission,* as the Law says. . . . what I am writing to you is *the Lord's command.*

313a. Only men who have all the qualifications that God has established may serve as pastors in our congregations.

1452) Acts 20:28. Keep watch over yourselves and all the flock of which the *Holy Spirit has made you overseers.*

1453) Acts 14:23. Paul and Barnabas appointed elders for them in each church [footnote: had elders *elected*].

313b. Only men whom the Holy Spirit has led the congregations to choose may serve as pastors in our congregations. (divine call)

314. From whom does a congregation get the authority to call a pastor?

1454) Matthew 16:19. *I will give you* the keys of the kingdom of heaven; whatever you bind on earth will be bound in heaven, and whatever you loose on earth will be loosed in heaven.

314. A congregation gets the authority from Christ to call a pastor.

315. What do the believers in a congregation call their pastor to do?

1455) Mark 16:15. Go into all the world and *preach the good news* to all creation.

1456) 2 Timothy 4:2,5. *Preach the Word* . . . ; correct, rebuke and encourage—with great patience and *careful instruction.* . . . do the *work of an evangelist,* discharge all the *duties of your ministry.*

1457) 1 Timothy 4:13. Until I come, devote yourself to the *public* reading of Scripture, to preaching and to teaching.

315a. The believers in a congregation call their pastor to preach and teach the Word of God publicly.

1458) Matthew 28:19. Go and make disciples of all nations, *baptizing them* in the name of the Father and of the Son and of the Holy Spirit.

1459) 1 Corinthians 11:24,25. This is my body . . . ; *do this* in remembrance of me. . . . This cup is the new covenant in my blood; *do this* . . . in remembrance of me.

1460) 1 Corinthians 14:33,40. God is *not a God of disorder* but of peace. . . . *Everything* should be done *in a fitting and orderly way.*

315b. For the sake of order the believers in a congregation also call their pastor to baptize and distribute Holy Communion.

1461) Matthew 18:18. Whatever *you bind* on earth will be bound in heaven, and whatever *you loose* on earth will be loosed in heaven.

1462) 1 Timothy 5:20. Those who sin are to be rebuked *publicly,* so that the others may take warning.

315c. The believers in a congregation also call their pastor to use the binding and loosing keys publicly.

316. How will a Christian congregation with its called pastor use the binding key?

1463) Matthew 18:17. If he refuses to listen to them, tell it to the church; and if he *refuses to listen even to the church, treat him as you would a pagan or a tax collector.*

1464) 1 Corinthians 5:4,5,13. *When you are assembled* in the name of our Lord Jesus . . . , *hand this man over to Satan, so that* the sinful nature may be destroyed and *his spirit saved* on the day of the Lord. . . . *Expel* the wicked man *from among you.*

316. A Christian congregation with its called pastor will use the binding key to exclude from the congregation those who are plainly impenitent that they may repent. (excommunication)

NOTE: See Question 308 for the reason why the use of the binding key in excommunication is an act of love, not hatred.

317. How will a Christian congregation with its called pastor use the loosing key?

1465) 2 Corinthians 2:6-8,10. The punishment inflicted on him by the majority is *sufficient for him.* Now instead, you ought to *forgive and comfort him,* so that he will not be overwhelmed by excessive sorrow. I urge you, therefore, to *reaffirm your love for him.* If you forgive anyone, *I also forgive him* . . . in the sight of Christ *for your sake.*

1466) Matthew 3:8. Produce fruit in keeping with repentance.

317a. A Christian congregation with its called pastor will use the loosing key to forgive and welcome back an excommunicated person who repents of his sin and is willing to amend.

1467) Isaiah 40:1,2. Comfort, *comfort my people,* says your God. Speak tenderly to Jerusalem, and *proclaim to her* . . . that she has received from the LORD's hand *double for all her sins.*

THE OFFICE
of the
PUBLIC MINISTRY

ordained by God	the minister must be	to minister publicly
(not just a human custom)	— qualified — called	— the Word and sacraments — the binding and loosing keys

"SERVANTS OF CHRIST"

1468) 1 Thessalonians 2:11,12. You know that we dealt *with each of you* as a father deals with his own children . . . , *comforting . . . you.*

317b. A Christian congregation asks its called pastor to use the loosing key to announce God's forgiveness publicly in our worship services and also privately to individuals. (absolution)

318. How valid and certain is this public use of the keys by a congregation with its called pastor?

1469) Matthew 18:18,20. *I tell you the truth,* whatever you bind on earth will be *bound in* heaven, and whatever you loose on earth will be *loosed in heaven.* For where *two or three* come together *in my name,* there *am I with them.*

1470) 1 Corinthians 5:4,5. When you are assembled *in the name* of *our Lord* Jesus . . . *and the power of our Lord Jesus* is present, hand this man over to Satan.

1471) 1 Corinthians 4:1. Men ought to regard us *as servants of Christ* and as those *entrusted with* the secret *things of God.*

318. The public use of the keys by a congregation with its called pastor is as valid and certain in heaven also, as if Christ, our dear Lord, dealt with us himself.

Other Forms of the Holy Ministry

In the preceding questions we took note of only one form of the holy ministry, namely, the office of a pastor. However, we noted in Question 312 that God has ordained the public ministry in the church. The passages quoted mention evangelists, teachers, elders, and overseers (bishops) in addition to pastors. Another office mentioned in the New Testament is that of deacon (1 Timothy 3:8).

From this we can see that God did not establish only one office of the public ministry, but he gave believers the liberty to set up various offices to meet whatever needs they may have (see Acts 6:1-7). A congregation may have only one person serving in the public ministry, a pastor. Or a congregation may have many serving them: one or more pastors, teachers, elders, evangelists, vicars, etc.

What God says about those who are pastors is true of all others who serve in the public ministry: (1) They must have the qualifications that God has established for those who serve in the church (see Answer 313a); and (2) no one may serve in the public ministry without a call by the Holy Spirit through the congregation (see Answer 313b). Each will serve according to what the congregation called him to do. A woman may be called to serve in any office where she is not required to exercise authority over men (1 Timothy 2:12).

When congregations join in an association or a synod to do such work as Christian education or mission work (see Question 246), they will call people to serve as professors, chaplains, missionaries, administrators, etc. Each will be serving in his call to meet the special needs of the association of congregations or the synod.

Whatever the form of the ministry, all who serve are called by the Holy Spirit through a group of believers to do the Lord's work.

CONFESSION

First: *What is confession?*

Confession has two parts. The one is that we confess our sins; the other, that we receive absolution or forgiveness from the pastor as from God himself, not doubting but firmly believing that our sins are thus forgiven before God in heaven.

Second: *What sins should we confess?*

Before God we should plead guilty of all sins, even those we are not aware of, as we do in the Lord's Prayer.

But before the pastor we should confess only those sins which we know and feel in our hearts.

Third: *How can we recognize these sins?*

Consider your place in life according to the Ten Commandments. Are you a father, mother, son, daughter, employer, or employee? Have you been disobedient, unfaithful, or lazy? Have you hurt anyone by word or deed? Have you been dishonest, careless, wasteful, or done other wrong?

Fourth: *How will the pastor assure a penitent sinner of forgiveness?*

He will say, "By the authority of Christ, I forgive you your sins in the name of the Father and of the Son and of the Holy Spirit. Amen."

319. What is the first part of confession?

1472) Psalm 32:5. I acknowledged my sin to you and *did not cover up* my iniquity.

1473) Luke 15:21. The son said to him, "Father, *I have sinned* against heaven and against you. I am *no longer worthy* to be called your son."

1474) Psalm 51:3,4. *I know* my transgressions, and my sin is *always before me. Against you,* you only, have I sinned and *done what is evil* in your sight, *so that* you are proved right when you speak and *justified when you judge.*

319. The first part of confession is that we admit that we are sinners who deserve God's punishment.

320. Why do we confess our sins?

1475) Joshua 7:19. (Joshua urged Achan to confess his sin.)

1476) Ezra 10:11. Now *make confession* to the LORD, the God of your fathers, and do his will.

1477) James 5:16. Therefore *confess your sins* to each other.

320a. We confess our sins because God in his Word urges us to do this.

1478) James 5:15,16. If he has sinned, *he will be forgiven.* Therefore confess your sins to each other.

1479) 1 John 1:9. If we confess our sins, *he* is faithful and just and *will forgive us our sins* and purify us from all unrighteousness.

320b. We confess our sins because we know and believe there is forgiveness for our sins.

321. What does God want us to say when we confess our sins to him?

1480) Psalm 51:5. Surely I *was sinful at birth,* sinful from the time my mother conceived me.

1481) Isaiah 64:6. *All of us* have become like one who is *unclean,* and all our righteous *acts are like filthy rags.*

1482) James 2:10. Whoever keeps the whole law and yet stumbles at just one point is *guilty of breaking all of it.*

1483) Psalm 19:12. Who can discern his errors? Forgive my *hidden faults.*

321a. God wants us to confess our complete sinfulness: both that we are sinful by nature and that we have sinned against him in thought, word, and deed.

1484) Isaiah 59:12. Our offenses are many in your sight, and *our sins testify against us.*

1485) Isaiah 59:2. Your iniquities have *separated you from your God.*

1486) Romans 3:12. All have turned away, they have together become *worthless.*

1487) Romans 6:23. The wages of sin is *death.*

321b. God wants us to confess that our sins have separated us from him and that we deserve only death.

322. How does God lead us to confess our sins?

1488) Romans 3:19,20. Whatever the law says, it says to those who are under the law, so that *every mouth may be silenced. . . . through the law* we become *conscious of sin.*

1489) Romans 7:7. I would *not have known what sin was* except through the law. For I would not have known what coveting really was *if the law had not said,* "Do not covet."

1490) Romans 7:19,24. What I do is *not the good* I want to do; no, the *evil* I do not want to do—this I keep on doing. What *a wretched man* I am!

1491) Psalm 38:3-6,18. Because of your wrath there is *no health* in my body; my bones have *no soundness* because of my sin. My guilt has *overwhelmed me* like a burden too heavy to bear. *My wounds* fester and are loathsome because of my sinful folly. *I am bowed down* and brought very low; all day long *I go about mourning. I confess my iniquity; I am troubled* by my sin.

322. God uses his law to lead us to know and feel our sins, so that we confess them.

323. What is the second part of confession?

1492) 2 Samuel 12:1-13. (When David confessed his sin, Nathan announced God's forgiveness to him.)

1493) Psalm 32:5. I said, "I will confess my transgressions to the LORD"—and *you forgave* the guilt of my sin.

1494) Proverbs 28:13. He who conceals his sins does not prosper, but whoever confesses and renounces them *finds mercy.*

1495) 1 John 1:9. If we confess our sins, he is faithful and just and will *forgive us our sins* and *purify us from all unrighteousness.*

1496) 2 Corinthians 2:7. You ought to forgive and *comfort* him, so that he will *not be overwhelmed by excessive sorrow.*

1497) Matthew 9:2. Jesus . . . said to the paralytic, "Take heart, son; *your sins are forgiven.*"

323. The second part of confession is hearing the comforting announcement that our sins are forgiven. (absolution)

324. When does our pastor make this comforting announcement to us regularly?

1498) Psalm 32:5. I said, "*I will confess* my transgressions to the LORD"—and *you forgave* the guilt of my sin.

1499) John 20:22,23. He [Jesus] breathed on them and said, ". . . *If you forgive* anyone his sins, *they are forgiven.*"

324. Our pastor makes this comforting announcement to us regularly in our worship services when he says, "By the authority of Christ, I forgive you your sins in the name of the Father and of the Son and of the Holy Spirit."

325. When is it helpful for us to make a private confession to our pastor?

1500) Psalm 38:4. My *guilt has overwhelmed me* like a *burden too heavy to bear.*

1501) 1 Thessalonians 2:11,12. You know that we dealt *with each of you* as a father deals with his own children, . . . *comforting . . . you.*

1502) 2 Timothy 4:2. Correct, rebuke and *encourage*—with great *patience* and *careful instruction.*

1503) Titus 1:9. He must hold firmly to the trustworthy message as it has been taught, so that he can *encourage others by sound doctrine.*

325. It is helpful for us to make a private confession to our pastor when we seek assurance of forgiveness for a sin that especially troubles the conscience.

CONFESSION

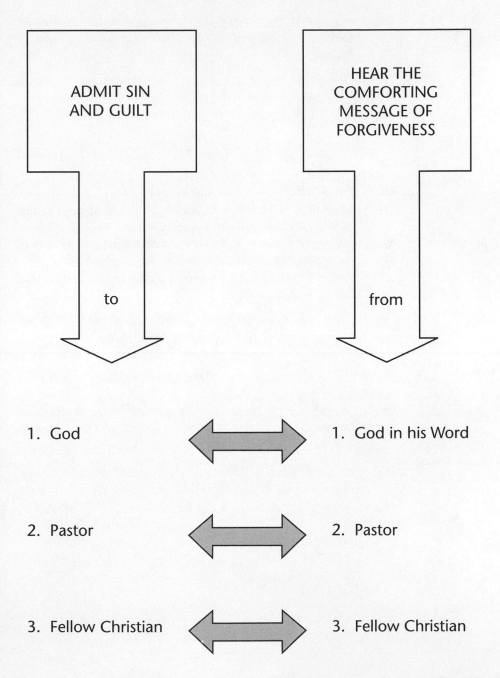

ADMIT SIN AND GUILT

HEAR THE COMFORTING MESSAGE OF FORGIVENESS

to

from

1. God

1. God in his Word

2. Pastor

2. Pastor

3. Fellow Christian

3. Fellow Christian

326. How will we receive the absolution spoken by our pastor?

1504) Matthew 16:19. *I will give you the keys* of the kingdom of heaven; . . . whatever *you loose* on earth will be *loosed in heaven.*

326. We will receive the absolution from our pastor as from God himself, believing that our sins are thus forgiven before God in heaven.

327. When does God want us to confess a sin to a fellow Christian?

1505) James 5:16. *Confess* your sins *to each other.*

1506) Matthew 5:23,24. If you are offering your gift at the altar and there remember that your *brother has something against you,* leave your gift there in front of the altar. First go and *be reconciled to your brother;* then come and offer your gift.

1507) Luke 15:21. Father, *I have sinned* against heaven and *against you.*

327. God wants us to confess a sin to a fellow Christian when we do something wrong against him.

328. How will we receive the absolution spoken by a fellow Christian?

1508) Matthew 16:19. *I will give you the keys* of the kingdom of heaven; . . . whatever *you loose* on earth will be *loosed in heaven.*

328. We will receive the absolution spoken by a fellow Christian as from God himself, believing that our sins are thus forgiven before God in heaven.

The
Lord's Prayer

PRAYER

329. What is prayer?

1509) Daniel 9:3,19. I *turned to the Lord God* and pleaded with him *in prayer.* . . . "O Lord, *listen!* . . . O Lord, *hear* and act!"

1510) Matthew 15:8,9. These people honor me *with their lips,* but *their hearts* are far from me. They *worship* me in vain.

329. Prayer is an act of worship in which we speak to God from our hearts.

330. Whose prayers does God hear?

1511) Isaiah 1:15. When you spread out your hands in prayer, *I will hide my eyes* from you; even if you offer many prayers, *I will not listen.*

1512) Hebrews 11:6. *Without faith* it is impossible to please God.

1513) John 16:23. My Father will give you whatever you *ask in my name.*

1514) 1 Peter 3:12. The *eyes of the Lord* are *on the righteous* and his ears are attentive to their prayer, *but* the face of the Lord is *against those who do evil.*

330. God hears only the prayers of those who are acceptable to him by faith in Jesus. (This is what it means to pray in Jesus' name.)

331. What kinds of prayers may a believer bring to God?

1515) 1 Timothy 2:1. I urge, then, first of all, that *requests,* prayers, intercession and *thanksgiving* be made *for everyone.*

1516) Philippians 4:6. Do not be anxious about *anything,* but in *everything,* by prayer and petition, *with thanksgiving,* present your *requests* to God.

PRAYER

is

WORSHIP

in which

BELIEVERS

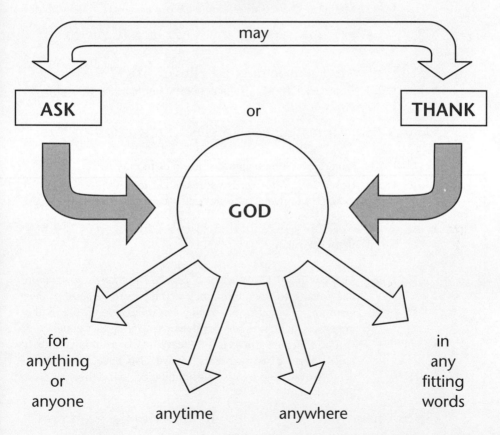

may

ASK or THANK

GOD

for
anything
or
anyone

anytime

anywhere

in
any
fitting
words

331. A believer may bring prayers of request or thanksgiving to God about anyone or anything.

332. When and where may a believer pray?

1517) 1 Thessalonians 5:17. Pray *continually.*

1518) Ephesians 6:18. Pray in the Spirit *on all occasions* with all kinds of prayers and requests.

1519) Matthew 6:6. When you pray, *go into your room,* close the door and pray to your Father, who is unseen.

1520) 1 Timothy 2:8. I want men *everywhere* to lift up holy hands in prayer.

1521) Matthew 28:20. Surely I am *with you always.*

332. A believer may pray at any time and anywhere.

333. With what words may a believer pray?

1522) 1 Samuel 1:10-16. (Hannah poured out her soul to God in her own words.)

333a. A believer may pray using his own words.

1523) Luke 11:1. (John taught his disciples to pray.)

1524) Hosea 14:2. *Take words* with you and return to the LORD. *Say to him:* "Forgive all our sins and receive us graciously."

333b. A believer may pray using words that are given to him by another person.

1525) Matthew 6:7,9-13. When you pray, *do not keep on babbling* like pagans, for they think they will be heard because of their many words. . . . *This . . . is how you should pray:* "Our Father in heaven, hallowed be your name, your kingdom come, your will be done on earth as it is in heaven. Give us today our daily bread. Forgive us our debts, as we also have forgiven our debtors. And lead us not into temptation, but deliver us from the evil one."

333c. A believer will surely use the words of the short prayer that Jesus gave us as a model. (the Lord's Prayer)

THE ADDRESS
Our Father in heaven.

What does this mean?

With these words God tenderly invites us to believe that he is our true Father and that we are his true children, so that we may pray to him as boldly and confidently as dear children ask their dear father.

334. What does Jesus want us to remember when he tells us to address God as "Our Father in heaven"?

1526) Galatians 3:26. You are all *sons of God through faith* in Christ Jesus.

1527) Galatians 4:4,5. God sent his Son, born of a woman, born under law, to redeem those under law, that we might receive *the full rights of sons.*

1528) 1 John 3:1. *How great is the love* the Father has lavished on us, that we should be *called children of God!*

334. When Jesus tells us to address God as "Our Father in heaven," he wants us to remember that by faith God is our true Father and that we are his true children.

335. Why does Jesus want us to remember the relationship we have with God by faith?

1529) Romans 8:15. You did *not* receive a spirit that makes you a slave again *to fear,* but you received the Spirit of sonship. And by him we cry, "Abba, Father."

1530) Ephesians 3:12. In him and through faith in him we may approach God *with freedom and confidence.*

1531) Matthew 7:9-11. Which of you, if his son asks for bread, will give him a stone? Or if he asks for a fish, will give him a

FATHER

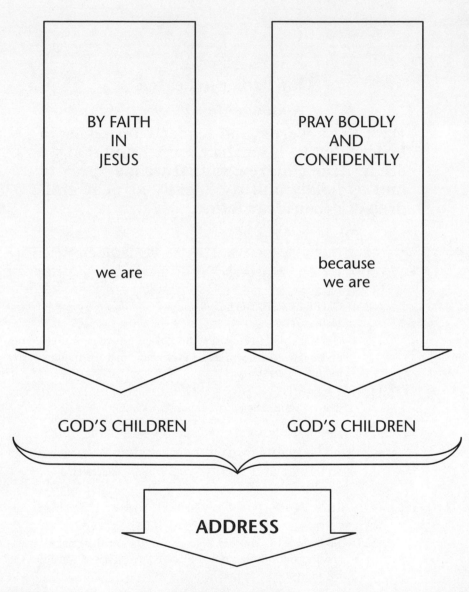

BY FAITH
IN
JESUS

we are

PRAY BOLDLY
AND
CONFIDENTLY

because
we are

GOD'S CHILDREN

GOD'S CHILDREN

ADDRESS

"Heavenly Father,
we are your
dear children!"

snake? If you, then, though you are evil, know how to give good gifts to your children, *how much more* will *your Father in heaven* give good gifts to those who ask him!

335. Jesus wants us to remember the relationship we have with God by faith, so that we feel free to pray to our heavenly Father as boldly and confidently as dear children ask their dear father.

336. In the Address, then, how does Jesus teach us to pray?

336. In the Address, Jesus teaches us to pray boldly and confidently.

THE FIRST PETITION

Hallowed be your name.

What does this mean?

God's name is certainly holy by itself, but we pray in this petition that we too may keep it holy.

How is God's name kept holy?

God's name is kept holy when his Word is taught in its truth and purity and we as children of God lead holy lives according to it. Help us to do this, dear Father in heaven! But whoever teaches and lives contrary to God's Word dishonors God's name among us. Keep us from doing this, dear Father in heaven!

337. What is God's name?

1532) Isaiah 42:8. I am *the LORD;* that is my name!

1533) Matthew 1:21. You are to give him the name *Jesus.*

1534) Exodus 34:5-7. The LORD . . . proclaimed his name, . . . *"The LORD,* the LORD, the *compassionate* and *gracious* God, *slow to anger, abounding in love and faithfulness, maintaining love* to thousands, and *forgiving* wickedness, rebellion and sin. Yet he does *not leave the guilty unpunished."*

1535) John 17:6,8. I have revealed you. . . . For I gave them *the words* you gave me.

337. God's name is his titles and everything else he has revealed to us about himself in his word.

338. Why can't we make God's name holy?

1536) Psalm 103:1. Praise *the LORD,* O my soul; all my inmost being, praise his *holy name.*

1537) Romans 1:2. He promised . . . through his prophets in the *Holy Scriptures.*

1538) Revelation 3:7. These are the *words* of him who is *holy and true.*

338. We can't make God's name holy because his name as it is revealed in his Word is holy in itself.

339. How do we keep God's name holy?

1539) Psalm 48:10. *Like your name,* O God, *your praise* reaches to the ends of the earth.

1540) John 17:17. Sanctify them by the truth; your *word is truth.*

1541) Jeremiah 23:28. Let the one who has my word *speak it faithfully.*

1542) Deuteronomy 4:2. *Do not add* to what I command you and *do not subtract* from it.

339a. We keep God's name holy by teaching his Word in its truth and purity.

1543) Ephesians 3:14,15; 4:1. I kneel before the Father, from whom *his* whole *family* in heaven and earth derives its name. . . . I urge you to live *a life worthy of the calling* you have received.

1544) Matthew 5:14,16. You are the light of the world. . . . let your light shine before men, that they may *see your good deeds* and *praise your Father* in heaven.

1545) 1 Corinthians 10:31. So whether you eat or drink or whatever you do, *do it all for the glory of God.*

1546) 2 Thessalonians 1:11,12. We constantly pray for you, that our God . . . may fulfill every good purpose of yours and *every act prompted by your faith.* We pray this so that *the name* of our Lord Jesus may be *glorified in you.*

339b. We keep God's name holy when we as the children of God lead holy lives according to his Word.

340. When is the name of God dishonored among us?

1547) Malachi 1:6-8; 2:7,8. (The priests despised God's name by teaching the people things that were contrary to God's Word.)

1548) 2 Peter 2:1,2. There will be *false teachers* among you. . . . Many will follow their shameful ways and will *bring the way of truth into disrepute.*

340a. God's name is dishonored among us when anyone teaches contrary to God's Word.

> 1549) Ezekiel 36:23. I will show the holiness of my great name, which has been profaned among the nations, *the name you have profaned* among them.
>
> 1550) 2 Samuel 12:7-14. (David's sins gave the enemies of the Lord an opportunity to despise God's name.)
>
> 1551) Romans 2:23,24. You who brag about the law, do you dishonor God by *breaking the law?* As it is written: *"God's name is blasphemed* among the Gentiles because of you."

340b. God's name is dishonored among us when anyone lives contrary to God's Word.

341. What, then, are we praying in the First Petition?

341. In the First Petition we are praying that God would help us teach and live his Word in the way which keeps his name holy.

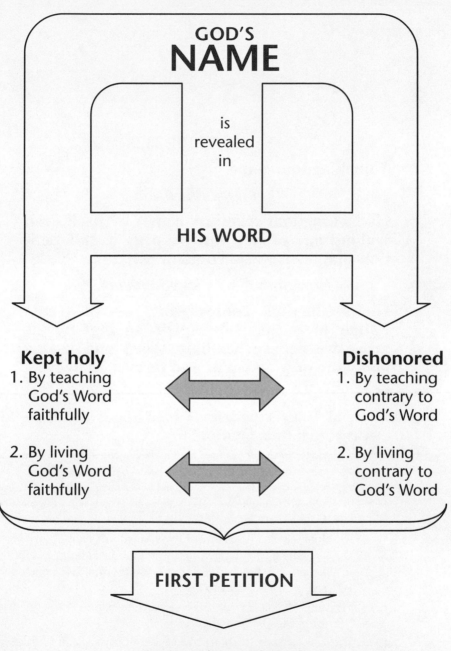

GOD'S
NAME

is
revealed
in

HIS WORD

Kept holy
1. By teaching God's Word faithfully

2. By living God's Word faithfully

Dishonored
1. By teaching contrary to God's Word

2. By living contrary to God's Word

FIRST PETITION

"Help us live and teach
your Word correctly!"

THE SECOND PETITION

Your kingdom come.

What does this mean?

God's kingdom certainly comes by itself even without our prayer, but we pray in this petition that it may also come to us.

How does God's kingdom come?

God's kingdom comes when our heavenly Father gives his Holy Spirit, so that by his grace we believe his holy Word and lead a godly life now on earth and forever in heaven.

342. What is the kingdom of God about which we are praying in this petition?

1552) Luke 17:20,21. Once, having been asked by the Pharisees when the *kingdom of God* would *come,* Jesus replied, "The kingdom of God *does not come with your careful observation,* nor will people say, 'Here it is,' or 'There it is,' because the kingdom of God is *within you.*"

1553) John 18:36,37. Jesus said, "My kingdom is not of this world. . . . *I am a king.* In fact, for this reason I was born, and for this I came into the world, *to testify to the truth.* Everyone on the side of truth *listens to me.*"

1554) John 10:3,4. He calls his own sheep by name . . . and his sheep *follow him* because they *know his voice.*

1555) Colossians 3:15,16. Let the peace of Christ *rule in your hearts.* . . . Let the *word of Christ* dwell in you richly.

342. The kingdom of God about which we are praying is Christ's rule in our hearts by his Word.

343. How does this kingdom come to us?

1556) 1 Corinthians 12:3. *No one can say, "Jesus is Lord,"* except by the Holy Spirit.

1557) Romans 14:17. The *kingdom of God* is not a matter of eating and drinking, but of righteousness, peace and joy *in the Holy Spirit.*

1558) Romans 9:16. It does *not . . .* depend on *man's desire or effort,* but on *God's mercy.*

1559) Romans 5:5. God has poured out *his love into our hearts by the Holy Spirit,* whom he has *given us.*

343. The kingdom of God does not come by what we do, but it comes by itself when our heavenly Father in his grace gives us his Holy Spirit.

344. Why do we pray for Christ to rule in our hearts?

1560) Matthew 11:28-30. Come to me, all you who are weary and burdened, and I will give you rest. Take my yoke upon you and *learn from me,* for I am gentle and humble in heart, and you will find *rest for your souls.* For *my yoke is easy* and *my burden is light.*

1561) John 8:31,32. To the Jews who had believed him, Jesus said, "If you *hold to my teaching,* you are really my disciples. Then you will *know the truth,* and the truth will *set you free.*"

1562) Romans 14:17. The *kingdom of God* is not a matter of eating and drinking, but of *righteousness, peace* and *joy* in the Holy Spirit.

344a. We pray for Christ to rule in our hearts because by his Word we learn to know and believe the truth of our salvation.

1563) 2 Corinthians 5:15,17. He died for all, that those who live should no longer *live* for themselves but *for him* who died for them and was raised again. . . . if anyone is *in Christ,* he is *a new creation;* the old has gone, the new has come!

1564) Galatians 2:20. *Christ lives in me.* The life I live in the body, *I live by faith in the Son of God,* who loved me and gave himself for me.

1565) Colossians 3:3,4. Your life is *now hidden with Christ* in God. When Christ, who is your life, appears, *then* you also will *appear with him in glory.*

344b. We pray for Christ to rule in our hearts because he enables us to lead a godly life now on earth and forever in heaven.

345. Why do we continue to pray for God's kingdom to come even though Christ already rules in our hearts?

> 1566) Mark 9:24. I do believe; *help me overcome my unbelief!*
>
> 1567) 2 Peter 3:17,18. Since you already know this, be on your guard so that you may not . . . fall from your secure position. But *grow in the grace and knowledge* of our Lord and Savior Jesus Christ.

345a. We continue to pray for God's kingdom to come because we want God to increase Christ's rule in our hearts by strengthening our faith.

> 1568) John 10:16. I have *other sheep* that are *not of this sheep pen.* I must bring them also. *They too will listen to my voice,* and there shall be one flock and one shepherd.

345b. We continue to pray for God's kingdom to come because we want God to extend Christ's rule to the hearts of many others who are not yet Christians. (prayer for missions)

346. What, then, are we praying in the Second Petition?

346. In the Second Petition we are praying that our heavenly Father would send his holy spirit, so that Christ may rule in our hearts and in the hearts of many others.

GOD'S
KINGDOM

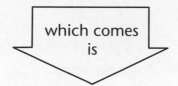

which comes
is

CHRIST'S
RULE
(in our hearts)

established	**results**
	in our believing the Word of Salvation
in our hearts	
by the Holy Spirit	and
through the Word	living a life devoted to Christ

SECOND PETITION

"Send the Holy Spirit to strengthen
Christ's rule in our hearts
and to spread that rule!"

THE THIRD PETITION

Your will be done on earth as in heaven.

What does this mean?

God's good and gracious will certainly is done without our prayer, but we pray in this petition that it may be done among us also.

How is God's will done?

God's will is done when he breaks and defeats every evil plan and purpose of the devil, the world, and our sinful flesh, which try to prevent us from keeping God's name holy and letting his kingdom come. And God's will is done when he strengthens and keeps us firm in his Word and in the faith as long as we live. This is his good and gracious will.

347.   What is God's good and gracious will?

> 1569)   Mark 16:15. Go into all the world and *preach the good news to all creation.*

> 1570)   Jeremiah 23:28. Let the one who has my word *speak it faithfully.*

347a. God's good and gracious will is that his Word be taught in its truth and purity to all people. (See Answer 339a.)

> 1571)   John 6:40. My Father's will is that everyone who looks to the Son and *believes in him* shall *have eternal life.*

> 1572)   1 Timothy 2:3,4. This is *good,* and *pleases God* our Savior, who wants *all men* to be *saved* and to come to a knowledge of the truth.

347b. God's good and gracious will is that all people believe in Jesus and be saved. (See Answers 343 and 344a.)

1573) 1 Thessalonians 4:1,3. We instructed you how to *live in order to please God.* . . . It is *God's will* that you should be sanctified.

1574) 1 Peter 2:15. It is *God's will* that *by doing good* you should *silence* the ignorant talk of *foolish men.*

347c. God's good and gracious will is that we should live a holy life. (See Answer 339b.)

348. How is God's will done in heaven and on earth?

1575) Psalm 103:20. Praise the LORD, you his *angels,* you mighty ones who *do his bidding,* who *obey his word.*

1576) Matthew 18:10. I tell you that their angels in heaven *always see the face of my Father* in heaven.

348a. In heaven God's will is always done by the angels.

1577) Psalm 115:3. Our God is in heaven; he *does whatever pleases him.*

1578) Ephesians 1:11. [God] *works out everything* in conformity with the *purpose of his will.*

348b. On earth God's will is done just as he plans it, even if we do not pray for it.

349. Who tries to prevent us from keeping God's name holy and letting his kingdom come?

1579) Matthew 4:1-11. (The devil tempted Jesus to lead him into sin, so that he could not be our Savior.)

1580) 1 Thessalonians 2:18. We wanted to come to you . . . but *Satan stopped* us.

1581) Matthew 18:7. Woe to *the world* because of the things that *cause people to sin!*

1582) James 4:4. Anyone who chooses to be a friend of the *world* becomes an *enemy* of God.

1583) Galatians 5:17. The *sinful nature* desires what is *contrary to the Spirit.*

1584) Romans 8:8. Those controlled by the *sinful nature cannot please God.*

349. The devil, the world, and our sinful nature (flesh) try to prevent God's will from being done.

350. How do the devil, the world, and our sinful nature (flesh) constantly try to prevent God's will from being done on earth?

1585) Genesis 3:1-6. (The devil led Adam and Eve into sin by leading them to doubt God's Word.)

1586) 2 Corinthians 11:3. I am afraid that just as Eve was *deceived* by the serpent's cunning, your minds may somehow *be led astray from* your sincere and pure devotion to Christ.

1587) 2 Corinthians 4:4. The god of this age has *blinded* the minds of *unbelievers,* so that they cannot see the *light of the gospel* of the glory of Christ.

1588) 1 John 3:8. He who does *what is sinful is of the devil,* because the devil has been sinning from the beginning.

1589) 1 Peter 5:8. Your enemy the devil prowls around like a roaring lion *looking for someone to devour.*

350a. The devil tries to prevent God's will from being done by leading people astray from God's Word, so that they live in unbelief and sin.

1590) 1 John 2:15,16. Do not love *the world* or *anything in the world.* If anyone loves the world, the love of the Father is not in him. For everything in the world—*the cravings* of sinful man, *the lust* of his eyes and *the boasting* of what he has and does—comes not from the Father but from the world.

1591) Luke 8:14. The seed that fell among thorns stands for those who hear, but as they go on their way they are *choked by life's worries, riches and pleasures,* and they do not mature.

1592) Luke 22:54-61. (Peter's fear of Christ's enemies led him to deny Jesus.)

1593) 1 Corinthians 15:33. Do not be misled: "*Bad company corrupts* good character."

350b. The people and things of the world try to prevent God's will from being done by leading people to ignore, forget, or deny Jesus.

1594) Romans 8:7. The sinful mind is *hostile to God.*

1595) Romans 7:19,25. What I do is not the good I want to do; no, the *evil* I do not want to do—this *I keep on doing. . . .* in the sinful nature [I am] a slave to the law of sin.

1596) Galatians 5:17,19-21. The sinful nature *desires* what is *contrary to the Spirit.* . . . The acts of the sinful nature are obvious: sexual immorality, impurity and debauchery; idolatry and witchcraft; hatred, discord, jealousy, fits of rage, selfish ambition, dissensions, factions and envy; drunkenness, orgies, and the like.

350c. The sinful nature (flesh) of all people tries to prevent God's will from being done by promoting a hatred of God's word and an enjoyment of sin.

351. How can God's will be done among us?

1597) 1 John 3:8. The reason the Son of God appeared was to *destroy the devil's work.*

1598) Psalm 17:14. O LORD, *by your hand save me* from such men, *from men of this world* whose reward is in this life.

1599) John 16:33. In this world you will have trouble. But take heart! *I have overcome the world.*

1600) Romans 6:6. We know that our *old self* was *crucified with him* so that the body of sin might be *done away with,* that we should no longer be slaves to sin.

351a. God's will can be done among us only when God breaks and defeats every evil plan and purpose of the devil, the world, and our sinful nature (flesh).

1601) James 4:7. *Submit* yourselves . . . *to God. Resist the devil,* and he will flee from you.

1602) 1 Peter 5:8,9. Your enemy the devil prowls around like a roaring lion looking for someone to devour. *Resist him, standing firm in the faith.*

1603) 2 Peter 2:20. They have *escaped* the corruption of the *world* by *knowing our Lord* and Savior Jesus Christ.

1604) Galatians 6:14. May I never *boast* except *in the cross of our Lord* Jesus Christ, through which the *world has been crucified to me,* and I to the world.

1605) 1 Peter 5:10. The *God* of all grace . . . *will . . . make you strong, firm* and steadfast.

1606) Ephesians 6:10-18. (The only way to stand firm in faith is by the power that God supplies when we put on his full armor.)

1607) 1 Peter 1:5. [You] *through faith* are *shielded* by God's power *until the coming of the salvation* that is ready to be revealed in the last time.

351b. God's will can be done among us only when God strengthens and keeps us firm in his Word and in the faith as long as we live.

352. What, then, are we praying in the Third Petition?

352. In the Third Petition we are praying that God's good and gracious will be done rather than the will of the devil, the world, and our sinful nature (flesh).

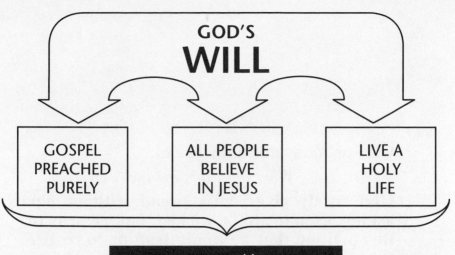

GOD'S
WILL

| GOSPEL PREACHED PURELY | ALL PEOPLE BELIEVE IN JESUS | LIVE A HOLY LIFE |

opposed by
Devil, World, Sinful Nature

but

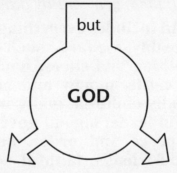

GOD

breaks and defeats them

strengthens and keeps us firm

THIRD PETITION

"Let your saving plan be done rather than the plans of the unholy three!"

THE FOURTH PETITION

Give us today our daily bread.

What does this mean?

God surely gives daily bread without our asking, even to all the wicked, but we pray in this petition that he would lead us to realize this and to receive our daily bread with thanksgiving.

What, then, is meant by daily bread?

Daily bread includes everything that we need for our bodily welfare, such as food and drink, clothing and shoes, house and home, land and cattle, money and goods, a godly spouse, godly children, godly workers, godly and faithful leaders, good government, good weather, peace and order, health, a good name, good friends, faithful neighbors, and the like.

353. What is meant by daily bread?

1608) Psalm 37:25,26. I was young and now I am old, yet I have *never* seen the righteous *forsaken* or their children *begging bread*. They are always *generous* and *lend freely*.

1609) Psalm 145:15,16. The eyes of all look to you, and you give them their *food* at the proper time. You open your hand and satisfy the *desires of every living thing*.

1610) James 2:15,16. Suppose a brother or sister is without clothes and daily food. If one of you says to him, "Go, I wish you well; keep warm and well fed," but *does nothing about his physical needs,* what good is it?

1611) Philippians 4:19. My God will meet *all your needs*.

353. By daily bread is meant food and all the other things that God promises to give us for our bodily needs.

354. To whom does God give daily bread?

1612) Psalm 145:15,16. The *eyes of all* look to you, and you give them their food at the proper time. You open your hand and satisfy the desires of *every living thing.*

1613) Matthew 5:45. He causes his sun to rise on *the evil and the good,* and sends rain on *the righteous and the unrighteous.*

1614) Matthew 6:8. Your Father knows what you need *before you ask him.*

354. God gives daily bread to all without their asking, even to all the wicked.

355. What does Jesus teach us Christians by this petition?

1615) James 1:17. *Every* good and perfect *gift is from above,* coming down from *the Father* of the heavenly lights.

1616) 1 Peter 5:7. Cast all your anxiety on him because *he cares for you.*

1617) Romans 8:32. He who did not spare his own Son, but gave him up for us all—how will he not also, along with him, *graciously give us all things?*

355a. Jesus teaches us to realize that everything we receive for our bodily needs is a gracious gift of our heavenly Father.

1618) Philippians 4:6. *With thanksgiving,* present your requests to God.

1619) Psalm 118:1. *Give thanks* to the LORD for he is good; *his love* endures forever.

355b. Jesus teaches us to receive all our bodily needs with thanksgiving.

356. Why does Jesus teach us to ask for bread for only today?

1620) Matthew 6:25-34. (Like the birds and the lilies, God wants us to trust him to supply our bodily needs each day and not to worry about tomorrow.)

1621) 1 Peter 5:7. *Cast all your anxiety on him* because he cares for you.

1622) James 4:13-15. Now listen, you who say, "Today or tomorrow we will . . . carry on business and make money." Why, *you do not even know what will happen tomorrow.* What is your life? You are a mist that appears for a little while and then vanishes. Instead, you ought to say, "*If it is the Lord's will,* we will live and do this or that."

1623) Luke 11:3. Give us *each day* our daily bread.

356. By teaching us to ask for bread for only today, Jesus teaches us to trust God to supply what we need each day and not to worry about the future.

357. What, then, are we praying in the Fourth Petition?

357. In the Fourth Petition we are asking our heavenly Father to provide our bodily needs day by day.

DAILY
BREAD

is

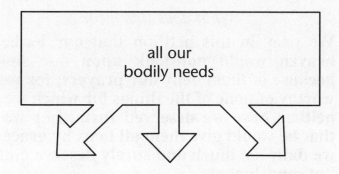

all our
bodily needs

| God's gracious gift | Received by us with thanksgiving | Which we trust God to supply each day |

FOURTH PETITION

"Provide our bodily needs
day by day!"

THE FIFTH PETITION

Forgive us our sins, as we forgive those who sin against us.

What does this mean?

We pray in this petition that our Father in heaven would not look upon our sins or because of them deny our prayers; for we are worthy of none of the things for which we ask, neither have we deserved them, but we ask that he would give them all to us by grace; for we daily sin much and surely deserve nothing but punishment.

So we too will forgive from the heart and gladly do good to those who sin against us.

358. What do we mean by sins?

1624) Matthew 6:14,15. If you forgive men when they *sin* against you, your heavenly Father will also forgive you. But if you do not forgive men their *sins,* your Father will not forgive your sins.

1625) Luke 11:4. Forgive us our *sins,* for we also forgive everyone who *sins* against us.

358. By sins we mean everything we have said, thought, or done wrong.

359. What do we know is true about ourselves because of our sins?

1626) Isaiah 59:2. Your iniquities have *separated you from your God;* your sins have *hidden his face* from you, so that he *will not hear.*

1627) 1 Samuel 6:20. *Who can stand* in the presence of the LORD, this *holy God?*

1628) Romans 3:10,12. There is *no one righteous,* not even one. . . . All have turned away, they have together become *worthless;* there is no one who does good, not even one.

1629) Genesis 32:10. I am *unworthy of all* the kindness and faithfulness you have shown your servant.

359a. Because of our sins, we know that we are worthy of none of the things for which we ask.

1630) Isaiah 59:12. Our offenses are *many* in your sight, and our sins *testify against us.* Our offenses are *ever with us,* and we acknowledge our iniquities.

1631) Colossians 3:25. Anyone who does wrong will be *repaid for his wrong,* and there is no favoritism.

1632) Romans 6:23. *The wages* of sin is *death.*

359b. Because we daily sin much, we know that we deserve nothing from God but punishment.

360. What are we asking when we pray for forgiveness?

1633) Psalm 51:1,2,9. *Have mercy on me,* O God, according to your unfailing love; according to your great compassion *blot out* my transgressions. *Wash away* all my iniquity and *cleanse me* from my sin. Hide your face from my sins and blot out all my iniquity.

1634) Ephesians 4:32. Be kind and compassionate to one another, forgiving each other, just as *in Christ* God forgave you.

360a. When we pray for forgiveness, we are asking God for Jesus' sake not to look upon our sins.

1635) Psalm 55:1,2. Listen to my prayer, O God, *do not ignore* my plea; hear me and answer me.

1636) Psalm 66:20. Praise be to God, who has *not rejected my prayer or withheld his love* from me!

1637) Psalm 69:16. *Answer me,* O LORD, *out of* the goodness of *your love;* in your great *mercy* turn to me.

1638) Isaiah 30:19. *How gracious he will be* when you cry for help! As soon as he hears, *he will answer you.*

360b. We are also asking God not to deny our prayers because of our sin but in his grace to give us all the things we ask for.

361. How do we show our thanks for God's forgiveness?

1639) Genesis 50:15-21. (Joseph forgave his brothers and gladly provided for them.)

1640) Ephesians 4:32. *Be kind* and compassionate to one another, *forgiving each other, just as* in Christ *God forgave you.*

1641) Matthew 18:32-35. "*I canceled all that debt* of yours because you begged me to. *Shouldn't you have had mercy* on your fellow servant *just as I* had on you?" In anger his master turned him over to the jailers to be tortured, until he should pay back all he owed. This is how my heavenly Father will treat each of you unless you *forgive* your brother *from your heart.*

1642) Luke 6:33,35,36. If you *do good* to those who are good to you, what credit is that to you? . . . But love your enemies, *do good* to them. . . . *Be merciful, just as your Father* is merciful.

361. We show our thanks for God's forgiveness as we forgive from the heart and gladly do good to those who sin against us.

362. What, then, are we praying in the Fifth Petition?

362. In the Fifth Petition we are praying that God in his grace would forgive all our sins and also lead us to forgive anyone who sins against us.

FORGIVENESS

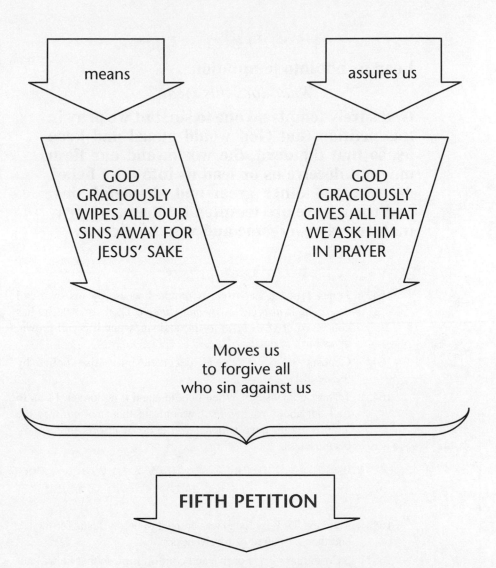

means

assures us

GOD
GRACIOUSLY
WIPES ALL OUR
SINS AWAY FOR
JESUS' SAKE

GOD
GRACIOUSLY
GIVES ALL THAT
WE ASK HIM
IN PRAYER

Moves us
to forgive all
who sin against us

FIFTH PETITION

"Graciously cancel our debt of sin
and lead us to do the same!"

THE SIXTH PETITION

Lead us not into temptation.

What does this mean?

God surely tempts no one to sin, but we pray in this petition that God would guard and keep us, so that the devil, the world, and our flesh may not deceive us or lead us into false belief, despair, and other great and shameful sins; and though we are tempted by them, we pray that we may overcome and win the victory.

363. What is meant by temptation?

1643) James 1:14,15. Each one is tempted when, by his own evil desire, he is *dragged away and enticed.* Then, after desire has conceived, it *gives birth to sin;* and sin, when it is full-grown, gives birth to death.

1644) Genesis 3:1-6. (Eve was deceived into false belief by the devil.)

1645) 1 Thessalonians 3:5. When I could stand it no longer, I sent to find out about your *faith.* I was afraid that in *some way* the tempter might have *tempted you* and our efforts might have been useless.

363a. By temptation is meant any situation in which a person may be deceived or led astray into false belief.

1646) Matthew 27:3-5. (Judas was enticed to betray Jesus for money and then despaired of forgiveness.)

1647) 2 Corinthians 2:7. Forgive and comfort him, so that he will not be *overwhelmed by excessive sorrow.*

1648) Romans 8:35. Who shall *separate us from* the love of Christ? Shall *trouble* or *hardship* or *persecution* or *famine* or *nakedness* or *danger* or *sword?*

363b. By temptation is meant any situation in which a person may be led astray into despair.

> 1649) Proverbs 1:10; 6:25; 12:26; 23:31; 30:8,9. My son, if *sinners entice you,* do not give in to them. Do not *lust* in your heart *after her beauty* or let her *captivate you* with her eyes. A righteous man is *cautious* in friendship, but the way of the wicked *leads them astray.* Do not *gaze at wine* when it is red, when it sparkles in the cup, when it goes down smoothly! . . . give me neither poverty nor riches. . . . Otherwise, I may *have too much* and disown you. . . . Or I may *become poor* and steal.
>
> 1650) 1 Timothy 6:9,10. People who *want to get rich* fall into temptation and *a trap* and into many *foolish and harmful desires* that plunge men into ruin and destruction. For the love of money is *a root of all kinds of evil.* Some people, eager for money, have *wandered from the faith* and pierced themselves with *many griefs.*

363c. By temptation is meant any situation in which a person may be led astray into great and shameful sins.

364. Who deceives us or leads us astray by temptation?

> 1651) Revelation 12:9. The great dragon was hurled down—that ancient serpent called the *devil, or Satan,* who *leads the whole world astray.*
>
> 1652) 1 John 2:16. For everything in the world—the *cravings* of sinful man, the *lust* of his eyes and the *boasting* of what he has and does—comes not from the Father but *from the world.*
>
> 1653) 2 Peter 2:18. They mouth empty, boastful words and, by appealing to the *lustful desires* of *sinful human nature,* they *entice* people.

364. The devil, the world, and our sinful nature (flesh) deceive us and lead us astray by temptation.

365. What do we know about our Father in heaven in regard to temptation?

> 1654) James 1:13. When tempted, no one should say, "God is tempting me." For God cannot be tempted by evil, *nor does he tempt anyone.*

TEMPTATION

is
**ANY SITUATION IN
WHICH WE ARE LED**

by
Devil, World, Sinful Nature

to
false
belief

to
despair

to
great
or
shameful
sin

GOD
CAN

KEEP
TEMPTATIONS
AWAY

or

HELP US
OVERCOME
TEMPTATION

SIXTH PETITION

"Help us so we are not overcome by
situations which might lead us to sin!"

365. We know that our Father in heaven does not lead us into temptation.

366. Why, then, do we ask our Father in heaven not to lead us into temptation?

1655) Matthew 26:41. Watch and pray so that you will not fall into temptation. The spirit is willing, but *the body is weak.*

1656) 1 Corinthians 10:12,13. If you think you are standing firm, *be careful that you don't fall!* No temptation has seized you except what is common to man. And *God is faithful;* he will *not let you be tempted beyond what you can bear.* But when you are tempted, he will also *provide a way out* so that you *can stand up under it.*

1657) Hebrews 4:15. We have one who has been *tempted in every way, just as we are*—yet was without sin.

1658) Hebrews 2:18. Because he himself suffered when he was tempted, he is *able to help those who are being tempted.*

1659) Romans 8:37-39. *In all these things* we are more than *conquerors through him who loved us.* For I am convinced that neither death nor life, neither angels nor demons, neither the present nor the future, nor any powers, neither height nor depth, nor anything else in all creation, will be able to separate us from the *love of God that is in Christ Jesus our Lord.*

366. We ask this of our Father in heaven because he alone has the power to guard and keep us from temptation or to help us overcome and win the victory over our temptations.

367. What, then, are we praying in the Sixth Petition?

367. In the Sixth Petition we are praying our heavenly Father to lead us, so that we are not overcome by any temptation.

311

THE SEVENTH PETITION
But deliver us from evil.

What does this mean?

In conclusion, we pray in this petition that our Father in heaven would deliver us from every evil that threatens body and soul, property and reputation, and finally when our last hour comes, grant us a blessed end and graciously take us from this world of sorrow to himself in heaven.

368. What is meant by evil?

1660) Genesis 1:31. God saw all that he had made, and it was *very good.*

1661) Genesis 3:16-19,23,24. (By the fall into sin, paradise was lost, and sorrow and suffering became part of life in the world.)

1662) Romans 8:22. We know that the *whole creation* has been *groaning* as in the pains of childbirth right *up to the present time.*

1663) Galatians 1:4. [Jesus] gave himself for our sins to rescue us from *the present evil age.*

368. By evil is meant all the bad things that are a part of our life on earth as a result of Adam's fall into sin.

369. How does the evil in the world affect our lives?

1664) Job 1:13-19; 2:7,11-13; 17:1; 19:13-20. (The suffering in Job's life included loss of his property and children, sickness that weakened his body to the point of death, and alienation from everyone.)

1665) Psalm 31:9-13. Be merciful to me, O LORD, for I am in *distress;* my eyes grow weak with *sorrow,* my *soul and my body* with grief. My life is consumed by *anguish* and my *years* by *groaning;* my *strength fails* because of my affliction, and my bones grow weak. Because of all my enemies, I am the *utter contempt of my neighbors;* I am *a dread to my friends.* . . . I have become like broken pottery. . . . there is *terror on every side;* they conspire against me and *plot to take my life.*

1666) Acts 14:22. We must go through *many hardships* to enter the kingdom of God.

369. The evil in the world brings many hardships into our lives because evil threatens our bodies and souls, property and reputation.

370. What does God do about the evil in the world?

1667) Psalm 91:10. No harm will befall you, no disaster will come near your tent.

1668) Psalm 121. (The Lord watches over us at all times to keep harm away.)

370a. God keeps evil away from us.

1669) Genesis 45:4-8; 50:20. (God permitted Joseph's brothers to do evil to him, but eventually God turned it into good for all of them.)

1670) Acts 2:23,36; 3:17,18. (God permitted the Jews to put Jesus to death, but by this God fulfilled his promise to save all people.)

1671) Romans 8:28. We know that *in all things God works for the good* of those who love him.

1672) 2 Corinthians 4:17. Our light and momentary *troubles are achieving for us an eternal glory* that far outweighs them all.

370b. When God permits evil to come into our lives, he makes it work for our good.

1673) 2 Corinthians 12:7-10. (Paul knew that whenever hardship came into his life, God's power would be at work to strengthen him.)

1674) Psalm 94:17-19. Unless the LORD had *given me help,* I would soon have dwelt in the silence of death. When I said, "My foot is slipping," *your love,* O LORD, *supported me.* When anxiety was great within me, *your consolation brought joy* to my soul.

313

EVIL

SATAN	GOD
1. Brought it into the world by the Fall	1. Keeps it from us
2. Uses it to make our lives hard	2. Permits it to come but — uses it for our good — helps us bear it
	3. Delivers us from it completely in heaven

SEVENTH PETITION

"Bring us safely through the
many hardships of life
to our heavenly home!"

1675) 1 Peter 5:10. The *God of all grace,* who called you to his eternal glory in Christ, after you have suffered a little while, will himself *restore you and make you strong, firm and steadfast.*

1676) Psalm 23. (especially verse 4) I will fear no evil, for *you are with me;* your rod and your staff, they *comfort me.*

370c. When God permits evil to come into our lives, he strengthens and supports us so that we are able to bear it.

371. When will God deliver us completely from all the evil of this world?

1677) 2 Timothy 4:18. The Lord will *rescue me* from every evil attack and will *bring me* safely to his *heavenly kingdom.*

1678) Numbers 23:10. Let me die the *death of the righteous,* and may *my end* be *like theirs!*

1679) Philippians 1:23. I desire to depart and *be with Christ,* which is *better by far.*

1680) Revelation 21:3,4. God himself will be with them and be their God. He will *wipe every tear from their eyes.* There will be *no more* death or *mourning* or *crying* or *pain,* for the *old order of things* has passed away.

371. God will deliver us completely from all evil when he grants us a blessed end and takes us from this world of sorrow to himself in heaven.

372. What, then, are we praying in the Seventh Petition?

372. In the Seventh Petition we are asking our heavenly Father to bring us safely through all the evil of this world to our heavenly home.

THE DOXOLOGY

**For the kingdom, the power, and the glory are
yours now and forever. Amen.**

What does this mean?

**We can be sure that these petitions are accept-
able to our Father in heaven and are heard by
him, for he himself has commanded us to pray
in this way and has promised to hear us.
Therefore we say, "Amen. Yes, it shall be so."**

373. **Why can we be sure that these petitions are acceptable to our Father in heaven?**

1681) Matthew 6:9. *This* is *how* you should pray: "Our Father in
heaven. . . ."

1682) Luke 11:2. He said to them, "When you pray, *say:* 'Father, hallowed be . . . '"

373a. We can be sure that these petitions are acceptable to
our Father in heaven because Jesus commanded us to
pray this way.

1683) 1 John 5:14. This is the confidence we have in approaching
God: that if we *ask* anything *according to his will,* he hears us.

1684) Matthew 6:33. *Seek first his kingdom* and his righteousness,
and all these things will be given to you as well.

373b. We can be sure that these petitions are acceptable to
our Father in heaven because in these petitions Jesus
teaches us to seek God's kingdom first as God wants
us to.

1685) 1 Chronicles 29:11. *Yours,* O LORD, *is* the greatness and the
power and *the glory* and the majesty and the splendor, *for
everything* in heaven and earth *is yours.*

373c. We can be sure that these petitions are acceptable to our Father in heaven because when we ask anything from him, we are giving all glory to God.

374. Why can we be sure that these petitions will be heard by our Father in heaven?

1686) Romans 8:32. He who *did not spare his own Son,* but gave him up for us all—how will he not also, *along with him, graciously give us all things?*

1687) Matthew 7:7,8. Ask and it *will be given* to you; seek and you *will find;* knock and the *door will be opened* to you. For everyone who asks *receives;* he who seeks *finds;* and to him who knocks, *the door will be opened.*

1688) John 14:13,14. I will do whatever you ask in my name, so that the Son may *bring glory to the Father.* You may ask me for anything *in my name,* and I will do it.

1689) James 4:2,3. You do not have, because you do not ask God. When you ask, you do not receive, because you *ask with wrong motives,* that you may spend what you get on your pleasures.

374a. We can be sure that these petitions will be heard by our Father in heaven because he promises to give us everything we ask in Jesus' name and to his glory.

1690) Exodus 7-11. (God showed his great power by delivering Israel out of Egypt by ten mighty plagues.)

1691) Ephesians 3:20. [God] is *able to do* immeasurably more than all we ask or imagine.

1692) Luke 1:37. Nothing is impossible with God.

374b. We can be sure that these petitions will be heard by our heavenly Father because he has the power to do far more than we ask.

375. Why do we close our prayers with the word "Amen"?

1693) James 1:6,7. When he asks, *he must believe and not doubt*, because he who doubts is like a wave of the sea, blown and

AMEN

**EXPRESSES
CERTAINTY**

that my
prayers
are

ACCEPTABLE

to the
Father
because

1. He commanded us
   to pray

2. We are praying
   for his kingdom
   and to his glory

HEARD

by the
Father
because

1. He promised to
   hear our prayers

2. We pray knowing
   he has the
   power to answer
   our prayers

DOXOLOGY

"We are sure you will hear and answer
our prayers!"

tossed by the wind. That man should *not* think he will *receive anything from the Lord.*

375. We close our prayers with the word "Amen" because we do not doubt but firmly believe that our Father in heaven will hear and answer our prayers.

376. What, then, are we saying in the Doxology?

376. In the Doxology we are saying that we are sure our Father in heaven will hear and answer these petitions.

CHRISTIAN QUESTIONS

For those preparing to receive the Lord's Supper

1. Do you believe that you are a sinner?

Yes, I believe that I am a sinner.

2. How do you know this?

I know this from the Ten Commandments, which I have not kept.

3. Are you sorry for your sins?

Yes, I am sorry that I have sinned against God.

4. What have you deserved from God because of your sins?

I deserve his wrath and displeasure, temporal death, and eternal damnation.

5. Are you convinced that you are saved?

Yes, such is my confidence.

6. In whom, then, do you trust?

I trust in my dear Lord Jesus Christ.

7. Who is Jesus Christ?

Jesus Christ is the Son of God, true God and man.

8. How many Gods are there?

There is only one God; but there are three persons: Father, Son, and Holy Spirit.

9. What has Christ done for you that you trust in him?

He died for me and shed his blood for me on the cross for the forgiveness of sins.

10. Did the Father also die for you?

He did not; for the Father is God only, the Holy Spirit likewise. But the Son is true God and true man. He died for me and shed his blood for me.

11. How do you know this?

I know this from the holy gospel and from the words of the Sacrament of Holy Communion.

12. Which are those words?

Our Lord Jesus Christ, on the night he was betrayed, took bread; and when he had given thanks, he broke it and gave it to his disciples, saying, "Take and eat; this is my body, which is given for you. Do this in remembrance of me."

Then he took the cup, gave thanks, and gave it to them, saying, "Drink from it, all of you; this is my blood of the new covenant, which is poured out for you for the forgiveness of sins. Do this, whenever you drink it, in remembrance of me."

13. Do you believe, then, that the true body and blood of Christ are in the Sacrament?

Yes, I believe it.

14. What moves you to believe this?

I am moved to believe this by the words of Christ, "Take and eat; this is my body. . . . Drink from it, all of you; this is my blood of the new covenant."

15. What does Christ want you to do when you eat his body and drink his blood in the Lord's Supper?

Christ wants me to remember and proclaim his death and the pouring out of his blood as he taught me: "Do this, whenever you drink it, in remembrance of me."

16. Why does Christ want you to remember and proclaim his death?

He wants me to do this so that (1) I learn to believe that no creature could make satisfaction for my sins, but only Christ, who is true God and man, could and did do that; (2) I learn to look with terror upon my sins and regard them as great indeed; (3) I find joy and comfort in Christ alone and believe that I have salvation through faith in him.

17. What moved him to die and make a complete payment for your sins?

He was moved to do this by his great love for his Father and for me and other sinners, as the Scriptures teach (John 14:31; Romans 5:8; Galatians 2:20; Ephesians 5:2).

18. Finally, why do you desire to receive Holy Communion?

I desire to do this so that I learn to believe that Christ out of great love died for *my* sins and that I also learn of him to love God and my neighbor.

19. What admonishes and moves you to receive Holy Communion frequently?

The command and the promise of Christ my Lord admonishes and moves me. Also, the burden of sin that lies heavy upon me causes me to feel a hunger and thirst for Holy Communion.

20. But what can a person do if he is not aware of the burden of sin and does not feel hunger and thirst for Holy Communion?

To such a person no better advice can be given than that, in the first place, he put his hand into his bosom and feel whether he still has flesh and blood, and that he by all means believes what the Scriptures say about this (Galatians 5:17,19-21; Isaiah 64:6; Romans 7:18).

Secondly, that he look around to see whether he is still in the world and keep in mind that there will be no lack of sin and trouble, as the Scriptures say (John 15:18-25; Matthew 24:9-13; Acts 14:22).

Thirdly, that person will certainly have the devil also about him. With his lying and murdering, day and night, the devil will let him have no peace. So the Scriptures picture the devil (John 8:44; 1 Peter 5:8; Ephesians 6:10-12; 2 Timothy 2:26).

21. What can you do if you are sick and are unable to come to Holy Communion?

Then I can send for my pastor to pray with me and to give me Holy Communion privately.

22. When is the proper time to do this?

The time to do this is not only when death is at hand, but earlier before all physical and mental power is gone.

23. Why would you want to do this?

I would want to do this to receive the assurance through Holy Communion that my sins are forgiven and that salvation is mine.

APPENDIXES

GLOSSARY

—A—

Abba. The word for "father" in the language of the Jews.

Abortion. The killing of an unborn child.

Abound. To be plentiful; to exist in large numbers or amounts.

Absolution. The announcement after a confession of sins that God has forgiven our sins because Jesus died for them. Absolution may be spoken publicly in a worship service or privately to an individual.

Abstain. To hold oneself back from doing something; to do without.

Acknowledge. To recognize the authority or claims of someone; to approve of someone or something; to accept.

Active Obedience of Christ. Christ's fulfillment of the law by keeping all the commandments perfectly for all sinners.

Address. The first words of the Lord's Prayer, indicating to whom the prayer is spoken.

Administrator. Someone who directs an organization or a department of an organization.

Admonish. To warn against or point out a sin.

Adultery. Sexual intercourse with someone other than the person to whom one is married; impure words or thoughts in respect to sexual matters.

Advent. "Coming"; 1. the season of the church year in which we celebrate the coming of Christ into the world as a man; 2. the coming of Christ in Word and sacrament; 3. the coming of Christ on judgment day.

Alien. Stranger; foreigner.

Alienate. To estrange; to make a stranger of.

Amen. "Yes, it shall be so!" A word used at the end of a prayer to express confidence that the prayer will be heard and answered.

Angel. "Messenger"; a bodiless spirit created by God to serve him.

Anguish. Agony; intense pain or distress.

Anoint. To pour oil on to show that someone or something is being set aside for the service of God.

Apology. "Defense." *The Apology* is a booklet written by Melanchthon to defend the Augsburg Confession.

Apostle. One of the special men personally chosen and sent out by Christ to preach the gospel.

Arrogance. Haughtiness; excessive pride.

Ascension. Christ's visible return to heaven 40 days after his resurrection.

Atone. To make a payment to remove the guilt of sin so that God will no longer be angry.

Atonement. A payment offered to remove the guilt of sin so that God and sinful man are reconciled (set at one). (See *Vicarious Atonement* and Question 181.)

Attribute. A quality that is characteristic of a person.

Authority. The power and right to do something.

—B—

Baal. The name of a false god of the Canaanites.

Babble. To speak nonsense.

Baptism. The sacrament in which water is used in the name of the triune God to bring us into the family of God.

Baptize. To use water by immersing, washing, pouring, or sprinkling (see Question 266).

Barren. Childless; unable to have children.

Beatitudes. The blessings spoken by Jesus in Matthew 5:3-12.

Believe. 1. To accept as true; 2. to trust or rely upon.

Betray. 1. To hand over (a friend to an enemy); 2. to reveal (a secret).

Bible. God's written Word; a collection of 66 books inspired by God.

Binding Key. The power and right given by Christ to his church to refuse to forgive the sins of those who are impenitent (see Questions 307 and 308).

Birthright. The right of the first-born son to receive a special blessing or inheritance.

Bishop. Overseer; a church leader who watches over a congregation.

Blaspheme. To speak of God in an evil or disrespectful way.

Blessing. 1. Any good thing given by God; 2. the words that promise good things to be given by God.

Born Again. Converted; having begun the new life in Christ (see *Rebirth* and Answer 223b).

—C—

Captivate. To hold the attention of; to fascinate.

Catechism. A book of instruction in the form of questions and answers.

Celestial. Heavenly.

Centurion. A Roman army officer in command of about one hundred soldiers.

327

Ceremonial Law. That portion of the law of Moses which instructed the Israelites how to worship God (see the narrative following Question 23).

Chaplain. A minister who takes care of the spiritual needs of people in a special setting (e.g., the armed forces, health institutions).

Christ. "Anointed"; the name of Jesus that refers to his office. In Hebrew the word for "the Anointed" is "Messiah."

Christian. 1. Belonging to Christ (adjective); 2. one who trusts in Christ alone for salvation (noun).

Church. 1. All those everywhere who believe in Jesus as the Savior (same as holy Christian church, invisible church, communion of saints); 2. a group of people who come together to hear the gospel (visible church, congregation, church body).

Church Fellowship. The sharing of worship and church work by which people express their unity of faith (see *Fellowship* and Question 246).

Circumcision. The cutting off of the foreskin of the male sex organ, which made an Old Testament man a member of God's family and obligated him to keep the Old Testament law.

Civil Law. That portion of the law of Moses which governed the Israelites as a nation. Since the time of Christ, God no longer requires that his church keep this part of the law.

Code. A collection of laws.

Commend. 1. To praise for a job well done; 2. to entrust or hand over to someone for safekeeping.

Commune. To receive the Lord's Supper (see *Communion*).

Communicant. Someone who receives the Lord's Supper (see *Communion*).

Communion. A coming together or having something in common. The church is called the communion of saints because all believers are united by the faith in Christ they have in common. The Lord's Supper is called Holy Communion because in it Christians are joined to the Lord and thus also to each other (see *Church; Holy Communion*).

Compassion. Sorrow for another's distress and a desire to help.

Conceive. 1. To think or imagine; 2. to become pregnant.

Concord. Agreement; harmony.

Condemn. To judge someone guilty of sin and deserving of punishment.

Confess. 1. To admit that one has sinned; 2. to tell what one believes.

Confession. 1. An admission of sin; 2. a statement of faith (see the narrative following Question 244).

Confirmation. A ceremony following instruction in which Christians confess their faith and are acknowledged as sufficiently instructed to receive Holy Communion.

Conform. To do something in a way that has been determined by someone else.

Conformity. Becoming or acting like someone else in his way of thinking and doing.

Congregation. A group of Christians who unite for the public worship of God.

Conscience. The voice God places in us that bears witness to his law (see Question 19).

Consecrate. To set aside for special use in the church.

Consolation. Comfort.

Conspire. To plot together.

Contempt. Scorn; the feeling that someone or something is bad or worthless.

Contrition. Fear and sorrow caused by a knowledge of one's sin.

Conversion. Turning from unbelief to faith in Christ (see Answer 223a).

Convert. To turn from unbelief to faith in Christ.

Corrupt. 1. To spoil or make bad (verb); 2. morally bad or rotten (adjective).

Covenant. A solemn agreement, especially one in which God promises to bless and save.

Covet. To desire something that God does not want us to have (see Question 117).

Crave. To desire intensely.

Create. To bring into existence; to make.

Creation. 1. The act of making; 2. that which is made.

Credit. To list on the plus side of an account. Faith in Christ is credited to the sinner as righteousness, thus cancelling the debt of sin.

Creed. A statement of what a person or group of people believes and teaches (see narrative following Question 147).

Crucify. To put to death by hanging on a cross.

Curse. To use God's name to wish evil on someone or something.

—D—

Damnation. Everlasting punishment in hell.

Deacon. "Servant"; someone chosen by a congregation to serve in the church, especially by helping the needy.

Debauchery. Giving in to sinful sexual desires to an extreme degree.

Deceive. To lead into sin or error by telling lies.

Decree. A command made by a ruler.

Defile. To make unclean or impure.

Deluge. To flood.

Delusion. A false belief or opinion.

Demon. A fallen angel. The demons are led by Satan in war against God and his believers. The demons are also called devils (see Question 168).

Desertion. The act of abandoning or leaving when one should stay; especially, the act of abandoning one's marriage partner.

Despair. The sin of losing all hope in God's goodness.

Detest. To hate; to dislike intensely.

Devil. 1. The leader of the fallen angels and chief enemy of God. The devil's name is Satan. 2. Any fallen angel. The devils are also called demons (see Question 168).

Discern. To recognize.

Disciple. One who follows in order to learn; frequently used of the twelve who followed Jesus most closely during his ministry. It can also be used of any Christian.

Discipline. A rebuke and/or punishment given in love to a wrongdoer to turn that person away from any further sinning (see Questions 72, 73, and 316).

Discord. Disagreement; lack of harmony.

Dismay. Fear or discouragement in the face of trouble.

Disrepute. Dishonor; bad reputation.

Dissension. Quarreling.

Distort. To twist so as to misrepresent the truth.

Divination. The attempt to learn hidden things or predict the future by using supernatural power.

Divine. Of God; having to do with God.

Divine Call. The call a person receives from a congregation or group of congregations to serve in the public ministry (see Questions 313-315 and the narrative following Question 318).

Divisive. Causing division or disagreement.

Divorce. To end a marriage officially in a court of law.

Doctrine. A teaching.

Dominion. Rule; the power of a lord to govern.

Doxology. An expression of praise to God.

—E—

Easter. The festival of the church year on which we celebrate the resurrection of Jesus. As a matter of church tradition, Easter is the first Sunday on or after the first full moon on or after March 21.

Elder. A man who is given certain spiritual responsibilities in a congregation.

Element. A part of a whole. The water in Holy Baptism and the bread and wine in Holy Communion are called "earthly *elements*" because they are only a

330

part of what is received in the sacrament.

Enlighten. To give light to; the Holy Spirit enlightens people by bringing them out of the darkness of unbelief into the light of faith (see Questions 224 and 225).

Enmity. Hatred; hostility.

Entice. To lure or attract to commit sin.

Epiphany. 1. Christ's appearance to people as the Son of God and Savior of the world; 2. the festival of the church year (January 6) on which we celebrate Christ's appearance as God's Son.

Epistle. A letter.

Esteem. To think highly of; to respect.

Eternal. 1. Having no beginning or end (God is eternal); 2. everlasting, having no end (eternal life, eternal death).

Eternal Death. Eternal separation from the blessings of God in the torment of hell.

Eternal Life. Enjoyment of God's blessings eternally in heaven.

Eucharist. "Thanksgiving"; same as *Holy Communion.*

Eunuch. A man who is physically unable to father children.

Evangelist. 1. Someone who shares the gospel with those who have not heard it; 2. writer of one of the four gospels.

Evil. 1. Moral badness; wickedness; 2. any bad thing that is part of our life on earth as a result of Adam's fall into sin.

Exaltation of Christ. That part of Christ's ministry beginning with his victorious descent into hell when he again made full use of his heavenly power and glory.

Exasperate. To make angry.

Excommunication. The act of excluding from the congregation those who are plainly impenitent that they may repent (see Question 316).

Exploit. To take advantage of.

Extol. To praise highly.

—F—

Faction. Strife; quarreling; dissension.

Faith. Trust; saving faith is trust in the true God and in the salvation that Jesus won for us.

False Prophet. Someone who claims to teach God's Word but whose teachings include doctrines that are not true (see Question 12).

False Visible Churches. Groups that teach or permit false doctrine but are still to be recognized as churches because Jesus is taught as the Son of God and the Savior of the world (see Question 244).

Fasting. The practice of voluntarily going without food for a certain period of time.

Fear of God. 1. Being afraid of God's anger; 2. awe and respect for God and his commands as a result of faith in him.

Fellowship. 1. Being united with others in the same faith; 2. an act of expressing this unity (e.g., by worshiping or praying together, doing mission work together, etc.; see Question 246).

Firstfruits. That part of a crop which is harvested first.

Fleeting. Passing swiftly; not lasting.

Flesh. 1. The muscular tissue of a body; 2. human nature; that which makes up a human person; 3. same as *Sinful Nature* (see Questions 126 and 127).

Folly. Foolishness, especially the foolishness of disobeying God's law.

Forgiveness of Sins. "Forgiveness"; the state of being forgiven or pardoned for our sins. God does not overlook our sins as though they do not matter, but he punished Jesus for them instead of us and declares us innocent. We receive this forgiveness through faith in Jesus.

Formula. A written statement of doctrine.

Fraud. Getting the possessions of others by dishonest dealing.

Fulfill. To bring to completion. Jesus fulfilled the law by obeying it perfectly. God fulfills his promises and prophecies by carrying them out.

Futile. Useless; without benefit or effect.

—G—

Gangrene. Decay of tissues that starts in one part of the body and spreads if left untreated.

Garland. Wreath.

Garment. An article of clothing.

Gentile. A non-Jew.

Glory. 1. Splendor of a very high degree. "The glory of the Lord shone around them" (Luke 2:9). 2. Adoring praise. "[Abraham] gave glory to God" (Romans 4:20).

Godless. Without faith in the true God.

Good Friday. The Friday before Easter on which we observe the death and burial of Jesus.

Good Works. Everything a believer does according to God's Word out of love and thanks for all of God's goodness (see Questions 227-230).

Gospel. 1. The good news that God in love sent Jesus to take away the sins of all people; 2. one of the first four books of the New Testament.

Grace. God's undeserved love that provides free forgiveness of sins, life, and salvation for all people.

Gracious. Showing divine grace; merciful.

Gradual. "A step"; in the order of service, a response of praise that leads from the Epistle to the Gospel.

Guilt. The state of someone who has done wrong and deserves to be punished.

—H—

Hallow. To regard as holy.

Heaven. 1. The sky; 2. the place of eternal life and perfect joy in the presence of God.

Hell. The place of eternal death and punishment where the devil and his angels and all who die as unbelievers are tormented.

Heresy. False doctrine.

Heritage. Something that is passed on from one generation to the next.

High Priest. The most important of the priests. According to the ceremonial law, only the high priest could enter the Most Holy Place on the Day of Atonement and atone for the sins of the nation. Jesus is our High Priest because he atoned for the sins of the world by offering himself as a sacrifice (see Questions 180 and 181).

Holy. 1. Pure; sinless. "Be holy because I, the LORD your God, am holy" (Leviticus 19:2). 2. Set apart for the holy God. "The seventh day shall be your holy day" (Exodus 35:2).

Holy Communion. The sacrament in which the body and blood of Jesus are given to us together with bread and wine for the forgiveness of sins.

Holy Spirit. One of the three persons of the triune God; also called Holy Ghost, Comforter, Counselor, Paraclete.

Homosexuality. The sin of having sexual relations with a person of one's own sex or of having a desire for such relations.

Hope. A confident longing for the things God has promised.

Hover. To remain in one place in the air.

Humiliation of Christ. The first part of Christ's ministry, when he usually chose not to make full use of his heavenly power and glory so that he might live and die in a lowly way (see Question 194).

Hypocrite. One who pretends to be a believer but is not.

—I—

Idol. A false god, especially one that is represented by a statue or image.

Idolatry. The worship of a false god (see *Open Idolatry; Secret Idolatry*).

Image of God. The holiness and knowledge of God's will in which Adam and Eve were created. The image of God was lost through the fall into sin, but it is restored through the work of the Holy Spirit (see *New Man* and Question 155).

Immanuel. "God with us"; one of the names of Jesus (Matthew 1:23).

Immerse. To put completely into water.

Immorality. That which is contrary to the moral law.

Impenitent. Not sorry for one's sins; not penitent.

Incarnation. The taking on of a human nature by the Son of God. In this way God became a man. It refers to the conception and birth of Jesus.

Inclination. A leaning or tendency; a liking or preference.

Indulge. To give in to desire.

Iniquity. "Failing to measure up perfectly" to God's law by breaking one of his commandments.

Inner Being. Same as *New Man* (see Question 130).

Inspiration. The miracle by which God "breathed into" the prophets and the apostles what he wanted them to write in the Bible. It is called *verbal inspiration* to show that God guided them to use the exact words he wanted them to write.

Institute. To establish; to found.

Intercede. To beg or plead in behalf of others.

Intercourse. The bodily joining of a man and a woman in sexual relations.

Introit. In the order of service, an opening psalm or opening sentences.

Invisible Church. The group consisting of all those everywhere who believe in Jesus as their Savior. They cannot be identified with absolute certainty because only God can see faith in the heart (see Question 239).

—J—

Justification. God's declaration that people are not guilty because Jesus has paid for their sins (see also *Objective Justification; Subjective Justification*).

Justify. To declare not guilty. This word pictures a judge in a courtroom who tells a criminal that there is no longer any charge against him (see Question 251).

—K—

Keys. The power and right given by Christ to the church either to forgive sins or to refuse to forgive sins (see also *binding key; loosing key*).

Kingdom of God. Christ's rule in the hearts of his believers through his Word.

—L—

Lavish. To give or bestow generously.

Law. 1. The commands that tell people what God wants them to do and not to do. 2. Sometimes in the Bible the word "law" refers to God's Word in general, even those parts that are not commands.

Lent. The season of the church year between the Epiphany season and Easter during which we give special attention to Christ's suffering and death; also called the passion season.

Lewdness. Indecency, lustfulness.

Loathsome. Disgusting.

Loosing Key. The power and right given by Christ to the church to forgive the sins of those who are penitent (see Question 309).

Lord. When this word appears in all capital letters, it stands for *Yahweh,* the name of God that emphasizes his grace and faithfulness to his promises.

Lord's Supper. Same as *Holy Communion.*

Lord's Table. Same as *Holy Communion.*

Lust. Sinful desire.

—M—

Malice. The desire to harm someone.

Marital. Having to do with marriage.

Maundy Thursday. "Thursday of the Commandment" (John 13:34); the day on which we observe the institution of the Lord's Supper.

Means of Grace. The gospel in Word and sacraments by which God offers and gives us the forgiveness of sins, life, and salvation (see the narrative following Question 264).

Mediator. One who serves as a go-between or negotiator between two parties.

Meditate. To think deeply.

Medium. Person through whom one tries to communicate with the dead or with evil spirits.

Mercy. God's kindness in not punishing sinners as they deserve but providing a Savior instead.

Mercy Death. A killing performed to end pain when there is no hope of recovery; also called euthanasia.

Minister. "Servant"; especially someone called to serve people with the means of grace.

Ministry. The office or work of a minister.

Miracle. A wonder or very unusual happening brought about by God beyond the natural order of things.

Mission Work. The sharing of the gospel with those who have not heard it.

Missionary. A person who is sent to preach the gospel, especially to those who have not heard it.

Moral Law. God's will for all people of all time; summarized in the Ten Commandments and the command to love (see Questions 23 and 24).

Most Holy Place. Room in the tabernacle or temple where the ark of the covenant was kept and where the high priest sprinkled blood once a year to make payment for the sins of Israel.

Myth. A story or teaching that seems to be historically true but is actually made up by some person.

—N—

Name of God. God's titles and everything else he has revealed about himself in his Word.

Natural Law. The law of God as it is written on the hearts of all people.

New Man. The new heart and mind that God creates in us by faith in Jesus. The new man delights in doing God's will and fights against the sinful nature. Also called *New Person; New Self; Inner Being; Spirit* (see Question 130).

New Person. Same as *New Man.*

New Self. Same as *New Man.*

—O—

Oath. A promise to do something, appealing to God as witness.

Observe. 1. To celebrate (a festival); 2. to keep or obey, such as to observe the law.

Offense. 1. A sin; 2. something that causes another believer to stumble in faith.

Offering. A sacrifice or gift brought to God.

Office. The work or service assigned to someone. In the church, the office of the public ministry is the work that the called ministers do. The office of Christ is the whole work Christ does as Prophet, High Priest, and King.

Old Adam. The same as the *Sinful Nature.* It is called the old Adam because it is an inherited condition going back to Adam and Eve (see Questions 126 and 127).

Old Man. Same as *Sinful Nature.*

Old Self. Same as *Sinful Nature.*

Omen. A happening regarded as a special sign foretelling the future.

Omnipotent. Almighty; all-powerful; able to do all things.

Omnipresent. Present in all places.

Omniscient. All-knowing; knowing everything past, present, and future.

Open Idolatry. To worship openly someone or something other than the triune God (see Question 36).

Orgy. A wild, immoral party.

Original sin. The guilt and sinfulness inherited by all people as a result of Adam's fall into sin (see also *Sinful Nature*).

—P—

Pagan. Unbeliever; heathen.

Palm Sunday. The festival of the church year (the Sunday before Easter) on which we celebrate Jesus' triumphal entry into Jerusalem.

Parable. A story told to teach a spiritual truth or lesson.

Paradise. 1. The Garden of Eden; 2. a name for heaven pictured as a beautiful park.

Partake. To receive a portion, especially of food.

Passion. 1. Suffering (e.g., the passion of Christ); 2. very strong feeling (the passions of the sinful nature).

Passionate. Having very strong feelings.

Passive Obedience of Christ. Christ's suffering of the penalties that we deserve for breaking God's law (see Answer 176b).

Passover. A yearly festival of the ceremonial law in which the Israelites sacrificed a lamb and remembered how God had rescued the nation from slavery in Egypt. The Passover lamb was a sign pointing to Christ, the Lamb of God.

Pastor. "Shepherd"; someone called to serve a group of Christians with the Word of God.

Penitent. Being sorry for sin and willing to stop sinning.

Pentecost. The festival of the church year on which we celebrate the special outpouring of the Holy Spirit on Jesus' disciples 50 days after Easter.

Perjurer. Someone who tells a lie when he has sworn to tell the truth.

Persecution. Troubles that the unbelieving people of the world cause for a Christian because they are enemies of Christ.

Persevere. To continue in spite of difficulties.

Perverse. Having a twisted mind that is set upon wrongdoing.

Pervert. Someone whose sexual desires are unnatural.

Petition. A request. Since there are seven requests in the Lord's Prayer, we call them the seven petitions.

Pharisee. A member of a Jewish religious group who claimed to keep more laws than the ones God commanded and thought that this made him right with God.

Physical. Bodily; not spiritual.

Praise. To speak joyfully and admiringly about God's goodness.

Prayer. An act of worship in which we speak to God from our hearts.

Prayer Fellowship. A way of expressing unity in faith by praying with others.

Precept. A command; a rule; a teaching.

Preservation. God's work of providing all that we need to keep our body and life (see Questions 158-160).

Priest. 1. One who is permitted to deal with God directly in prayer and in the use of God's Word and sacraments (see *Priesthood of All Believers*); 2. one who is chosen to lead the people in worship and to offer sacrifices for them.

Priesthood of All Believers. The priestly office held by all believers, which gives them the right to pray to God directly and to use his Word and sacraments (see Question 305).

Profane. To treat something that is holy with disrespect; to dishonor.

337

Propers. The parts of the order of service that change from Sunday to Sunday, such as the Gradual, Introit, collect, and Scripture readings.

Prophecy. Any message from God spoken or written by a prophet; often a message foretelling the future.

Prophet. One who speaks a message from God.

Prostitute. A person who commits sexual sins for pay.

Provision. A supply.

Prudent. Wise; having sound judgment.

Public Ministry. The teaching of God's Word and the administering of the sacraments by workers (pastors, teachers, and others) who have a divine call. These workers act as representatives of the group of Christians who called them (see Questions 312-315 and the narrative following Question 318).

—Q—

Quickening. Making alive; raising from the dead. This is one way to picture the miracle of faith that the Holy Spirit works in us.

—R—

Radiant. Bright; shining.

Ransom. 1. Payment given to free people from captivity (noun); 2. to free from captivity by paying a price (verb).

Real Presence. The miraculous presence of Jesus' real body with the bread and of his real blood with the wine in Holy Communion.

Realm. Kingdom.

Rebirth. Being born again. This is one way to picture the miracle of faith that the Holy Spirit works in us (see Answer 223b).

Rebuke. To scold someone for doing wrong.

Reconcile. To restore someone to peace and harmony with another.

Reconciliation. The restoration of peace between God and man as a result of Christ's death.

Redeem. To ransom; to buy back; to pay a price in order to free from slavery or captivity.

Redemption. Christ's work of ransoming all people from the slavery of sin, death, and the devil by paying the price of his blood, suffering, and death.

Regeneration. Same as *Rebirth*.

Render. 1. To give; 2. to cause to become; to make.

Renewal. The Holy Spirit's work of making us new by creating a new man inside of us through the gospel.

Renounce. To give up; to intend to have nothing to do with.

Repentance. A "change of mind" about one's sin. The Bible uses the word "repentance" in two senses: 1. sorrow over sin and desire to stop sinning; 2. sorrow over sin and faith in the forgiveness of sins.

Repentant. Same as *Penitent.*

Resurrection. Coming to life after death; refers especially to Christ's return to life on Easter and to the raising of all the dead on the Last Day.

Reveal. To "unveil"; to make known something hidden.

Revenue. A country's income from taxes, which is used to pay public expenses.

Revile. To use bad language about someone; to call bad names.

Righteous. Sinless; morally perfect.

Righteousness. Sinlessness; moral perfection. God has righteousness and demands righteousness from us. Through faith in Christ his righteousness is given to us.

Robbery. Taking the possessions of others by force.

—S—

Sabbath. Hebrew word for rest.

Sabbath Day. The day of rest. According to the ceremonial law, the Israelites were commanded to rest from their work on the seventh day of the week (Saturday).

Sacrament. A sacred act that Christ established for his church, in which an earthly element is used together with God's Word, as a means of offering, giving, and sealing to us the forgiveness of sins and thus also life and salvation.

Sacrament of the Altar. Same as *Holy Communion.*

Sacrifice. The killing of a living being (usually an animal) as an offering to God. The most important purpose of sacrifice was for atonement (see *Atone*).

Saint. "Holy one." Every believer in Christ is a saint because through faith in Christ he has the holiness of Christ (see Question 236).

Salvation. Rescue or deliverance; especially the rescue from sin, death, and the devil accomplished by Jesus, the Savior.

Sanctification. The work of the Holy Spirit through the means of grace. For the two different ways in which the Bible uses the word, see *Sanctify.*

Sanctify. To make holy, used in two different ways in the Bible: 1. to call someone out of the unbelieving world to be holy by bringing that person to faith in Christ, enlightening him, and keeping him in the faith (sanctify in the wider sense); 2. to lead a believer to hate sin and be eager to live a holy life filled with good works (sanctify in the narrow sense).

Sanctuary. A holy place set apart for the worship of God. Both the tabernacle and the temple are called a "sanctuary."

Satan. "Adversary"; a name of the devil.

Scripture. "Writing." Usually the word "Scripture(s)" refers to the Bible.

Second Birth. Same as *Rebirth.*

Secret Idolatry. Giving someone or something first place in one's heart instead of God (see Question 37).

Self-righteousness. Same as *Work-righteousness.*

Sensuality. Allowing oneself to have sinful bodily pleasures.

Sin. "Missing the bull's eye" of God's law by breaking one of his commandments.

Sin of Commission. Doing something that God forbids.

Sin of Omission. Not doing something that God wants us to do.

Sinful Nature. A mind and heart inclined only toward evil. All men have a sinful nature because they are born of sinful parents. Also called *Original Sin; Flesh; Old Adam; Old Self; Old Man* (see Questions 126 and 127).

Slander. False statements that harm someone's reputation.

Sorcery. Witchcraft; the magic of one who is aided by the devil.

Soul. The spiritual being which, when united with a body, makes a living human person.

Sovereign. 1. Having the highest ruling power (adjective); 2. highest ruler (noun).

Spell. A form of words believed to have magical power.

Spirit. 1. A bodiless personal being (e.g., God, angels, the devil, demons); 2. "the Spirit" often means the Holy Spirit; 3. the new man that is given to believers by the Holy Spirit; 4. sometimes "spirit" means the same as soul.

Spiritist. Someone who supposedly communicates with the spirits of the dead.

Spiritual Death. Separation from the spiritual blessings of God. All men are born spiritually dead and remain that way until the Holy Spirit quickens them, that is, calls them to faith in Christ.

Sponsor. Someone chosen to speak at the baptism of a baby, who is to be concerned with the spiritual welfare of the child as he grows up. Sponsors are not mentioned in the Bible and are not necessary for a valid baptism (see the narrative following Question 271).

Statute. A law.

Steadfast. Firm; unmovable.

Subdue. To take control of.

Substitute. One who takes the place of another.

Suicide. The sin of killing oneself.

Superstitious. Trusting in powers that God has forbidden.

Sustain. To hold up or support; to keep alive.

Swear. To use God's name to assure someone that the truth is being told.

Synod. A group of congregations that unite to help each other in the Lord's work.

—T—

Tabernacle. The tent used by the Israelites as a place of worship from the time of the giving of the law on Mt. Sinai until the building of Solomon's temple.

Temple. God's house; a building where he dwells and is worshiped. Believers are called the temple of God because he lives in them.

Tempt. To try to lead someone into sin, false belief, or despair.

Temptation. Any situation in which someone may be led into sin, false belief, or despair.

Testament. A covenant. The Old Testament books of the Bible cover that portion of history when the old covenant (the law of Mt. Sinai) was in effect. The New Testament books describe the new covenant that Jesus established by fulfilling the law perfectly and by dying to earn the forgiveness of sins (see Questions 6 and 7).

Testify. To speak as a witness.

Testimony. A statement of what one knows to be true. Frequently testimony refers to God's Word or a portion of it.

Theft. Taking the possessions of others secretly.

Time of Grace. The time of one's life on earth that God gives to an individual as his only opportunity to come to faith in Jesus and be saved (see Question 80).

Transform. To change.

Transgression. "Crossing the forbidden line" of God's law by breaking one of his commandments.

Trespass. Same as *Transgression.*

Tribulation. Suffering; affliction.

Trinity. The triune God.

Triune. Existing as both three (tri-) and one (-une). The triune God is three persons but only one God (see Question 148).

—U—

Unblemished. Spotless; faultless.

Uncircumcision. Not being circumcised; sometimes used as a picture of unbelief and disobedience.

Unrighteous. Morally imperfect; sinful; contrary to God's will.

Unrighteousness. Lack of righteousness; sinfulness.

—V—

Valid. Legally binding; acceptable.

Verbal Inspiration. See *Inspiration.*

Vicar. A student training for the ministry who serves a congregation under the direction of a pastor.

Vicarious. Performed by taking the place of another; substitutionary.

Vicarious Atonement. The sacrifice of Jesus in our place, accepted by the Father as payment for our sins (see Question 181).

Visible Churches. Groups of people who gather to use the means of grace (see Questions 242-244).

Vision. Something that is seen by other than normal sight, such as in sleep or in a trance.

—W—

Wickedness. Great sinfulness.

Witch. A woman who seeks supernatural power by making an agreement with evil spirits.

Witchcraft. The attempt to do things by the power of the devil (see Question 48).

Witness. 1. Someone who is an observer. The apostles were witnesses of Jesus' resurrection. Witnesses at a baptism observe the baptism to verify that it took place (noun). 2. The testimony that an observer gives. To bear witness means to give testimony (noun). 3. To testify; to speak as one who has seen (verb).

Word of God. That which God has said either directly, or through angels, prophets, or apostles. The Bible is the written Word of God.

Workmanship. A product; something that has been made.

Work-righteousness. Trying to earn righteousness before God by one's own works (see Question 254).

Worship. Any thoughts, words, or actions that we direct toward God as a way of praising him.

Wrath. Intense anger.

Written Law. The law of God as it is written in the Bible.

—Z—

Zion. The hill on which Jerusalem stands. "Zion" is also used as a name for the church.

PRONOUNCING VOCABULARY

Aaron	AIR-un
Abednego	uh-BED-neh-go
Abel	AY-bul
Abiram	uh-BY-rum
Abraham	AY-bruh-ham
Absalom	ABB-suh-lum
Achan	AY-can
Adam	ADD-um
Ahab	AY-hab
Ananias	an-uh-NY-us
Antioch	AN-tea-uk
Arimathea	air-uh-muh-THEE-uh
Baal	BAY-ul
Balaam	BAY-lum
Balak	BAY-lack
Barabbas	bar-AB-bus
Barnabas	BAR-nu-bus
Bathsheba	bath-SHE-buh
Bereans	Burr-EE-uns
Caiaphas	KAY-uh-fuss
Cain	KANE
Canaanite	KANE-uh-night
Centurion	sen-TOUR-ee-uhn
Corinth	CORE-inth
Corinthians	cor-INTH-ee-uns
Cornelius	core-NEE-lee-us
Daniel	DAN-yell
Dathan	DAY-thun
David	DAY-vid

Egypt	EE-jipt
Eli	EE-lie
Elijah	ee-LIE-juh
Elisha	ee-LIE-shuh
Elymas	EL-ih-mus
Endor	EN-door
Esau	EE-saw
Ethiopian	EE-thee-OH-pea-uhn
Eunuch	YOU-nock
Eve	EEV
Gabriel	GAY-bree-el
Gaius	GAY-us
Galatians	gah-LAY-shunz
Golgotha	GUL-ga-tha
Goliath	go-LIE-uth
Gomorrah	guh-MORE-ruh
Hannah	HAN (*a* as in *bat*)-nuh
Herod	HAIR-ud
Hymenaeus	hi-men-EE-us
Isaac	EYE-zack
Isaiah	eye-ZAY-uh
Jacob	JAY-cub
Jairus	jah-EYE-rus
James	JAMZ
Jericho	JERR-ik-koh
Jerusalem	jerr-RUE-suh-lem
Jezebel	JEZ-uh-bell
Job	JOHB
Joel	JOE-el
John	JON
Jonathan	JON-uh-thun
Joseph	JOE-zef
Joshua	JOSH-ooh-uh
Judas	JEW-das
Lazarus	LAZ-zuh-rus
Lot	LOT (*o* as in *odd*)

Machpelah	mack-PEA-luh
Martha	MARR-thuh
Melanchthon	mel-LANK-thun
Meshach	ME-shack
Moses	MOE-zuz
Nabal	NAY-bul
Naboth	NAY-buth
Naomi	nay-OH-my
Nathan	NAY-thun
Nazareth	NAZ-zur-reth
Nebuchadnezzar	NEB-uh-kud-NEZ-zur
Noah	KNOW-uh
Onesimus	oh-NES-ih-mus
Paradise	PEAR-uh-dies
Paul	PAUL
Pergamum	PURR-gah-mum
Peter	PEA-turr
Pharisees	FAIR-ih-sees
Philadelphia	fill-uh-DEL-fee-uh
Philetus	fie-LEE-tus
Philip	FILL-up
Philippi	fill-LIP-eye
Philippians	fill-LIP-eh-unz
Pontius Pilate	PON-chuz PIE-let
Potiphar	POT-uh-fur
Rome	ROME
Ruth	ROOTH
Samaritan	suh-MARE-ih-tun
Samuel	SAM-you-ell
Sapphira	sah-FIE-rah
Sardis	SAR-dis
Saul	SAUL
Shadrach	SHAY-drack
Shimei	SHIM-ih-eye
Silas	SIGH-lus
Sinai	SIGH-nigh
Sodom	SOD-um

Solomon	SOLL-uh-mun
Stephen	STEE-fun
Thomas	TOM-us
Uriah	you-RYE-uh
Zacchaeus	zak-KEY-us

INDEX OF TOPICS

Numbers refer to answers. Asterisk (*) indicates that the topic is found in the paragraph(s) following the answer.

—B—

Body of Christ
name for holy Christian church
235,238
present in Holy Communion
287,288

Books of the Bible 8*

Born Again
see *Rebirth*

Bread
earthly element in Holy Communion 264*,286-288
daily bread 353-357

Burial of Christ
part of humiliation 195
commemorated on Good Friday
59*

—C—

Call to Faith 220-223
work of Holy Spirit 221
through means of grace 222,
240
pictures for it 223

Call to Public Ministry
see *Divine Call*

Capital Punishment 81

Catechism
a confession of the Lutheran
church 244*
Luther and the, page 24 of the
Introduction
our use of, page 24 of the
Introduction

Ceremonial Law 23*

Certainty
of truth of Bible 11
of God's promises 151b
of Christ's blessings for us 199-
203
of eternal life 192,212,
257b,274,292

of forgiveness of sins 256,257,
292,302a,325
of God's answer to the Lord's
Prayer 373-376

Chaplains 318*

Characteristics of God
known from creation 2
revealed in his Word 150
Jesus has them 172b
Holy Spirit has them 219b

Charity
helping those in need 83b,101b
kindness toward everyone 83a,
112c

Children
gift of God in marriage 89c
need to be baptized 271
instruction in God's Word 246c

Children of God 334,335

Christ
meaning of title 177
true God 36b,172,175,176
true man 173,175,176
work of 184-193
humiliation of 194-196
exaltation of 197-208
belonging to 209-212
appearing of 59*
crucifixion of 195
descent into hell 198,200
incarnation 174
intercession 204b
sacrifice of 77b,124b,181
see also *Active Obedience of;
Ascension of; Birth of; Blood of;
Body of; Burial of; Coming of;
Conception of; Death of; Judgment Day; Kingdom of; Office
of; Passive Obedience of;
Redemption; Resurrection of;
Second Coming of; Sitting at*

—F—

Faith
what it is 151
makes us children of God 152b,334
basis of Christ's judgment 208
receives the blessings of Christ's redemption 213
worked by the Holy Spirit 215, 216
Holy Spirit uses means of grace 222
opposed by devil, world, sinful nature 233
Holy Spirit keeps us in it 234
known only by God 239
importance of 255
of little children 271c
created or strengthened in Baptism 277b
strengthened in Holy Communion 294b,302b
makes us prepared for Holy Communion 298
God wants all to come to it 347b

Faithfulness
in use of our possessions 102
in our work for our employer 104b
of God 150c

Fall into Sin
devil led Adam and Eve into sin 167
original sin 127
ruin of creation 166
evil in our lives 368

False Prophets
see *False Teachers*

False Teachers
use God's name to lie 46

dishonor God's name 340a
fellowship forbidden with 248, 249

False Testimony 111

False Visible Church
how recognized 243,244,244*
fellowship forbidden with 248, 249
members may be saved 250

Family
providing for 101a
see *Parents; Husband; Wife; Children*

Family of God 268

Fasting 297

Father, God the
first person of Trinity 152
our Father by faith 152b,334-336
Christ receives equal glory with 36b

Fear of God
what it is 35a
expresses our thanks 40
fear of his wrath 138

Fellowship 245-249
church fellowship 246a,299
prayer fellowship 246b
in Christian education 246c
in mission work 246d
forbidden with those who persist in falsehood 248,249, 301d

Festivals
see *Special Days*

Flesh
see *Sinful Nature*

Forgiveness of Sins 251-257
accomplished by Jesus 16a,290
Jesus died to take away sins 39b,51b,61b,77b,85b,97b, 106b,115b,124b

in God's promises 11b,151b
in the righteousness of Christ
255
Truth
of God's Word 11a,57
opposed by devil 169
confessed by Lutheran church
244*
teaching God's Word in its truth
339a,347a
love for it 249a

—U—

Unbelief
will be judged by Christ 208
is a darkness 224
Unbelievers
condemned to hell on Last Day
260
their prayers are not heard 330
Unfaithfulness, Marital 90c
Unity of Faith
in the communion of saints 238
expressed in fellowship 245
expressed in Holy Communion
299,302c
Use of the Keys
see *Keys*

—V—

Verbal Inspiration 10
Vicarious Atonement 181,189
Vicars 318*
Victory
of Christ over sin, death, and
devil 183,200,202a
our victory over temptation 366
Virgin Birth 174
Visions 12a

—W—

Wastefulness 103a
Water in Baptism 264*,266,267
Wife
helper to husband 89a
is to honor and love her husband 94b
Will of God 347-352
what it is 347
done by angels 348a
done on earth 348b,351
opposed by devil, world, and
sinful nature 137,349-351
prayer that God's will be done
352
equivalent to the moral law 23*
see *Law*
Wine
earthly element in Holy Communion 264*,286-288
Wisconsin Synod 244*
Wisdom of God 2
Witchcraft 48
Witnesses of Baptism 271*
Women in Public Ministry 313a,
318*
Word of God
Bible is 8*,9-12,151a
is living and active 9
to be placed above the word of
others 35a
despising God's Word 56,60
hearing God's Word
55,58a,58b,59b,62
sharing God's Word 58c
is holy and true 57
made all things 153
taught by prophets and Jesus
178,179
to be taught in its truth and
purity 244,244*,339a,347a

INDEX OF SCRIPTURE PASSAGES

References are made to question numbers. Asterisk (*) indicates that the passage is found in the paragraph(s) following the answer.

Proverbs

1:3,5,8,9—67
1:10—95,363
3:5—37
6:16-19—111
6:23—74
6:25—363
8:13—35
10:12—112
11:9—108
11:13—110
11:25—104
12:26—363
13:24—72
14:35—71
15:26—118
16:8—103
16:28—109
17:6—89
17:9—110
18:10—42
18:22—87
19:5—110
19:18—73
20:9—123
21:6—103
21:19—90
22:1—108
22:6—246
22:16,22—103
23:13—73
23:20,31-33—82
23:22—70
23:31—363
25:9—110
28:13—323
30:5—57
30:8,9—363
30:11,17—71
31:8,9—112

Ecclesiastes

5:1—56
12:7—157,258

Song of Songs

1:15,16—89
4:1-7—89
5:10-16—89

Isaiah

1:15—330
5:8—119
30:19—360
32:17—225
40:1,2—317
41:10—234
42:8—34,41,337
43:11—25
45:12—154
45:21—34
50:10—35
53:5—134,186
53:5,6—189,252
53:6—61
55:6—80
55:10,11—241
55:11—242,250
57:21—135
59:2—321,359
59:12—321,359
61:1—179
61:10—210,225
64:6—144,231,321
66:24—260

Jeremiah

1:7—178
14:14—12,46
17:5—37
23:24—150
23:28—339,347
23:31—46
31:34—251

Lamentations

3:22—170
3:22,23—257

Ezekiel

11:19,20—130
18:4—135
33:11—170
36:23—340

Daniel

3:1-18—35
6:1-4—104
6:1-23—35
6:10,11—49
6:16-23—161,162
9:3,19—329
12:2—192,259

Hosea

4:1-3—66
14:2—333

Joel

1:3—246
2:28—217

Malachi

1:6-8—340
2:10—152
2:7,8—340
3:8-10—101

NEW TESTAMENT

Matthew

1:18-20—195
1:18-20,24—88*
1:20—174
1:21—41,337
1:22,23—174